BERLIN

and POTSDAM

Second Revised Edition
1995

TABLE OF CONTENTS

HISTORY AND CULTURE

BERLIN BY DAY

EXPERIENCING BERLIN

BERLIN BY NIGHT

FEATURES

GUIDELINES

GREATER BERLIN

0   5 km

LIST OF MAPS

BERLIN

On its Way to Becoming a European Metropolis

It is said that you are not simply a Berliner, you *become* one. People who quote this saying usually have moved to Berlin from elsewhere and like to think of themselves as real Berliners. What is true about this saying is that Berlin has always been more than just a city; the word Berlin has always stood for an idea, a feeling and ultimately for a powerful myth that all too often obscured the city's real character.

The Berlin myth originated during the Roaring Twenties; what consolidated the legend was the basement culture of the post-war period, the Berlin Wall and the Cold War, the Kreuzberg riots and being the capital of East Germany, and finally the fall of the Berlin Wall and reunification. Since recently, the "wild East" with its experimental galleries and bars and the avantgarde scene on Prenzlauer Berg has people spellbound.

All this makes up Berlin, but it isn't the whole truth. Berlin, on its way to being a modern European metropolis, gives the impression of being a city searching for its own identity.

Berlin seems to have gotten lost somewhere between its glorious and legendary history, insecure present and by no means safe future. Some say that the Berlin Bear is spinning on its own axis, directionless and dizzy as a result of the many rapid changes.

Berlin's unsuccessful application for the Olympic Games in the year 2000

Preceding pages: The angel on the victory column. Post-card display. A pop concert in front of the Reichstag. Gedächtniskirche at night. Winter landscape on the Havel. Left: Anything goes in Berlin.

showed how frantic the politicians' attempt was to give Berlin the vision of a glorious future. This future is to be the capital of the Federal Republic of Germany, turnstile between Western and Eastern Europe, and Europe's cultural metropolis. These ideas must be furnished with contents and deeds – and it's proving to be Berlin's Achilles heel.

The hopeful longing with which Berliners are waiting for the Federal Government and its Parliament to move from Bonn to Berlin and the way they are welcoming new investors shows how far removed Berlin is from the relaxed confidence of other metropoles such as Paris or London. Is Berlin simply a city in historical free fall?

Berlin – the Unified City

Only a few years after the fall of the Berlin Wall, the city itself has still not been unified. The people in the East and West still think and live differently, even if their children are growing up as Berliners. The experiences each half of the city went through during the three decades of brutal separation were diametrically opposed and that past is still omnipresent.

There was West Berlin, which, after the Wall went up on August 13, 1961, became an artifical island in the middle of the Communist sphere of influence, an outpost of democracy and open-mindedness. It was often called the Window on the West. In reality, this is where the Cold War was fought and it formed the interface between East and West. For Berliners in both parts of the city, the experience was at first hand and took place on their own doorstep, making it part of their everyday life.

But during the course of time, West Berlin learned how to live in the shadow of the Wall: young students and artists who had moved to Berlin from West Germany had not left any family and friends

on the other side of the Wall. Hence West Berlin became a niche for drop-outs, a place where people experimented with new life-styles and shaped a different future for themselves. Almost all the important alternative impulses that eventually spread throughout the whole of West Germany came from Berlin: student revolts and extra-parliamentary opposition, the Green Party, squatters and punks. West Germany – and the rest of the world, too – was soon forgotten by the Berliners.

West Berlin imagined itself to be the hub of the universe – after all, the world was watching, even if the intervals were becoming longer and longer. At the same time, West Berlin was becoming more and more provincial. Building speculators and narrow-minded politicians dominated city life, scandals and affairs became the order of the day.

Above: Backyard tranquility in a cement jungle. Right: A typical Berliner.

Meanwhile, on the other side of the Wall, a completely different city was evolving. East Berlin was artificially redesigned and became the representative "capital of the GDR", in a vacuum, so to speak. In the East, the other part of the city was simply disregarded. West Berlin – or Berlin (West) as GDR jargon had it – only existed on the subway charts and city maps as a large, blank area. The other part of the city beyond the Wall was no-man's-land for the GDR.

Instead, Unter den Linden, an avenue rich in tradition, was converted into a parade ground for cheering squadrons of workers. Alexanderplatz with its new high-rises from the 60s was to become the center of the peaceful, socialist Republic.

But East Berlin's outlying areas told a different story. The old, 19th century tenement blocks fell into disrepair, the infrastructure remained on the level it was during the 50s – East Berlin was a sad grey drabness smelling of brown coal. The pompous self-display of the GDR regime was staged one last time in 1987 during the city's 750-year celebrations. Two years later, everything was a shambles, as policemen marched against the rebellious "we-are-the-people" demonstration on Unter den Linden.

The peaceful GDR revolution triumphed on November 9, 1989, when the border crossing at Bornholmer Straße was opened. That night, and during the following nights, people danced exuberantly on the broad Wall in front of the Brandenburg Gate, broke through the Wall at various points and celebrated wild parties on the streets. Once again, the world was watching Berlin.

During the two years after the Wall fell, Berlin became the testing ground for Germany's reunification. Something was happening to Germany – and at first the change passed virtually unnoticed as the geographical distance between Bonn and Frankfurt/Oder was too great. The ones

who were the first to feel it – once again – were the Berliners. The transports of delight of the autumn of 1989 did not last long. After a short period of getting to know one another, the Berliners in the West and in the East pulled back to their own neighbourhoods in rapidly growing disillusion. The reunification celebrations in October 1990 were the last joyful act in this unified and free city. Since then, much has changed in Berlin.

Coarse Charm: Berlin Mentality

Berlin and the Berliners have become the victims of their own clichés: their lippiness and bellicosity, Berlin nights and Kreuzberg, Laubenpieper and islanders, cheekiness and provincialism. The list could be extended for as long as you like; people come to Berlin expecting a city that will confirm all of their preconceived notions.

These people then stroll along the Ku'-damm and are in for a surprise. They come across the cheeky busdriver and the square but affable Laubenpieper, the man with the warm Berlin heart, and the active old lady who may well have been one of the women who cleared away the rubble after the war (the legendary *Trümmerfrauen*).

However, in recent years, this cliché has turned stale. Only since the reunification has Berlin's charm revived, mainly thanks to the East Berliners. The neighbourhoods of East Berlin had managed to maintain the kind of working-class and petty bourgeois culture as well as the Berlin lippiness and the typical wit of the metropolitan which is no longer found in West Berlin. Drinking one's *Molle* mit *Korn* (beer and a shot of spirits) and taking your family to the country or to the city swimming pools on Sundays is a habit that has not changed in a hundred years. A genuine dialect can be heard on Berlin's streets once again, quite different from the ostentatious, phony dialect with which people who moved to Berlin would like to cover up the fact that they aren't real Berliners.

Although lippiness is once again typical of Berlin, it has also become more international. In the way that Berliners have for hundreds of years been knocking together their own dialect from the languages of their immigrants, so they accept today the languages now established in everyday life, particularly Turkish and Polish.

Perhaps the Berlin mentality is changing back to what it used to be. Crude yet spirited, cheeky and rebellious, Berliners are again behaving the way they did before the war. This is also a result of reunification; the new fast pace of everyday life in a metropolis is so overwhelming that people instinctively use coarser manners to protect themselves. Today, as one hundred years ago, Berlin lippiness is a kind of protection which all too often hides a genuine friendliness. The nature of the Berliner differs drastically from the reservedness of the northern Germans, the loud heartiness of the inhabitants of the Rhineland or the cosy conviviality of the Bavarians.

Berliners are unpredictable. Perhaps that is why Goethe referred to them as an "audacious race" and Berlin a place where "you have to have hair on your teeth and occasionally be a bit coarse to keep your head above water."

The visitor to Berlin has to come to a decision: One either loves Berlin or hates it. Berlin keeps a firm grip on its visitors and citizens, as life in the city is too fast-paced and the intensity of urban life too overwhelming.

If the visitor revisits this city on the Spree, he may notice that each time he goes there, the welcome will be a bit different. Sometimes his stay will be delightful, the next time he may feel repelled by the city and its people, probably because Berlin is such a chaotic and contradictory place.

Right: The futuristic skyline of the Alexanderplatz, a traditional social hub of Berlin.

The fact that people totally disagree about Berlin may be its greatest forte. As long as a city is provocative, it is also interesting and will keep the visitor spellbound.

The Future is Already Waiting

Great things are in store for Berlin: If you take a trip to Berlin in the 90s, you will immediately notice the large numbers of construction cranes on the horizon. During the course of its history, the city has often been rebuilt – in both senses of the word. But the construction boom that Berlin is presently experiencing is the greatest one to date. By the year 2000, almost fifty billion Deutschmarks will be spent on construction in the new metropolis, and whole new districts and centers are being created on the drawing board.

The most celebrated construction site is the historical Potsdamer Platz, where Mercedes Benz and Sony are now erecting huge office-cities. The new government and parliamentary buildings are planned to be built around the Reichstag in the Tiergarten area. Several corporations are erecting department stores and service centers on Friedrichstrasse, once the capital's most prestigious shopping street. It is hoped that in a few years time Friedrichstrasse will regain its full glory as Berlin's Fifth Avenue. Around the Alexanderplatz, the socialist brutalist architecture is now being torn down and replaced by new, elegant high-rises. All in all, the area being demolished and rebuilt is as large as the downtown area of Munich.

Simultaneously, the city is experiencing a difficult transitional period: the Cold War had given it a special status, which it has now lost. When the Allied troops and the Red Army left East Berlin in 1994, the post-war period found its symbolic end in Berlin. Yet the West Berliners confess that they miss the Al-

lied troops. In spite of sporadic tensions arising over the years, the Berliners had gradually learned to hold "their" Allies in high esteem.

Since then, Berlin has become even more "normal", which is something particularly visitors notice – the change doesn't seem quite so marked to the Berliners. Maybe they don't really want to know. It is more than obvious that Berlin lost some of its special flair and status when it started to resemble the majority of other German cities.

The planned merger of Berlin and Brandenburg into one large state will probably completely redefine the character and role of the city: as yet, many Berliners still only have a vague perception of their immediate surroundings.

Nevertheless, Berlin is still larger, more diverse, more aggressive and more Eastern than most cities in Germany and central Europe.

Since the fall of the Berlin Wall in 1989, the city and its 3.5 million inhabitants has attracted even more immigrants from Germany and elsewhere. It's getting crowded in Berlin. Life on the Spree is becoming more colorful, diverse and even more cosmopolitan, but at the same time it is getting more aggressive and noisier.

The crime rate in the city has stayed almost the same since the beginning of the 90s, yet most people feel increasingly unsafe and threatened in subways and undergrounds or out on the streets at night. The social problems in Berlin have undoubtedly intensified: the city is broke, yet it is faced with an army of unemployed people, especially in East Berlin, where tourists will see instances of extreme poverty, even on the prestigious Ku'damm.

Maybe these are all the first harbingers for the metropolization of a major city: in the coming years, Berlin may outgrow its role as the "little sister" to the world cities of New York, London and Paris. Berlin is still sustaining itself on its historical myth, and yet it is on its way to becoming a European metropolis.

TWO VILLAGES ON THE SPREE

The present-day area of Berlin had already been settled by various Slavic tribes beginning in the 6th century A.D. They came in from the east during the era of the great migrations, and gradually reclaimed the swampy, remote forest regions along the rivers. In the area of present-day Berlin the Heveller, named after the river Havel, had constructed a fortress at Spandau, and the Sprewaner, named after the river Spree, a castle on the present Köpenicker Schlossinsel, or Castle Island.

Around 1100 increasing amounts of land throughout Germany began to be cleared and settled, and German princes also attempted to expand into the territories east of the Elbe River. The Ascanian Prince Alfred the Bear subjugated the Slavs in a single campaign, and, in 1137, took their most important fortress, the Brennabor at the river Havel, making it into his residence. He and his successors settled their dominion in a planned manner and extended it as far as the Oder River: The March of Brandenburg thus came into being. Then, sometime during the first half of the 13th century, the towns of Berlin and Cölln were founded between Spandau and Köpenick.

They were located on a narrow, shallow place on the Spree, ideally suited for a ford and a harbor. There were no articles of incorporation for either of the cities. The name Cölln first appeared in 1237 on a document referring to a witness, a priest named Symeon of Cölln. Incidentally, this document provided the basis for the celebration of the city's 750th anniversary, even though the name Berlin isn't mentioned at all. That name first appeared in a document from 1244. Berlin officially became a city in 1251; Cölln was so designated ten years later.

Left: Elector Joachim II (1535-1571), oil painting by Lucas Cranach, about 1551.

Just where the name Berlin originated is unknown. Possibly it is a compound of the Slavic words *bar* (pine forest) and *rolina* (farmland). But another theory suggests that settlers brought the name with them from the west.

Soon, Berlin and Cölln became economic centers, in that they stood on the intersection of the important trade routes linking Frankfurt on the Oder to the west, and the route from the Baltic coast going south. Both towns served as shipping points for lumber and rye from the March, fish from the north, pelts from Russia and increasingly precious spices.

The Ascanians accelerated economic development by granting merchants exemptions from duties and giving Berlin the right to its own mint, supreme jurisdiction within its boundaries, as well as the depot laws which decreed that traders who were travelling through should sell a portion of their wares in Berlin.

Civic Freedom and Royal Seat

In doing so, the Ascanians undertook nothing against the interests of the city's patricians who generally came from merchant families, and dominated the Magistrate (the municipal authority). During the 14th century, the roughly 8000 residents of the twin city could, despite great obstacles, proclaim their dominant position in the March of Brandenburg. In 1307 Berlin and Cölln merged, even building a third city hall on the Lange Brücke (Long Bridge) which connected the two cities over the Spree. Nonetheless, the twin city must have seemed rather modest when compared to the episcopate cities on the Rhine.

Berlin was almost completely levelled by fire twice during this period, and the Black Plague that ravaged Europe also paid a lethal visit. Nevertheless, in spite of these calamities, the city was able to survive relatively intact the feuds raging between the noble houses in the March of

21

Brandenburg after the passing of the last Ascanian prince in 1319. At the beginning of the 15th century, the battles in Brandenburg became increasingly fierce. Of course, the land was elevated to an electorate in 1356, but robber barons invaded and plundered Brandenburg, and they did overlook Berlin either. The militia was defeated and the city occupied. In 1412 King Sigismund sent his closest advisor, Burgrave Friedrich von Hohenzollern of Nürnberg, to Brandenburg with the task of pacifying the rebellious noble families. Friedrich defeated the robber barons, liberated Berlin in 1414 and was named margrave and elector for his efforts. His rule signalled the beginning of the 500-year-long ties between Berlin and the Hohenzollerns, under whom the city lost many rights. His successor, Friedrich II, used internal conflicts among the citizenry as a pretext for subjugating the city's proud and independent patricians:

Above: The Great Elector Friedrich Wilhelm welcoming the French Huguenots to Berlin.

The Magistrate was stripped of power; old rights of the city abrogated, goods and estates seized. The Berliners did not put up with the situation for very long. In the famed *Berliner Unwillen* (indignation) of 1448, they decided to rise up against the elector. However, their militia was again defeated and the city had to publicly declare its vassalage. The electoral soldiery thereby put an end to all attempts at autonomy on the part of the citizenry. The elector also had his position of power vividly portrayed in a new seal for the city of Berlin: Naturally it showed the Berlin bear, however the Hohenzollern eagle was perched in a victorious pose on its back.

Berlin was then systematically expanded into a royal seat: Friedrich I had already started with the construction of a castle in 1443, which his successors constantly remodelled. The Hohenzollerns had hunting lodges built in Grunewald and Köpenick and recruited court officers from their homelands Franconia, Swabia and Thuringia. The assemblies of the

March also took place in Berlin starting in the mid-15th century.

By 1550, the population had grown to about 12,000, and the luxury of the royal court also made its way into the city. The intellectual climate was enlivened by the first schools, printing presses and a newspaper. Indeed, in the course of the 16th century the Berliners managed to regain some of their erstwhile municipal rights, in particular their own jurisdiction, since the electors needed money and sold many rights back to the city.

The Reformation swept through Berlin more peacefully than elsewhere. In 1539 Elector Joachim II converted to Lutheranism, albeit under pressure from the estates of the March. The Plague raged in Berlin several times during this period, and the Thirty Years' War (1618-1648) also exacted its tribute. Because the local rulers could not quite decide which side they were on, Protestant or Catholic, Swedish troups and imperial armies repeatedly invested Brandenburg. The outlying areas of Berlin suffered as a result, half of the population fled and gradually the city fell into decay.

The Great Elector and the Huguenots

Elector Friedrich Wilhelm acceeded to the throne in 1640 at the age of 21. During his rule he attempted in particular to strengthen the economic power of the province and extend its influence. The weakened Brandenburg of the day consisted of the March as well as regions in Westphalia and the Duchy of Prussia in present-day East Prussia. In this disjointed land, the Great Elector (so named after his 1675 victory over the Swedes at Fehrbellin) established a centralist administration. He curtailed the rights of the landed estates and the cities. He installed a military governor in Berlin and Cölln in 1658, who, as highest-ranking officer of the electorate in the twin city, took over many municipal duties besides

police power. Friedrich invigorated construction activity with tax reductions and a new building code. For his officers he even founded two new, independent cities: Friedrichswerder to the southeast of Berlin and later Dorotheenstadt. These plans were certainly quite expensive, so that in 1667 he had to introduce a general excise tax, the *Akzise*. In addition Berliners were forced to take on construction tasks at the new fortifications which had been laid in a star-shaped form around the city. The economies in these new cities flourished, however. The first manufacturing plants based on the French example were established and crafts became increasingly specialized.

In 1669 the Baltic and North Seas were connected with each other via a new canal between the Spree and Oder rivers: The traffic of goods between the coastal cities and wealthy Silesia could thus also be carried out via Berlin.

The Great Elector also understood how the economic upswing could be given an additional stimulus with a skillfully thought-out immigration policy. Starting in 1671 he admitted wealthy Jewish families from Vienna into the March (who could, however, only practice their religion under certain conditions), and, following the famed Edict of Potsdam (1685), primarily Huguenots. 20,000 of these French Protestants fled from their Catholic homeland to Brandenburg; 6000 settled in the Berlin area, particularly in the two new cities. The Huguenots formed an independent society, but their culture, language and especially their skills as craftsmen influenced the life of Berlin. You can still find traces of the Huguenots today. Some examples are the French Cathedral and the French *Gymnasium* in Berlin (1689), which is the oldest extant school.

Friedrich also directly supported the arts and sciences. His collection of paintings created the basic stock for Berlin's future museums, and he established the

first public library, which in 1686 already included some 20,000 volumes. By the time of his death in 1688, he had created four blossoming cities on the Spree, of which Berlin alone numbered 20,000 inhabitants. His wise policies put Berlin on the road to becoming the capital city.

The successor to the Great Elector, Friedrich III, continued in the same vein as his predecessor. In 1701 he elevated himself to the rank of king and ascended the Prussian throne as Friedrich I.

In 1709 he consolidated the four cities of Berlin, Cölln, Friedrichswerder and Dorotheenstadt into the greater municipality of Berlin; in so doing he cleverly succeeded in setting limits on the old civic rights by giving the larger city a new, restrictive municipal constitution. He had the old city castle beautified, bringing the most important master builders of his time to the Spree: Andreas

Above: Frederick the Great, quintessence of the enlightened despot. Right: The Tea-house in the Sanssouci complex.

Schlüter, Arnold Neuring and Eosander von Göthes, who all shaped the new appearance of the city with their Baroque structures. The cultural life also changed, becoming more that of a capital city. In 1694 the Academy of Arts was founded and later the Academy of Sciences, whose first president was the philosopher Wilhelm Leibniz. When Friedrich I died in 1713, he left behind a city with upward aspirations, a population of 60,000 and numerous magnificent buildings. However, the price for this urban development was a gigantic mountain of debt.

Berlin as the Center of Prussiandom

The new king, Friedrich Wilhelm I, introduced a strict and frugal rule to the court. Court officials were reduced in number, servants released from their duties, officers' salaries cut. Where once the court had shaped the face of the city and its economy, it was now require-ments of the army for which the city lived and produced. Friedrich wasn't named

24

the "soldier king" for nothing. He enlarged the Prussian army from 40,000 to over 80,000 men, the fourth most powerful military force in all of Europe. Berlin soon took on the appearance of one big military camp: Many soldiers were housed in private quarters, the pleasure gardens and the Tempelhofer Feld were turned into exercise grounds.

In 1740 Friedrich II ascended the throne. Old Fritz, as he came to be called, was a split personality: On the one hand he was a flute-playing king who received Voltaire in Sanssoucci, a modern monarch under whom the Enlightenment gleamed in Berlin with such personalities as Friedrich Nicolai, Moses Mendelssohn and Lessing. He was the kindly and humane leader who abolished torture and laid the first stones for the founding of a constitutional state, the art-lover of refined tastes whose architect Wenzeslaus von Knobelsdorff improved Unter den Linden to a boulevard with such magnificent buildings as the Opera and St. Hedwigs Cathedral. However, Friedrich had another, darker side. He was also the absolutist monarch, who, with high import duties and systematic state support, geared up the Prussian economy for war. With its new weaving mills, Berlin became the city with the largest German textile production. However, this policy served only the military because Friedrich proved to be a cold-blooded power politician who wanted to propel his country into the circle of Europes' great powers at all costs. To this purpose, he put his subjects through a series of grievous wars which almost ruined the country. When Friedrich II died in 1786, Berlin was nevertheless still the center of Prussia and, with its 150,000 residents, could claim membership in the club of the great cities of Europe.

The next decades, though, brought about the collapse of Old Fritz' state. The French Revolution caused the downfall not only of monarchies, but also of the very idea of an absolutist state.

Ultimately Prussia succumbed to the attack of Napoleonic troops. In 1806 the

25

Grande Armée staged a triumphal march right through the Brandenburg Gate and occupied Berlin. The French reorganized the city administration and even set up the forerunner of a city parliament. These ideas were picked up by Prussian reformers such as Baron vom Stein in 1809 after the French had withdrawn. With his legislation the interests of the state and the city were separated by the institution of Berlin's own assembly of councils. This resulted directly in the first mayoral elections of 1809.

The cultural life of the city gained noteworthy lustre, side-by-side with those new political and civic structures. In 1810 the Friedrich Wilhelm University was founded by Wilhelm von Humboldt. Its registration soon numbered 2000 students, making it, at the time, the largest in Germany. Berlin attracted the greatest minds of the era, such men as Alexander von Humboldt, Hufeland, Hegel, Schleier-

macher and Neander. This development continued into the following decades, when writers such as Heinrich Heine, E.T.A. Hoffmann or Bettina von Arnim, the painter Adolph Menzel and philosophers such as Leopold von Ranke or Johann Gottlieb Fichte flocked to Berlin. In the field of architecture it was Karl Friedrich Schinkel who, beginning in 1815, finally turned Unter den Linden into a boulevard worthy of a capital.

The citizenry entirely devoted itself to the arts in the years following the Wars of Liberation; cafés, operas and concert attendance epitomized the spirit of the period. And brilliant, intellectual conversation animated the salons of Rahel Varnhagen and Henriette Herz. However, a retreat into culture was also the resigned answer of the citizenry to its unfullfilled political hopes. One certainly cannot speak of enlightened and liberal politics in Prussia during this period.

As the Restoration increased its grip, the reformers of yesterday became the persecuted of today.

Above: Men, women and children on the barricades in 1848, fighting for civil rights.

1848: The Failed Revolution

When the new king of Prussia ascended the throne in 1840, a great hope for political reform, swept through the expectant society. His liberal gestures were only of short duration – soon the land was being governed by the same tyrannical Prussian regime which suppressed each and every political activity of the citizens and took no note of the interests of most classes. Dissatisfaction among the people became greater, especially in Berlin, where many associations were formed allegedly to cultivate sports or the intellect, but in truth as a way to solidify a political opposition. And, as discontent festered, social tensions also increased. The 1844 rebellion of weavers in Silesia also reached Berlin, where large sections of the populace also lived in great poverty, especially in the city's outskirts. In 1847 the city had to devote 40 percent of its expenditures to relief for the poor. Yet the urgent social problems continued to grow unabated, a fact which was then made public in newspapers and books as well. In the same year the *Kartoffelrevolution* (Potato Revolution) took place: After a bad harvest had pushed up prices, enraged Berliners stormed the market stalls.

One year later, influenced by the new revolution that was shaking France, the citizens, craftsmen and workers of Berlin plucked up their courage. They wanted to negotiate with the king about changes in the constitution, but the Prussian crown showed no inclination whatsoever to waste its breath discussing polital matters with its people. A demonstration before the Brandenburg Gate resulted in the first casualties when the police advanced on the crowd. The military marched into the city in order to re-establish law and order. Once again, on March 18, 1848, a large demonstration took place, at which the freedoms of assembly, press and speech were demanded as well as a pull-out of the military from the city. As these demands were called out, troops advanced against the crowd and opened fire. The demonstrators set up barricades, and in turn attacked the soldiers. The battle lasted almost a full day, until the king called on the citizenry for peace in a proclamation beginning: "To my dear Berliners." As a symbol of his good faith he had the military withdraw and promised reforms. How heavy the pressure must have been on the monarch became readily apparent when he paid his last respects to the 183 people who had been shot, and whose coffins were laid out in state on the Gendarmenmarkt.

Friedrich Wilhelm actually kept his promises, guaranteeing the freedoms of assembly and press – even the uneven voting system was reformed, giving the less fortunate more power for their ballot. The Berliners revelled in the new freedoms. Newspapers flooded the city, and people openly discussed politics in the cafés; in the salons political associations were formed, the forerunners of the future parties. However, the experiment of the first German Parliament in Frankfurt fell apart in May 1848. Nor could the Prussian National Assembly dominated as it was by conservative merchants and industrialists come to any sort of agreement on a new constitution.

In December 1848 Friedrich Wilhelm brought the experiment to an abrupt end by forcing the Prussian National Assembly to adopt a new constitution which contained liberal elements – which his successor later rescinded. Furthermore, this second version reintroduced the tax-based voting system, which now applied to Berlin's Municipal Parliament as well: Only 5 percent of the roughly 430,000 inhabitants were thus allowed to cast their ballots. Police President von Hinckeldey suppressed the liberal opposition with rigorous censorship of the press and police terror. The reactionaries had claimed victory in Berlin.

THE SPLENDOR AND MISERY OF A WORLD CITY

Beginning in the mid-19th century, Berlin grew to become Europe's largest center of industry. No other city in Germany or Europe underwent such a headlong and turbulent industrial development. The political and social results were also more blatant here than anywhere else. Engineering and metal working especially contributed to the city's economic upswing. The factories required an ample supply of workers; as a result the population increased at first to 450,000 (1860), then to 1 million (1877) and ultimately to 2 million (1905).

However, the shadow side of this growth loomed ever larger. The workers had to toil up to 16 hours a day, frequently under inhumane conditions; the wages were only enough for survival when all members of the family worked, and child labor was no rarity those days.

The rapid population growth posed immense problems to the city, since it had to build affordable housing as quickly as possible. Between 1860 and 1870 the total number of residences doubled to 166,100. On the outskirts of Berlin entire quarters such as Moabit, Wedding or sections of Schöneberg popped up out of the ground as if by magic. Land speculators and contractors became wealthy by throwing up cheap housing complexes and leasing them at excessive prices. Berlin became the city of rental barracks, in which the families of workers often had to live in one room. On top of that, most of the apartments were very dark due to their small interior courtyards, and they often lacked sanitary facilities.

After its victory over Austria in the Austro-Prussian War (1866), Prussia had put the second great German power out of the running. In the same year the North

Left: A working class family in a Berlin tenement at the end of the 19th century.

German states also consolidated into the North German Confederation, which was dominated by Prussia. The chancellor was Otto von Bismarck, whose goal, however, was the unification of all German states – a wish which was to be fulfilled in 1870/71. The German states – again under Prussian command – achieved a victory over France in the brief but fierce war. This most significant of 19th-century European wars of unification forced the German states together and lead directly to the founding of the German Empire. In the Hall of Mirrors in Versailles, on January 18, 1871, King Wilhelm I, King of Prussia, was proclaimed Kaiser of Germany.

The Berliners themselves remained quiet on receiving the news of German unification. The prospect of their city becoming the capital of Germany didn't spark great euphoria. Furthermore, Berlin's hospitals and sick bays were full of Prussia's wounded; the economy of the city had also been crippled by the rapid conversion to and from war production.

As the capital of the Reich, Berlin attracted emissaries not only from the other German states, but also from foreign countries who constructed their embassies here. In addition, political parties established their central offices in Berlin. Social democracy, with a major following in Berlin, was especially successful and important for the city. One of the main reasons for the easy propagation of Socialist ideas was the poor living conditions of the city's proletariat. Despite Bismarcks *Sozialistengesetze* (Socialist Laws) which banned the Social Democrats, the party continued to enjoy great popularity in Berlin. Its leaders such as August Bebel and Karl Liebknecht were among the most important politicians of the Reich. Bismarck was also unable to fully coopt the proletariat with his – for those days – modern social laws. Conditions in the poorer quarters of Berlin were too miserable for this. In sharp con-

trast to the rest of the Reich, support for the Social Democratic Party (SPD) among Berliners persisted. In 1890 the party received more than half of all the ballots in Berlin, and after 1893 five of the city's six representatives in the Reichstag (the Parliament) were Social Democrats.

An economic renascence also coincided with the founding of the German Reich, which created a gigantic unified economic region with millions of consumers. Germany experienced a tremendous economic boom which was further enhanced by five billion francs in war reparations exacted from the French. In the midst of this upturn, as the new capital, Berlin profited most heavily from these founding years. Banks, insurance firms and joint-stock companies moved to the Spree or were founded in Berlin – in 1872 alone some 250 firms, 40 of which were in the construction business.

Above: Prussia's pomp and glory – Emperor Wilhelm I at a parade in Berlin.

In the second half of the 19th century the city underwent an increasingly rapid industrialization. Appearing alongside the traditional branches of industry such as engineering and the processing of textiles were new sectors such as electrical engineering and the chemical industry. Siemens & Halske introduced the first electrically-powered locomotive in 1879; the AEG (Allgemeine Elektrizitäts-Gesellschaft) was founded; chemical giants like Schering took their places beside older companies such as Borsig.

The industrial upswing was accompanied by correspondingly rapid, and not altogether easy, development of the city. Since the middle of the century Berlin had become more self-assured with regard to the Prussian state. Berlin's pride manifested itself in the new representative Rotes Rathaus, the Red Town Hall (thus named after the color of its bricks), which was constructed from 1861 to 1869 near Alexanderplatz.

Since Berlin had become the capital, many things also improved for its citizenry.

A sewer network (still functioning today) was finally installed, as well as new water works and, in 1885, the first electrical power plant went into operation. The city now added the construction of roads and street cleaning to its tasks, concerned itself with laying out parks and gardens, and arranged for Berlin's better provisioning with the building of a new market and a central livestock yard and slaughterhouse. In 1873, the first municipal hospital was opened in Friedrichshain.

Berlin's transportation system changed along which the growth and modernization of the city. Increasingly, the old horse-drawn omnibus disappeared; by 1902 all routes had been electrified. By 1877 the ring railway (*Ringbahn*) had already been put into service. It connected the various main railroad stations with each other. At first the carriages were pulled by steam locomotives, later electric ones. And, starting in 1905, the first automobiles appeared in the streets; in 1913 the first German *Autobahn,* the AVUS, was constructed through the Grunewald district.

Berlin and the Wilhelminian Era

During the period Berlin developed into a world-class metropolis, Germany was first ruled by Kaiser Wilhelm I; in 1888 – the so-called "year of the three Kaisers" – Friedrich III ruled for 99 days. He was succeeded by the man who was to be Germany's last Kaiser, Wilhelm II (1859-1941), and whose name left its stamp on an entire epoch.

The young, energetic Kaiser, whose first act was to fire Chancellor Bismarck, had himself and the dynasty celebrated with parades and marches before the Stadtschloss (City Castle). The Berlin of this epoch consisted of plucky officers with spiked helmets who displayed their militarism for all to see and of timorous philistines of the sort described by the chronicler of the times, Heinrich Mann,

in his 1918 novel *Der Untertan* (*The Subject*). There was, however, also another side to Berlin with artists both real and fake, corrupt politicians, money-hungry financiers of dubious repute, and social climbers whom Heinrich Mann parodied in his 1900 novel *Im Schlaraffenland* (*In Never-Never-Land*).

The literary world of Berlin attracted many talents, among them Theodor Fontane (1862-1914) and Gerhart Hauptmann (1862-1946). In painting, Berlin artists also forged new paths: In the *Brücke* (Bridge) movement expressionist artists such as Emil Nolde, Ernst Ludwig Kirchner and others joined forces. The leading exponents of the Secession, Max Liebermann (1847-1935) and Walter Leistikow worked in Berlin. Max Reinhardt produced numerous works on the city's stages. The Philharmonic Orchestra was founded in 1882; new theaters and opera houses opened. Scientists such as Max Planck (1858-1947), Albert Einstein (1879-1955), Fritz Haber (1868-1934) and Robert Koch (1843-1910) – many of them Nobel Prize winners – taught at Berlin's universities.

Berlin seemed to have a great future ahead of it. However, with his aggressive foreign policy and tremendous arms build-up Wilhelm II brought the German Empire into ever sharper conflict with the other great powers of Europe. With their equally aggressive arms build-up, France, England and Russia did their share to make Germany feel hemmed in. A chain reaction lead to the outbreak of World War One in August 1914.

Kaiser Wilhelm II called out to the jubilant Berliners in front of the Stadtschloss: "I no longer know any parties, I know only Germans." However, belief in a quick victory soon fell apart and German patriotism began to waver as the initial successes of the Great War gave way to the muck and the mire. Besides the enormous blood toll, fighting a slow-moving, material-intensive war on two fronts

against a much larger enemy exhausted the country's moral and finances. The winter of 1917 was the hardest the Berliners had ever seen. Everything was rationed: An adult received only 70 grams of meat and 20 grams of butter per week!

In April 1917, 300,000 workers at Berlin's armaments plants went on strike; in August the populace plundered the weekly markets; the victory of the Russian Revolution helped to mobilize the proletariat. As Germany's military situation became increasingly hopeless the seamen of the German fleet mutinied in November 1918, thus precipitating the events. On November 9, Kaiser Wilhelm II had to abdicate, workers and soldiers took up arms and councils were formed. Germany and Berlin looked to the Reichstag, but its members were unable to act until, on the same day, the Social Democrat Philipp Scheidemann proclaimed the

Above: Holding an important position during the Spartacus Rebellion in January 1919. Right: Bustling city life on Friedrichstrasse.

German Republic in the Reichstag. At the same time, the Spartacist leader Karl Liebknecht proclaimed a Socialist Republic from the City Castle.

The Twenties: Days of Gold and Chaos

The political confusion in the new Republic lasted until late March 1920. Up until then the Communists, Social Democrats and reactionaries struggled for power in the country. In January 1919, the so-called Spartacus Rebellion broke out in Berlin's newspaper district on Kochstrasse and Friedrichstrasse. It suffered a bloody defeat at the hands of troops loyal to the government.

In the process, two of the most important ringleaders, Karl Liebknecht and Rosa Luxemburg, were shot by soldiers of the Freikorps, a militia made up of World War I veterans, with reactionary leanings. The 1919 elections to the National Assembly had turned out a solid majority for the democratically oriented

parties but in March of the same year it became apparent how unstable the new order was. Units of the Imperial Army under a quite unknown officer by the name of Kapp carried out a putsch and occupied Berlin. The rest of the Imperial Army refused to obey the government and did nothing to stop the rebellion. It was a strike by Berlin workers that ultimately brought an end to Kapp's political ambitions.

The first years of the Weimar Republic continued to be tumultuous. On June 24, 1922, Foreign Minister Walter Rathenau (1868-1922) was shot on the street by assassins from the extreme right wing. This attack was the climax in a wave of 376 political murders which shook the Republic from 1918 to 1922. By the way, 354 of these murders were committed by right-wing extremists; most of the perpetrators were never convicted.

On November 9th, 1923, a group of arch-reactionary politicians and army officers around the still obscure Adolf Hitler attempted a putsch in Munich. This time he could be headed off, sentenced and sent to prison.

The economic situation reflected the political disorder: Germany had to come to grips with millions of soldiers returning from the fronts, an exhausted industry that had been adapted for war production and heavy reparations. The German economy stumbled from one crisis to the next. In 1923 the galloping inflation hit its peak, with the U.S. dollar costing 170,000 reichsmark (July), then 12 million (August) and finally 12 billion (October), until ultimately a new currency, the *Rentenmark*, was introduced.

After the new currency was put into circulation the economy slowly began to recover and the unemployment rate dropped. Berlin was ready for a new start. A 1920 urban reform had drastically increased the size of the city. Berlin and seven additional cities in the vicinity, almost 60 villages and 27 farming communities were consolidated into a single, gigantic administrative district called Greater Berlin. At this point 3.8 million people lived here; only ten years later the population crossed the 4 million mark.

The face of the metropolis was transformed yet again. As ever the housing complexes remained the dominant feature. On the Alexanderplatz and Potsdamer Platz modern office high-rises in the lucid Bauhaus style were erected. In the outlying districts model residential complexes were built following the same principles, an example being the renowned *Hufeisensiedlung* (Horse-Shoe settlement) in Britz (1925-1927). The transportation network in the city was finally brought up to world-class level. Ernst Reuter, then responsible for the city's transportation, rapidly extended the subway system (U-Bahn) and managed the amalgamation of all the transportation firms into the joint-stock *Berliner Verkehrs-Aktiengesellschaft*, the BVG, which, in 1928, united all of Berlin's means of transportation under one roof. During these days Berlin became the "little sister" of the great metropolises of Paris, London and New York. In many aspects Berlin even came to set examples for these cities.

These few years between 1918 and 1933 gave rise to the myth of Berlin, identifying the city with an entire epoch, referred to as the "Golden Twenties." Berlin's unique reputation was justified in many ways. But alongside its distinguished rank as a nucleus of culture, technology and the sciences, there was the suffering of the thousands forced to exist in conditions of abject poverty, the constant yo-yoing of daily politics and the equally unstable economy. Berlin was marked with blatantly clashing social contrasts. All the glamor and misery of an epoch came together here. Perhaps it was these contrasts combined with an aggressive, hectic atmosphere which attracted artists and literary figures.

Right: Monetary inflation and loose living – scenes from the Golden Twenties.

They met together in Berlin's countless cafés and restaurants, the most famous of which was the gloomy Romanisches Café on Auguste-Viktoria-Platz where the Europa-Center stands today. There were "swimmer" and "non-swimmer" sections (so to speak) for the regular guests and the curious upstarts wishing to begin their careers here. In fact, such literary figures as Arnold Zweig, Bert Brecht, Walter Benjamin, Leonhard Frank, Wolfgang Koeppen, Klaus and Erika Mann, Kurt Tucholsky, Joachim Ringelnatz and Erich Kästner drank their coffee in the Romanisches Café. Journalists like Carl von Ossietzky, Herbert Ihering and Alfred Kerr sometimes wrote their critiques and articles there. With the nearly 150 newspapers and countless magazines which were being published in Berlin the city became the center of the German press.

Just as in literature and political journalism, all directions of the visual arts were also represented in Berlin. Some of them, such as the anarchistic Dadaism and the austere Futurism, first unfurled to their full impact in the city. Such painters and sculptors as Karl Hofer, Max Beckmann, Ernst Barlach, Georg Kolbe, Fritz Klimsch and George Grosz found their motifs here. Like no other artist, Grosz captured the zenith and decline of the twenties with his Berlin collages.

Berlin's music scene was very much that of a world-city as well: Wilhelm Furtwängler, Bruno Walter and Otto Klemperer directed the Berlin Orchestra; Erwin Piscator and Leopold Jessner directed their great theater successes here. Berlin was also the capital of German film. The UFA built Europe's largest film studios in Babelsberg. UFA's film stars resided there and in Potsdam, but they took their entertainment in Berlin. Heinrich George, Elisabeth Bergner, Fritz Kortner, Werner Krauss and many others stood before the camera here. Future Hollywood, Greta Garbo, Marlene Dietrich

and Peter Lorre, among others, also began their careers in Berlin. Political cabarets and large-scale variety shows were other new developments. The two largest houses, the Wintergarten and the Scala, constantly tried to out-do each other with their rather daring revues. The Berlin of the Weimar Republic knew no closing hours, no censors, no stultifying morality laws. As a result the city quickly acquired a reputation as a den of iniquity where everything was allowed. However, the shrill and colorful hedonism and craze for amusement of the period began to seem more and more like a dance on a volcano because the political situation was growing more threatening.

Berlin and National Socialism

After 1926 the German economy gradually weakened. In the following years increasing numbers of firms went bankrupt resulting in mass firings. In October 1929 the western industrialized nations were shaken by the crash of the New

York stock exchange. Black Friday was the final warning signal of the approaching crisis.

The collapse of the financial system ultimately had its nefarious effect on the German economy. Even major Berlin firms like the Borsig plants released all of their employees. After a hard winter, in February 1930, there were 450,000 unemployed in Berlin; in May the first riots took place. Thirty people died.

The state unemployment benefits were too low to prevent a political radicalization of the masses. In the Rotes Rathaus and the Reichstag the elections of that year produced no solid majorities, while the first street-fighting occured between Nazis and Communists. The number of unemployed rose to 600,000 by 1932. A full 25 percent of all Berliners were then living on welfare.

In the same year the National Socialists (NSDAP) reaped its best results to date in the elections on July 31: 37.4 percent of eligible voters cast their ballots for the "brown" party (only 28.6 percent

35

in Berlin). Thus the NSDAP became the strongest party, and after the Reichstag was again dissolved and new elections held – with two further governments miscarrying – President Hindenburg named Adolf Hitler the new Chancellor on January 30th, 1933.

On the evening of that same day the SA, Hitler's paramilitary organization known as the brown shirts, marched in a torchlight procession through the Brandenburg Gate, passing before Hitler, who was standing at a window of the Chancellery. Max Liebermann, the Jewish painter and president of the Prussian Academy of the Arts, lived nearby and on this occasion is supposed to have said: "*Ich kann gar nicht so viel fressen, wie ich kotzen möchte.*" (I can't eat nearly as much as I would like to vomit). Several days later the torchlight parades were repeatedly staged for the cameras of the weekly film news *Wochenschau*. The Nazis used ter-

ror to increase pressure on the ministers and other politicians of the democratic parties. On February 27, 1933, the Reichstag burned. Up to this day no one knows exactly who set the fire, but all indications point to the Nazis, who exploited it for their own propagandistic purposes. Indeed, that very night Hitler declared that the Communists had set the fire and that an overthrow from the left was looming in the immediate future. Under this pretext some 5000 members of the opposition were arrested in the following nights, especially in Berlin. Also, on the next day the Reichstag passed an "emergency decree for the protection of the people and the state" that gave Hitler comprehensive powers.

In March 1933 elections were held anew, since the National Socialists wanted to have public approval of their policies. However, the turnout was disappointing for the Nazis: They received only 43.9 percent of the ballots; in Berlin only 34.6 percent – the Communists were still the second-strongest party in the city! None-

Above: A perfectly arranged mega-spectacle – Jan. 30, 1933, Hitler seizes power.

theless, Hitler also managed to cripple the parliament with the *Ermächtigungsgesetz* (Law of Empowerment). Only the remaining Social Democrat ministers voted against it; the mandate of the 81 Communist members of parliament had been withdrawn beforehand. With the death of Hindenburg in August 1934, Hitler designated himself Führer und Reichskanzler (leader and chancellor).

Terror and Resistance in Berlin

Already in the first days after Hitler's appointment as chancellor in January 1933, the Nazis in Berlin had established spontaneous concentration camps and opened a big one in Sachsenhausen to the north of Berlin.

There were about 150,000 Jews living in Berlin at that time (in comparison, there were only 500,000 in all of Germany). Only 5000 of them were able to hide in Berlin; some 55,000 were killed in the concentration camps; the others had succeeded in fleeing.

Many of Berlin's intellectuals and artist were of Jewish extraction. They and members of the opposition had to either flee or go underground. Kurt Tucholsky, Max Reinhardt, Else Lasker-Schüler and Hans Sahl managed to leave Germany in time. Other prominent people, such as Carl von Ossietzky and the major Berlin publishers Samuel Fischer and Rudolph Mosse were killed by the Nazis or died from sheer bitterness.

Step by step, starting in 1933, the rights of Jews were restricted, until they lost all rights under the 1936 Nürnberg Laws. And, on the so-called *Reichskristallnacht* (Night of the Broken Glass) on November 9, 1938, Jewish businesses were ransacked and plundered, and synagogues set ablaze. 12,000 Berlin Jews were deported in that night and the days following.

Berlin had become the center of power for the Third Reich. The headquarters of

the SS and the Gestapo were located on the Prinz-Albert-Strasse and the Wilhelmstrasse in Kreuzberg; the Luftwaffe was situated in a monumental new building, and on the Vossstrasse Hitler had a new chancellery constructed.

These palatial buildings were only the beginning. Starting in 1937, Hitler's chief architect, Albert Speer, began taking his plans for the future Berlin from the blackboard to reality. As "Germania" the city was to become the capital of a National Socialist world empire; the center was to be a seven-kilometer-long north-south artery cutting straight through Berlin; it was to be fringed with immense government buildings; at each end great halls were to rise skyward. With their heights of around 300 meters they would have had room for 180,000 people, the perfect arena for the massive propaganda productions of the Nazis. Compared to these proportions the Brandenburg Gate would have seemed like little more than a diminutive side-entrance. These orgiastic phantasms of Hitler's grand delusion were destroyed by World War Two.

While the National Socialists in Berlin fanned the flames of state terror, the city simultaneously became the center of the (even though limited) German resistance. Alongside the SPD and the German Communist Party (KPD), which were active in the underground distributing flyers and illegal publications almost until the beginning of the war, the two churches stirred up opposition. Officially both confessions had come to some agreement with Hitler, but some priests and theologians of the *Bekennende Kirche*, an opposition church movement, struggled against the rule of the Nazis. The priest Martin Niemöller, who preached in Dahlem, Dietrich Bonoeffer and others paid for their courage with long internments in the concentration camps, or with their lives. Parallel to them, secret organizations such as the *Rote Kapelle*

(Red Chapel) smuggled Jews out of the country, and members of the opposition found kindred spirits in the "Kreisauer circle."

The most significant circle of resistance formed around Carl Goerdeler, the former mayor of Leipzig. Besides Goerdeler it was particularly the upper ranks of the military, such as Colonel-General Ludwig von Beck and officers in the various ministries, who planned putsches against Hitler.

However the assassination attempt on July 20, 1944, committed by Colonel Claus Schenk Graf von Stauffenberg, failed. Members of the Kreisau Circle were arrested; on the same evening Count Stauffenberg and others were summarily shot in the inner courtyard of the Bendlerblock. Almost 200 people paid with their lives for the attempted assassination of Hitler.

Above: Roland Freisler in the People's Court. Right: Berliners search for food among bombed out houses.

38

A Hail of Bombs and Chaos

While Hitler spread terror across Germany, he systematically built up the armaments industry. In matters of foreign policy he increasingly took over the initiative; with the propaganda slogans of *Lebensraum* for Germany he demanded concessions from the neighboring European countries. With a mixture of skillful demands for peace and coldly calculated threats, he managed to impose his will on Europe before turning to open aggression. However, the Berliners didn't rejoice when German troops attacked Poland on September 1st, 1939. In contrast to 1914, there were no huge parades on the streets of Berlin – the people were stunned, frightened and depressed.

This slowly changed with Germany's victories up to 1941, although during these years life in Berlin became progressively more difficult. Even in the first year of the war, rationing coupons were introduced for foodstuffs; the economy had also been converted to war produc-

tion. The stylish, pleasure-seeking Berlin of the pre-war years was already a vague thing of the past by 1940. More and more the city resembled a grey military encampment with nightly black-outs.

In the summer of 1940 the German Luftwaffe began bombarding civilian targets in England. The Royal Air Force struck back; on August 25 and 26, 1940, the first bombing attacks on Berlin took place. 222 Berliners had lost their lives in these bombardments by the end of 1940; from then on the British and, later, American bombers flew one mission after the other. The heaviest attack of all took place in February 1943: 2643 tons of bombs were dropped on Berlin. In that year 400,000 Berliners became homeless. During the entire war some 49,600 people died in the hail of bombs on Berlin alone.

In April 1945 the Red Army accelerated its advance on Berlin from the east; the bombed-out city had meanwhile sunken into chaos, the infrastructure was destroyed, the administration disinte-

grated. Straggling troops, civil militia and refugees wandered through the devastated streets and put up a last suicidal house-to-house battle against the Red Army in late April 1945. Meanwhile, the upper echelons of power of the Thousand Year Reich cowered in their bunkers. Adolf Hitler finally shot himself on April 30, 1945 in his bunker beneath the chancellery. The other Nazi commanders and generals either died or fled. The fighting in Berlin continued until May 2, when City Major General Weidling surrendered. Six days later the German army was just about finished; on May 8, Germany's unconditional and total surrender was signed at the Soviet headquarters in Berlin-Karlshorst.

However, the suffering of Berlin's population was to continue into the last days of the war: The Russian army plundered, raped and often wantonly murdered civilians as well. This was in revenge for the gruesome massacres that the Wehrmacht and the SS had committed in the Soviet Union.

FROM ZERO HOUR TO THE
FALL OF THE WALL

At the end of the war Berlin was the largest single area of ruins in Europe. Of all its former power and splendor, this was the only superlative that could possibly apply to the one-time imperial capital. 28.5 square kilometers of densely constructed urban area had fallen victim to allied bombing and shelling by the Red Army; 75 million cubic meters of debris were piled high in the streets. The true scale of the destruction was only discernible from the air. The balance looked as follows: Of some 250,000 buildings, a meagre ten percent had made it through the war undamaged. Almost 48,000 were completely destroyed or irreparably damaged; the remaining 70 percent had suffered more or less serious damage.

On assuming the highest authority in the city, the Red Army had also taken over primary responsibility for both the woes and well-being of the civilian population. Approximately 2.5 million people, of which there were almost twice as many women as men, were hovering on the edge of a catastrophic famine in this city of ruins. Peoples' Commissar Anastas Mikojan, acting on behalf of the Moscow War Commission, organized on-location deliveries of aid. "Everywhere, women, children and the elderly are begging members of the Red Army for a piece of bread," he reported on May 18, 1945, in *Pravda.*" The people are eating grass and the bark of the trees."

Families of refugees from the east, who had left their homes and belongings to flee from the Red Army, strayed through the desert of rubble in their search for food and shelter. Hygenic conditions were catastrophic, dysentery and typhus raged. Cut off from the outer world, shattered and pillaged, Berlin had

Left: The memorial to the Berlin air lift in Tempelhof, a symbol of freedom.

arrived at the nadir of civilization. That it was able to get back on its feet was due more than anything to the indefatigable nature of its inhabitants.

The Russian troops had scarcely moved on when the huge clean-up began in the outlying areas. By the end of May the first subways and streetcars started running. Gas and electricity were restored, though intermittently at best. The new cultural stirrings were promising. In the Titania Palast in Steglitz the players of the Philharmonic gathered to perform on May 26th. One day later, the Renaissance Theater celebrated its post-war première, and in mid-June the Chamber of Creating Artists (*Kammer der Kunstschaffenden*) opened an exhibition with the works of painters and sculptors who had been ostracized under the Nazis. The *Reichstrümmerfeld*, or imperial field of rubble as the Berliners called their home town with a healthy portion of black humor, had once again come to life.

The Sector-City

For two months the Soviet conquerors ruled Berlin alone. Exiled German Communists, purposely flown in from Moscow, recruited reliable party activists for the new city administration. They were supposed to represent all of the anti-fascist powers – at least for the sake of outward appearances – under an impartial mayor. However, the decisive posts were filled with their own confidants.

On June 5th, 1945, the Allies established a Supreme Control Council for occupied Germany, with its seat in Berlin. The city was put under the supervision of the Four Powers, as had been decided by the Big Three on September 12, 1944. The governmental protocol concluded in London concerning the zones of occupation in Germany envisaged a status as "special region" under international law for the territory of Greater Berlin under inter-allied administration. In contrast to the other zones it

would be occupied by the forces of all three powers (four, after the inclusion of France).

Even before the end of April, General Eisenhower's forward line had pushed up to the Elbe through the Red Army's planned occupation zone. On July 4, in the course of an exchange of troops, the Americans were the first to march into Berlin, followed by the British and the French. The Control Council moved into headquarters in the former Supreme Court at the Schöneberger Kleistpark. The large conference hall where in August 1944 the notorious Nazi peoples' court (*Volksgerichtshof*) had sentenced to death the men who had attempted to assassinate Hitler on July 20 1944 became the place where the four military governors met at regular intervals. Their adjudication served as the basis for all questions affecting Germany as a whole.

Above: Mayor Ernst Reuter on November 9, 1948. Right: The Anhalter Railway Station, still a ruin to this day.

The inter-allied command in Dahlem played the same role for Berlin. Unanimous decisions – there was no other kind – were conveyed to the Mayor, Dr. Arthur Werner, for implementation. At the very first meeting, the Soviets were able to push through their position that prior orders of their military command would remain in effect until further notice.

The allies subdivided the entire Berlin occupation zone into sectors for the quartering of the various troops. As might have been expected, the western allies took over the western half, with a total of 12 districts. Remaining in Soviet hands – almost the same size in area – were the eight eastern district, including the traditional center of the city.

The miseries of the post-war period continued to be the same, regardless of which victor ran what sector. Chronic hunger was written on the faces of many people. Adult men had an average weight of 57 kilograms, women 53 kilograms. Out of dire need, tens of thousands of Berlin women hired themselves out to clear the rubble, clean the bricks and so on. In the graduated rationing system, workers clearing the rubble were given class two foodstuff cards. For the rest of the population there was the notorious class five "graveyard card" providing only 1200 calories per day. The only way to survive was either to go to the country to scrounge for food, or to barter on the black market. The winter of 1946/47 was a particularly harsh setback, with temperatures of 20°C below zero – lasting weeks. There were no coal rations available. Transportation, the economy and culture came to a standstill; the municipal council established public warming shelters. 1142 people were found starved and frozen in their homes.

For the first time since May 1933, Berlin elected a city parliament on October 20, 1946. Meanwhile, in the surrounding eastern zone, the Socialists had been put out of action as an independent political

power as a result of their forced unification with the Communist Party. The Social Democrats were successful in resisting the merger by means of a strike ballot, but only in Berlin's western sector. The newly-formed Communist SED suffered a humiliating defeat in both the overall results and in the Soviet sector. With 19.8% – compared with 46.4% for the Social Democrats – they wound up back in third place behind the Christian Democrats (CDU), which received 22.2%. The Liberal Democrats (LDP) received 9.3%. Thus, the bottom line was that a convincing majority had decided in favor of the West and a social system based on individual liberty.

The Soviets didn't take their loss of power in the democratically elected legislative body sitting down. On June 24, 1947, the municipal assembly elected Ernst Reuter, the leading spokesman of Berlin's Social Democrats, as governing mayor. But the Russian commander thwarted his assumption of office with a veto, so that Reuter's deputy, Louise Schröder (SPD), had to take on the difficult post. The Soviet Union transformed its zone into a people's democracy following the Stalinist model. The western powers aspired toward a parliamentary federal government. In the Council of Foreign Ministers the Soviet Union insisted upon unreasonable war reparations and a say in the future of the Ruhr River Valley. On the other hand, within his sphere of influence Stalin blocked the Marshall Plan for the reconstruction of Europe, leading to the division of the continent. As a result, the western powers decided to merge their zones – as the initial political stage in founding a state with a unified economic and currency system.

Blockade and Airlift

Against this background, trouble arose in the Allied Control Council on March 20, 1948. As a protest against the western powers' unilateral decisions to hammer together a modern German state, Marshall Sokolowski declared the work of

the Four Powers' supreme committee ended. The Soviet delegation in the commanders' headquarters cleared their desks – for good – on June 16.

Meanwhile the Communists' war of nerves against the presence of western troops continued full blast. Since the lines of communication ran through the eastern zone, the Soviet Union clearly possessed the greater direct leverage. The through traffic to and from Helmstedt depended upon previous arrangement with the military commanders. The supervision and maintenance of the Autobahn and railroads was the exclusive reponsibility of the eastern side. Only the use of the three flight corridors had been formally regulated by arrangement within the Control Council at the end of 1945. The systematic impairment of the military and civilian interzonal traffic signalled the beginning of the first Berlin crisis in the spring of 1948.

Above: Montgomery and Zhukov in Berlin.
Right: A "raisin-bomber" about to land with nutritional pay load.

It escalated into an open test of strength on June 23, when Marshall Sokolowski decided to enact a currency reform for the greater area of Berlin analogous to that of the eastern zone. The western Allies declared the order null and void within their areas of command. They simultaneously arranged for the introduction of the new German mark of the western zones of occupation as the legal currency in their three sectors.

At midnight, the lights went out in the western sector – the electricity coming in from the other zone had been cut off. In the same night, the Soviet military administration called a halt to all road and rail transportation between the western zones and Berlin. Inland navigation also fell victim to this arbitrary blockade.

Military Governor Lucius D. Clay warned his superiors in Washington that if Berlin should fall, West Germany would follow. On July 1 President Harry S. Truman announced the decision that the Allies would be staying in Berlin. The western half of the city, with a population of 2.1

million, had food supplies to last 30 days. There was still enough coal on hand for 45 days. For the necessities of survival, allied experts calculated a transportation requirement of at least 4500 tons per day. If it was to be done at all, the defense of Berlin boiled down to an airlift. From the outset, both the Americans and the British were in the same boat. Mayor Ernst Reuter vouched for the steadfastness of his fellow Berliners. The situation certainly helped the victors and the vanquished of the besieged city to pack away their enmities and become allies.

Operation Vittles developed from an improvised shuttle operation to a major logistical undertaking. To relieve pressure on Tempelhof and Gastow, a new third airfield in Tegel was hastily set up from scratch in a record three months. With meager rations of dried food, but unbroken morale, the "islanders" endured the fourth post-war winter without coal or light. Less than 100,000 Berliners registered in the Soviet sector for the sake of food and fuel. On the "Easter Parade" of April 15 and 16, 1949, the airlift reached its zenith: 12,940 tons of supplies were flown in on 1398 flights. Behind the scenes at the United Nations building in New York, secret talks were already underway to end the deadlock. On May 12, at one minute before midnight, the barriers swung up again.

Altogether during the nine months of the blockade the western Allies had transported 1.7 million tons of supplies into the city on about 213,000 flights. 70 allied airmen and eight German assistants gave their lives in service toward a common goal. In the democratic world the name Berlin won a new reputation. Whereas at the war's end it was associated primarily with the monstrous crimes of the Hitler regime, during the blockade the former capital of the Third Reich became a symbol of the western determination for freedom. The price, however, was the division of the city.

The Cold War in Berlin

The unified municipal administration of Berlin had broken up in the autumn of 1948 in the midst of the maelstrom of the currency dispute. The Communist SED drove the majority of the parliamentary assembly out of the East Berlin city hall with the help of pre-arranged demonstrations. In the constitutionally mandated new elections of December 5, which could now be held only in the western sector, 64.5% of all voters confirmed Ernst Reuter as Berlin's spokesman. Meanwhile, hailing itself as the vanguard of a "Democratic Bloc," the SED had wrested unto itself the sole authority in the Soviet sector. Friedrich Ebert (SED), son of the former president during the Weimar Republic, became the head of the East's separate municipal council. For the next 41 years Berlin remained a divided city. This process was accentuated by the founding of the Federal Republic of Germany and the German Democratic Republic. Each half of the

45

city was linked with one of the two different states, which belonged to two opposing geopolitical camps.

The Parliamentary Council had included Greater Berlin in Bonn's area of authority. The western allies suspended the corresponding passage in article 23, under condition that Berlin would exercise no vote in the upper and lower houses of Parliament "and will not be governed by the federal government either." Thus West Berlin could not become a full-fledged state under the Four Powers Agreement of 1944/45.

Five months after the Bonn constitution took effect, the German Democratic Republic celebrated its founding with a torchlight parade on Unter den Linden on October 7, 1949. All of the Soviet zone's administration, political authorities and cultural establishments had already been concentrated east of the Brandenburg Gate. According to article 2 of the GDR's constitution, all that was needed was the proper label to proclaim East Berlin the capital of the second German state.

The municipal government of West Berlin made its temporary offices in the Schöneberg City Hall, which features a liberty bell donated by the American people. On October 1, 1950, the new constitution took effect, defining Berlin as "German nation and city at the same time." The subsequent elections to Berlin's Chamber of Deputies on December 3 resulted in a tripartite Senate of SPD, CDU and FDP (Free Democratic Party), under the leadership of Ernst Reuter. During the preceding dangers, he had become a charismatic father-figure for the people of Berlin. A sudden heart failure snatched the "man with the beret," as he was popularly known, away from his work on September 29, 1953.

The political divisions and West Berlin's isolation became increasingly perceptible during the fifties. The east-west conflict even overshadowed everyday life. In May 1952 the Soviets prohibited residents of the three western sectors from entering the eastern sector. Tens of thousands of West Berliners found themselves shut out from their garden houses and family gravesites on the other side of the city border. During the same year the inner-city telephone lines were severed. In the next year bus and streetcar transportation followed suit. However, the subways and suburban trains continued across the city. Hundreds of thousands commuted daily (from the east) over the open sector borders, and such repeated trips from one system to the other encouraged comparisons.

After the blockade, West Berlin faced a huge mountain of economic and social problems. It had lost its function as a capital city, its backlands and the greatest portion of its industry. In 1950 every third person was on welfare. The island-city was declared an official distress area, but then primped up into the "showcase of the West" with financial shots-in-the-arm from the federal government and the USA. Once again, the Kurfürstendamm with its palatial cinemas shone in its old neon gleam. The alluring shop windows and the unrestrained western lifestyle didn't fail to exert their magnetism on the people in the east.

The SED regime adorned itself with a showpiece boulevard. 80 meters in width, with eight-to-ten storied residential complexes constructed in the Stalinist monumental style, the "first Socialist street of Berlin" – the *Stalinallee* – arose from the rubble of the old Frankfurter Allee. The workers' rebellion of June 17, 1953, flared up right on this prominent construction site, to protest against a drastic increase of their expected job-performance quotas, on the previous day masons and carpenters had marched from the Strausberger Platz to the ministry headquarters on the Leipziger Strasse. Calling for the government to re-

Right: Workers defend themselves against Soviet tanks on June 17, 1953.

sign and for free elections, they aired their built-up anger over the repressive regime of the despised SED General Secretary Walter Ulbricht ("The pointy-beard (*Spitzbart*) must go!"), calling for free elections and the resignation of the government. A general strike was announced for the next day. On the morning of June 17, tens of thousands of striking workers flooded into East Berlin's governmental district. Two young demonstrators took the red banners down from the Brandenburg Gate. Severe clashes occured with the *Volkspolizei* (the People's Police); shots were fired. At 1p.m. the Soviet military commander declared martial law. Russian tanks bloodily crushed the uprising in East Berlin and other places in the budding Communist "workers'and peasants' state." The number of fatalities is unknown to this day.

The Construction of the Wall

There was only one way left for the residents of East Berlin and the GDR to visibly demonstrate their dissatisfaction. "Voting with ones' feet", it was called, and that was most easily done through Berlin. During 1953 approximately 332,000 refugees, an absolute record number at the time, turned their back on the GDR. From 1954 until the end of 1958 the loss of population due to emigration mounted to some 1.5 million, of which half were in the age group 25 and under. Nearly two-thirds of these people had been gainfully employed: jobs in the industry and the trades were particulary affected. This resulted in an increasing shortage of workers and specialists in East Germany, much to the detriment of the state treasury and the planned economy. SED boss Ulbricht later estimated the losses at 30 billion marks.

Republikflucht (*Flucht*=flight) was declared a punishable act; the direct crossing of the border into the Federal Republic became more difficult from year to year. The *Volkspolizei* intensified their border checks for traffic to Berlin, however, the loopholes into the "four-sector

from November 27, 1958 to that effect, Moscow sent the Western Allies an ultimatum to negotiate the retreat of their troops within six months. Khrushchev let the ultimatum expire, but the situation remained tense. A conference of foreign ministers in Geneva broke up without results in 1959. At a summit meeting held in Vienna in early June 1961, with the new president of the United States, John F. Kennedy, in attendance, Khrushchev threatened to solve the "West Berlin problem" within one year by means of a separate peace treaty with the GDR.

In the US Senate, Kennedy proposed additional military expenditures of 3.4 billion dollars, and strengthened the army from 870,000 to 1 million men. In order to eliminate the last trace of doubt about US determination, he summarized his administration's position on Berlin on July 25 in the *Three Essentials*. These consisted of: 1) The Allies right to maintain a presence in Berlin; 2) Free access to the city; and 3) Berlin's viability and the freedom of its population.A hysterical war of propaganda on both sides caused the number of refugees to increase explosively in the summer of 1961. From mid-July on there were no weekdays fewer than 1000 new arrivals. The economic collapse of the GDR was only a matter of time. In early August, at a secret conference of party leaders from the Warsaw Pact states, the decision was made to build the Berlin Wall.

In the night of August 12 to 13, the border of the eastern sector was transformed into a huge army camp. Armed groups of factory workers, the *Volkspolizei* and soldiers of the National Peoples' Army mounted guard. Under the protection of tanks and armored vehicles, rolls of barbed-wire were laid out, pavements torn up and concrete posts driven. Aroused by radio news reports, Berliners hurried to the scene of events. In impotent fury they had to look on as a bustling, lively city with its familiar, interwoven

city" could not be plugged so easily. Night after night at' the close of the late news, *RIAS*, the Radio in the American Sector, broadcast how many refugees had reported to the official agency dealing with asylum-seekers in West Berlin in the past 24 hours. 90,862 came in 1959; in 1960 there were 152,291. The majority were flown to West Germany at the cost of the federal government.

The SED leadership urged their protectors in the Kremlin to eliminate the "troublemaker West Berlin." The USSR took a second run at driving the western powers out of Berlin. The land blockade had become a dulled weapon. In response to the wishes of the allies the Berlin Senate stockpiled enough supplies to last a year. The Soviet government and party leader Nikita Khrushchev demanded the transformation of West Berlin into a "free, demilitarized city." Simultaneously, in a memorandum

Above: Erecting the wall on August 13, 1961. Right: John F. Kennedy and Mayor Willy Brandt after Kennedy's speech.

neighborhood tapestry was torn apart. Erich Honecker, then in charge of security matters in the Central Committee of the SED, directed the action, which had been prepared by the General Staff. The West was taken by surprise, quite literally in its sleep. On this critical Sunday morning in the conference room of the Allied Command three perplexed city commanders waited in vain for instructions from their capitals.

The Allies confined themselves to belated protests. That they sat still – practically without lifting a finger – during the forcible division of the city, was deeply shocking to the Berliners. It demonstrated that, in fact, the American guarantees ended at the sector boundaries. As a symbol of encouragement, President Kennedy sent Vice President Johnson to Berlin in his stead. The Pentagon also sent a 1500-man task force over the interzonal Autobahn. Exgeneral Clay, the steadfast hero of the 1948/49 airlift, returned on special assignment from Kennedy to the focal point of the Cold War. Disputes

with GDR border posts concerning the uncontrolled access to East Berlin for American civilians heated up to a critical confrontation by October 1961. American and Russian tanks faced each other at the Friedrichstrasse border crossing.

Here, at Checkpoint Charlie, which later became an almost mandatory feature in any spy thriller from the Cold War, Nikita Khrushchev waved affably over the borderline. Five months later President Kennedy appeared on the opposite side. His triumphal visit on June 23, 1963 – which attracted 1.3 million people – reached its peak at a rally before the Schöneberg City Hall with his world famous proclamation: "Ich bin ein Berliner!" (I am a Berliner.)

The Divided City

More than ever the residents of the walled city needed moral encouragement during these years. The trauma of August 13 and the feeling of isolation weighed heavily on peoples' minds and souls.

49

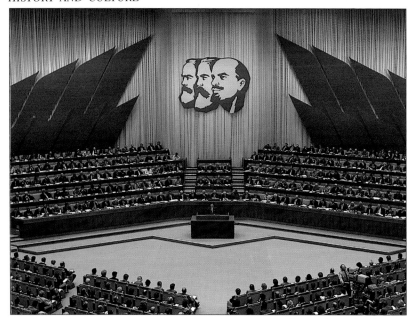

After almost 28 months of division, a complicated agreement between the Senate and the GDR was reached on passes which permitted West Berliners to visit their relatives in the east for Christmas 1963. In 1966 another agreement on the same level established six visiting periods. After this, West Berliners were only permitted to travel "yonder" for urgent family matters.

Through a "Tristate Concept" which treated West Berlin as an "independent political unit," Soviet diplomacy tried to separate the island-city from Bonn. When, despite protests from the east, the Bundestag conferred in the new *Kongresshalle* on April 7, 1965, Russian jet fighters terrorized the population with supersonic booms. Carefully planned pin pricks directed against transit and air traffic – just short of a blockade – repeatedly made plain the vulnerability of the western outpost, which could survive econ-

Above: The annual SED party conference in East Berlin, the proud capital of the GDR.

omically and financially only through billions of marks in subsidies from the Federal Republic's capital Bonn.

The GDR's economy stabilized in the shadow of the Wall; the reconstruction of East Berlin began to make visible progress. The immense 365-meter-high television tower, visible from every point on the compass, ushered in the "New Socialist Design" of the city center around the Alexanderplatz. Year by year the GDR perfected the 165-km-long fortified line surrounding West Berlin. By the fourth generation the Wall had grown to a height of 4.2 meters. Like some grotesque tapeworm, the ugly and monstrous inner-city concrete wall chewed a wide swath 45 km in length for itself through the sea of buildings.

Nonetheless, inhabitants of the GDR repeatedly managed to overcome the militarily secured border installation, some in rather adventurous ways. The number of memorial crosses on the West Berlin side grew from year to year. The first year of the "anti-fascist protection wall" was especially bloody. Of the 10,315 days of the Wall's existence, 30 of the altogether 80 known or nameless escapees who paid with their lives died during that first year. Reality and symbol in one, the monstrous edifice has gone down in history as a monument of inhumanity and – albeit only on the western side – the largest graffiti gallery in the world.

In the years of greatest threat a rigorous anti-Communism had smothered all of the internal contradictions inherent in the society of a city on the cold-war front. This changed when, in the mid-sixties, a world-wide youth revolt with roots in the USA broke out. The generational conflict with the older "blockade-Berliners" flared up particularly over the issue of Americans in Vietnam. The anti-authoritarian university students went out into the streets against the protecting power USA. With its fresh impetus, the rise of the protest generation revitalized the anachronistic island city. The scintillating subculture of the alternative scene had its wellspring in the turbulence of the 1968 rebellion. Its members became involved, through public initiatives, in the politics of the city, and by 1981 could boast for the first time a representative in government from their own list of candidates.

The front lines of the Cold War also started to move. The superpowers began pursuing a policy of détente. Under Willy Brandt, the Social-Liberal coalition government introduced a "New Eastern Policy" (*Neue Ostpolitik*). During the bilateral treaty discussions held in Warsaw, Moscow and East Berlin, the ambassadors of the victorious powers came together in the old Control Council buildings in order to defuse the political crises in the center of Europe. Regardless of their varying legal positions, in the Berlin Accord of September 3, 1971, both sides accepted the status quo as the basis for a pragmatic balancing of their respective interests. They put their common responsibility for the whole of Berlin into practice through establishment of an alternating dispatch of military patrols and co-operation in the inter-allied air traffic control center. Additional agreements on the inner-German level provided for a regulated coexistence in practical matters. One of the agreements finally secured the unhindered operation of through-traffic.

The GDR authorities agreed to refrain from arbitrary checks on people and cars. In the following 15 years, the number of travellers to and from Berlin using the roads tripled from 7.8 to 23.9 million annually. Telephone connections were restored between the two halves of the city. In addition, the restrictions on visitors from West Berlin were eased. The exchange of permanent missions normalized relations between Bonn and East Berlin. From a showplace of confrontation the city was transformed into a test ground for peaceful coexistence, but the gash through Berlin remained. Tourists from the West visiting the divided metropolis during the seventies and eighties found two fundamentally different political communities. Despite everything which separated them, though, the two Berlins were interwoven with each other like Siamese twins.

On the one side was a big city pulsating around the clock, an open-minded cultural metropolis of two million people. West Berlin, still Germany's largest industrial center and the seat of numerous federal agencies, sought and found new tasks as a super-regional center for service industries. Politically, legally and economically incorporated into the structure of the Federal Republic, by international law the city-state was under the sovereignty of the three western powers, a fact which was reflected in a number of occupation laws, for example the "temporary identity card" for West Berliners and the omission of compulsory service in the armed forces. East Berlin, with another 1.2 million resi-

dents, was the showcase of the SED state. Erich Honecker, who took power in the State Council offices after Ulbricht was deposed, interpreted the preferential improvement of the GDR capital as a "concern of the entire republic." Prussian heritage came back into favor under the native Saarlander, whose principal aim was to indoctrinate the citizens of the GDR with a separate national identity. In 1981 the equestrian statue of Old Fritz returned to its customary place in Berlin's historic center, and the great architectural monuments of Classicism rose again in their old magnificence. "Socialist Berlin" self-assuredly held separate festivities for the 750th anniversary of the city in 1987.

Berlin – Unified Again

The senescent SED leadership stood firm on its policy of separation, although

Above: Selling GDR flags at the Brandenburg Gate – symbol of the collapse of the GDR. Right: A job well done!

entirely different signals were coming from Moscow's General Secretary Mikhail Gorbachev. While the world around them was changing under the banner of *glasnost* and *perestroika*, the population of the GDR waited in vain for reforms. Blind to the mistakes of "real existing Socialism," on January 18, 1989, Honecker boasted that the Wall through Berlin would "still be standing in 50 and even in 100 years, if the reasons at hand had not yet been eliminated." However, power slipped away from the obstinate cronies in the SED Politburo more rapidly than expected. Honecker and the old guard made their last public appearance on October 7 at a pompous military parade for the 40 anniversary of the German Democratic Republic. No real mood of jubilation could be drummed up, however, due to the spectacular mass exodus underway at the time. At the beginning of September, Hungary had opened its western borders to citizens of the GDR. Each day thousands took advantage of the chance to flee. Others followed the route through the Federal Republic's embassies in Prague and Warsaw, and in the GDR the rapidly sprouting opposition would not allow itself to be intimidated any more with police terror. A powerful movement swelled up from peace and environmental groups, carrying their protest against Stalinist conditions into the street with the cry: *"Wir sind das Volk!"* (We are the people!) On November 4, more than one-half million people marched through the streets of East Berlin's inner-city in support of democracy and freedom of expression. Then Czechoslovakia became the second "brother country" to open up the Iron Curtain. Egon Krenz, Honecker's successor, saw that a radical change of course was necessary.

In the early evening of November 9 1989, the GDR television network broadcast a press conference following the 10th plenary session of the SED Central Committee. Toward the end, Information Secretary Günter Schabowski mentioned almost in passing that the GDR had opened its borders. "Private travel abroad" could be applied for immediately, without special preconditions.

It took several more hours before the sensational importance of this news got around, but from then on there was no stopping the flood. The East Berliners hurried *en masse* to the sector border crossings; everyone wanted to be among the first at the opening. The border guards finally capitulated before the onrush. They opened up the gates and let everyone through. On the same night tens of thousands from the eastern section of the city took the chance for an excursion through the Wall. On the other side they were received by jubilant throngs of West Berliners. Champagne corks popped, complete strangers embraced each other, and nobody was ashamed of shedding tears. Soon the Ku'damm was full of Trabis and Wartburgs, the automotive symbols of the GDR. Before the Brandenburg Gate the crowds danced

atop the Wall. The whole event was broadcast to the wider world via live television, Berlin celebrated the "most jubilant people's festival in its history." Walter Momper, governing mayor of West Berlin, rejoiced over the end of the city's division: "This is the day we've awaited for 28 years." Those who hadn't learned of the historic events of the previous night until listening to the radio the next morning thought they had awoken in another city. The Wall was gone.

This was the end of the Cold War and the post-war period. Since then Berlin has grown back into being one city again. And with the 1991 decision of the German Bundestag to move parliament and government to Berlin the city has regained its status of national capital. However, the Berliners don't expect the arrival of the first members of parliament until the next century. As a sovereign, free and unified city and, since 1994, with no special status under occupying powers, Berlin is on its way to becoming a normal European metropolis.

BOULEVARDS AND
SQUARES

KURFÜRSTENDAMM
BRANDENBURG GATE
UNTER DEN LINDEN
ALEXANDERPLATZ

THE KURFÜRSTENDAMM

There is scarcely anyone who does not associate Berlin with the **Kurfürstendamm** almost immediately. Every larger German city has its own distinguishing landmark, usually a church, cathedral, castle or fortress. Berlin alone is associated straight away with a street – the Kurfürstendamm, a chic strip familiar to the man of the world, for one reason or another at any rate.

The Kurfürstendamm is Berlin's most magnificent boulevard, a shopping dorado and a center for entertainment. In Berlin it is called plainly and somewhat insolently the **Ku'damm**. Since the re-unification of Berlin the Ku'damm has been glamourizing itself again. The old mixture of cosmopolitan flair and provincial narrowness led to its rapid decline. Now, however, hotels, cinemas, department stores and shops are undergoing expensive renovations in order to keep up with Friedrichstrasse in the east which is recapturing its pre-war flair.

The Ku'damm already existed in 1542, though it was known then as the *Knüp-*

Preceding pages: The ICC at night. The Zehner bridge spanning the Tegeler Fliess. Left: Skyline showing the Gedächtniskirche and the television tower.

peldamm. Back then it was a scarcely paved riding path for the electors who rode from the Stadtschloss (City Castle) on Unter den Linden to their hunting lodge in Grunewald. This state of affairs remained unchanged for centuries, until 1871, when the chancellor of the newly-founded German Empire, Otto von Bismarck, returned to Berlin from Paris. He had seen the Bois de Boulogne in the French capital and admired the Champs Elysées. He wanted to create an equally splendid boulevard for the German capital as well. The Iron Chancellor fought for almost ten years until finally the "Kurfürstendamm Association" was established in 1882 with the aim of transforming the riding path into a showpiece avenue.

Bismarck had a very precise conception of his magnificent road: It was to be 3.8 kilometers long from Grunewald to the Zoo, with a width of 56 meters, featuring a riding path in its middle and lined on both sides with splendid apartment buildings. These lordly edifices, richly decorated with balconies and turrets, ornamented with cornices and intricate stucco work, provided an ideal living situation for well-to-do tenants. The marble staircases and columned halls richly decorated with mirrors and sculpted figures showed off the wealth of the occupants. Only Bismarck's fondest dream, an equestrian monument of himself on "his" boulevard, has remained unfulfilled to this day.

Around the Breitscheidplatz

Those who want to truly experience the Ku'damm and the city of Berlin ought probably begin their stroll on the **Breitscheidplatz**. This plaza was formerly the Auguste-Viktoria-Platz, but after the Second World War it received the name of the SPD Reichstag representative Rudolf Breitscheid, who was killed in a concentration camp.

The plaza is dominated by the **Kaiser Wilhelm Memorial Church** (Gedächtniskirche), constructed between 1891 and 1895 in memory of Kaiser Wilhelm I, and almost completely destroyed in World War Two. The ruins, which are called *Hohler Zahn* (hollow tooth) by tongue-in-cheek locals, would have been torn down after the war if things had gone according to the wishes of the then-Senator for Housing and Construction. However, polls taken at the end of the fifties turned out in favor of preserving the church. In 1961, a new church, designed by Prof. Egon Eiermann, was constructed on the ruins of the tower. One can of course argue over the beauty of the new structure, but not over the fascinating bluish play of light in its interior.

Today's church-ensemble is not meant to commemorate any monarch, but rather the horrors of war. Its steps have been used as a forum for vigils, rallies and happenings for many years. These gatherings have frequently had a rather unreal appearance before a background of glowing advertisement signs. Across from the church, the Mercedes star shining on the roof of the Europa Center is brighter than all the other illuminated billboards on the plaza.

In front of the Europa Center stands the **Weltkugelbrunnen** (Globe Foun-

tain) designed by Joachim Schmettau. It supposedly circulates some 400,000 liters of water per hour. In the summer there are swarms of people at, in front of and not infrequently *in* the fountain; sometimes the atmosphere recalls that of a popular festival. People meet each other here, chat, perform street theater, and cool their feet in the splashing water. In short: Everyone does just about as they please and no-one gets upset about it. The same applies to the punks and the homeless who wait around here, often the whole day long, and ask passers-by for a spare mark or two.

The people of Berlin are tolerant and aware of the fact that a big city has many faces, including those of poverty, which

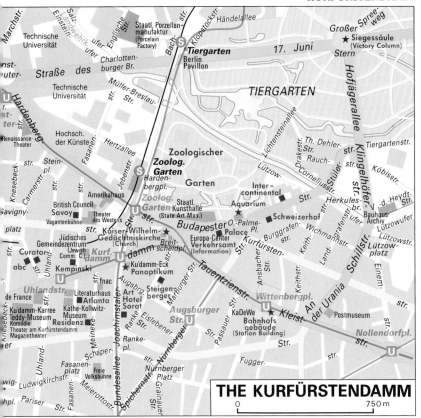

THE KURFÜRSTENDAMM

0   750 m

can be seen here right alongside the extravagant world of consumerism of the **Europa-Center.** By the way, a genuine Berliner never says center, but always *zenter* (z=ts). In the previous century the Wilhelmshallen, which featured the renowned **Romanisches Café,** stood on this location. In the Golden Twenties, Berlin's bohemian culture, the poets and thinkers, caricaturists, designers, theater critics, actors and actresses all came together here. In the post-war years, life on the Breitscheidplatz was a good deal quieter. The Romanisches Café had succumbed to the hail of bombs, and on the barren plot surrounding the plaza there were wooden shacks and the tent of a traveling wrestler.

The Europa-Center wasn't built until 1965. Incidentally, it was also the first write-off speculation project in the city. There are about 100 stores, restaurants, the casino **Spielbank Berlin,** the cabaret **Die Stachelschweine**, the **La vie en rose** revue theater, the **Multivisionskino**, a movie house, in which you can see a fast-motion history of Berlin. The **Royal Kinos** with what is supposedly the largest projection screen in Europe, and Berlin's largest sauna provide for an ample variety of diversions and amusement. Certainly there are a great number of shops and boutiques in the Europa-Center and on the Ku'damm, but the small retailers are being increasingly forced out by high commercial rents.

DM 400,- (approx. US$ 250,-) per square meter is about the norm nowadays, which is second only to Paris. This did not put off the US movie colossus, Warner Brothers, which opened the largest **studio store** on the continent in the Europa-Center. Even anyone who does not like stuffed animals should drop by: the four-horse chariot from atop the Brandenburg Gate and the Victory Column are interpreted here in a novel way.

Today a stroll around the various levels of the complex is enjoyable in any weather. In earlier days you often had to brave the bad weather in the draughty yard and be properly bundled up for your contemplation of the shops. As compensation, there was a skating rink in the middle of the courtyard. Later, the entire area was covered with a glass dome and the skating rink gave way to an artificial waterfall.

Above: Breitscheidplatz, the heart of the western part of the city. Right: The Globe Fountain, known as the "Wasserklops".

Another eye-catcher in the Europa-Center is the **Uhr der fliessenden Zeit** (Clock of Flowing Time), a technological artwork constructed by the Parisian physicist Bernard Gitton. In this 13-meter-high sculpture various colored liquids demonstrate drop-by-drop how quickly time slips away. The Berliners' predilection for jocular nicknames didn't stop here. They call it *Fruchtsaft-Automat* (fruit-juice machine). The Europa-Center is also one place to get a bird's eye view of the city. You can take an elevator to the 22nd floor, where an **observation platform** and the **i-punkt-café** offer an impressive panoramic view of Berlin.

The building with a flat roof extending along the north side of the plaza on the **Budapester Strasse** is the **Staatliche Kunsthalle** (State Art Gallery), under which there is a shopping arcade with various souvenir and jewelry shops as well as a bookstore and the office of the **Berliner Festspiele** (festival). To the right is a futuristic blue sphere. Here a

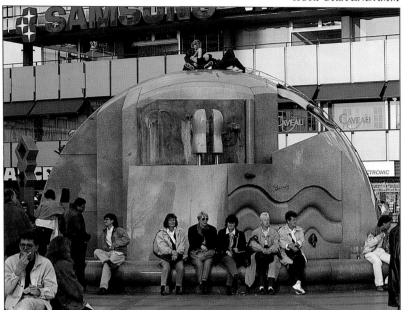

disco now tries to enliven people from Neukölln and tourists with striptease and hands-on experience of naked men.

The Wittenbergplatz and the KaDeWe

The Breitscheidplatz connects the Ku'-damm and the Tauentzien with each other; the latter leads to the Wittenbergplatz and the Kaufhaus des Westens (Department Store of the West), called simply **KaDeWe** by the locals.

In contrast to the Ku'damm, the **Tauentzien** is strictly a shopping street, on which an especially large number of boutiques and the better-known fashion chains have settled. Several of the generally unremarkable buildings are to be enlarged and elaborately redecorated in the next few years.

The crowning glory of this shopping strip is the **KaDeWe**, whose labyrinthian interior extends over 24,000 sqare meters of retail space. When the store was opened in 1907 by businessman Adolf Jahndorf, the Berliners warmed up to it very quickly, although the city's west side was not yet the shopping paradise it is today. In 1927 the department store merged with the Hertie chain, becoming its flagship and having continually expanded since then. Even its almost total destruction during the Second World War couldn't shake the reputation of the store, and by 1956 it already shone with its old lustre. Over the last few year this most financially successful of German department stores has been renovated once more: two great atriums which had been walled up since the war have been reopened and clad with sandstone slabs. Glass elevators glide silently up to the 7th floor where the store's conservatory, with its palms and waterfalls, offers gastronomic pleasures high above the roofs of Berlin. A huge glass dome lets in light from the blue sky.

The Wittenbergplatz itself is dominated by the building of the **U-Bahn** (subway station). The station was constructed from 1911 to 1913 according to the plans of Alfred Genander, a star architect of the period. After the first subway line was built between Stralauer Tor and the Zoo, the spot was occupied by little ticket booths, which were also designed by Genander. When he then received the contract to build a "first class high-speed railway station," he designed the structure in neoclassical style. Unfortunately, the beautiful stone building fell victim to the bombs of World War Two. The heaviest of the damage was not repaired until 1951.

At the beginning of the eighties, the station was finally put under historical preservation and painstakingly renovated for some 3.5 million DM. Using old photographs, the Art Nouveau ornamentation and the yellow and turquoise majolica tiles were faithfully restored to their original shape.

A Stroll down the Ku'damm

The way back to the Ku'damm leads by a gleaming metallic sculpture on the median at the corner of the **Marburger Strasse**: two oversized chain links, each broken in two places. This work of art, named *Berlin,* was created by the artist couple Matschinsky-Denninghoff, and symbolizes the long division of the city. The sculpture is on long-term loan from the Deutsche Bank to Berlin; it was a contribution for the city's 750th anniversary festivities. In 1987 eight sculptures virtually transformed the Ku'damm and Tauentzien into an open-air gallery. Only three of the pieces remain; the two others are located on the western end of the Ku'-damm.

Our stroll down the Ku'damm starts with Kurfürstendamm Nr. 11, behind the Breitscheidplatz on the right side of the street. The first house numbers disap-

peared in a wondrous manner as a result of a re-routing of the street. Until 1925 the Ku'damm began behind the Europa Center and the present-day Budapester Strasse was its last section.

All the construction sins committed during the fifties and sixties are, unfortunately, all too plainly visible on both sides of the street, creating a regrettable backdrop for the present-day Ku'damm. Alfred Messel, the builder of the old Wertheim department store on the Leipziger Platz (one of the most beautiful in the city) would probably have a heart attack at the sight of the concrete blocks of the current **Wertheim**. Nevertheless, next to the department store is one of these formerly magnificent buildings, the **Café Möhrling** and the cinema halls of the **Marmorhaus** (House of Marble) and the **Gloria Palast**. Cafés and the major first-run cinemas have made the Ku'-damm an attractive entertainment boulevard since the 1920s.

The Marmorhaus is one of Berlin's oldest cinemas. It was opened in 1913 as a palatial luxury cinema and until recently had declined into a lacklustre assemblage of projection halls. Today this movie palace, now renovated, is once more popular with moviegoers again.

Also, the **Café des Westens** in the Ku'-damm-Eck on the corner of Joachimstaler Strasse and the **Café Kranzler** diagonally opposite are famous indeed. Naturally the Café des Westens no longer has anything in common with the old "Café Grössenwahn" (megalomania), and the Kranzler – a Berlin institution for 150 years – has lost much of its polish since World War Two. Irate critics even claim that the Kranzler has degenerated into a cake-and-coffee joint for Berlin's retirees, primarily the widows from Wilmersdorf, and a revolving door for groups of tourists. Nonetheless, going to the café-bakery is still among the Berliners' favorite activities, and what is better than lounging around in front of the Café

Right: The "Clock of Flowing Time" at the Europa Center, nicknamed Fruit-Juice Machine by the Berliners.

Möhring or the Kranzler in the summertime and experiencing the tumult on the Kurfürstendamm?

The **Ku'damm-Eck** is a thoroughly inconspicuous newer building serving as refuge to a hodgepodge of businesses, including pornographic cinemas, discount stores and the **Berliner Panoptikum** (a wax museum). The gigantic electronic news billboard features not only the latest world news, but also, in the evenings, greetings from Berliners in love, personal adds and even poems and cartoons.

The Café Kranzler is not far from the **Hotel Kempinski**, another Berlin institution. On the way is the new **Aschinger**, a restaurant famous for pea soup. It was formerly located at the Zoo but fell victim to the age of fast food and so went on with its efforts to satiate fans of hearty Berlin food at a new location, in the **Haus Wien** right on the Ku'damm.

The Hotel Kempinski is situated on the corner of the Fasanenstrasse, possibly the most stylish side-street leading off the Kurfürstendamm. Many luxurious businesses have established themselves here in the last few years, especially in the **Fasaneneck** and the **Uhlandpassage**. Berlin's **Jewish Community Center** is located on the way to the Kantstrasse. Berlin's largest synagogues once stood here, but only the entrance arch remained after the temple's destruction by the Nazis in 1938. It was incorporated into the current modern building. In the opposite direction are the **Käthe-Kollwitz Museum**, which honors the Berlin artist with a permanent exhibition, and the **Literaturhaus**, which caters to literary fans with readings and exhibits. Those seeking a break from the overfilled Ku'damm cafés can withdraw to the dignified **Café Wintergarten**.

On the corner of the Ku'damm and Fasanenstrasse it is worth paying a visit to the cosy **Café Leysieffer**, which is located in the former Chinese embassy, and taking a look in **King's Teagarden**, where you can make a selection among more than 200 varieties of tea to strains of classical music. Next door, the **Astor**

beckons to a night of film-viewing in its splendid halls. Further on in the direction of the Halensee is the **Uhlandstrasse**, on the corner of which stands the **Maison de France**, the French cultural center for West Berlin. In the same building, the **Cinéma Paris** (one of the better cinemas on the Ku'damm) presents Gallic film culture. The **Galerie Brusberg**, one of the most renowned art galleries in Berlin, is housed in a gleaming white building opposite.

Twinkling in tones of orange and red on the median just past the Uhlandstrasse is the **Mengenlehre** (set theory) **Clock**. Across the **Ku'damm-Karree** is a shopping arcade with pubs for tourists, small stores, a second-hand bookshop and a cute teddy bear museum.

Just as with every complex of newer buildings on the Ku'damm there is not the least bit of atmosphere in the Ku'-damm-Karree, though the owners plan to

beautify the arcade both inside and out with many plants and a lot of glass.

Rising up from the median of the Bleibtreustrasse stands the **Pyramide** by Josef Erben with a height of 13 and breadth of 40 meters. This sculpture is also a remainder from the 750th anniversary festivities.

The buildings on the four corners of the intersection with the **Wielandstrasse** have either been reconstructed or are in original condition. One of these buildings was almost totally destroyed by a hotel fire – just after it had been renovated at a cost of millions of deutsche marks; only the façade remained. It has been painstakingly restored during reconstruction of the building.

One block further, on the **Leibnizstrasse**, there is another magnificent example of a manorial residence of old Berlin, the **Iduna House**. In this case, however, only the façade has been retained in its original condition, the rest is all new construction. Across the street you can take a break on the comfortable

Above: Sitting in a Ku'damm street café.
Right: An artist earning his pay on the street.

benches next to the bronze **Entenbrun-nen** (Duck Fountain).

Passing by the **Olivaer Platz** and the **Adenauerplatz** you arrive at the **Lehniner Platz** where you can scarcely overlook the **Schaubühne's** architecturally remarkable building, designed by Erich Mendelsohn between 1926 and 28. The renowned Schaubühne is without a doubt one of the best theaters in the world.

Finally, where the Kurfürstendamm ends beyond the **Halensee Bridge** at the Rathenauplatz, the Grunewald residential area begins. At the Rathenauplatz there is one further monument from the "art-boulevard:" Action artist Wolf Vostell set some old Cadillacs on end next to each other and embedded them in concrete. It is slated to disappear soon. The demolition costs have been estimated at about 60,000 DM; when added to the artists' honorarium (50,000 DM) and the installation costs (120,000) the yield is quite a large sum, exceeding the value of the work itself by a large margin. It's too

bad that the East German Trabant in concrete, which some practical joker put next to the Vostell sculpture one night, has disappeared again. Someone paid 10,000 DM to give it a loving home.

Via Kantstrasse to the Zoo Station

The **Kantstrasse**, running parallel to the Ku'damm, can be reached by any Ku'damm side-street you choose. Along Kantstrasse you can find many interesting shops, pubs and other establishments, some of which are quite inexpensive. Over the last few years, 43 specialty shops have settled here, offering cheap electrical goods to foreigners (who, of course, don't have to pay the usual sales taxes).

Savignyplatz, on either side of the Kantstrasse, is certainly worth a look, as are the numerous shops and cafés – especially under the S-Bahn viaducts. This rectangular park was named after the Prussian Minister of Justice and legal scholar Friedrich Karl von Savigny

(1779-1861). The plaza was given a fresh shine for Berlin's 750th anniversary celebrations. The 19th-century pavement mosaic was carefully restored all around the square. The small park was also given a face-lift. And so Savignyplatz has once again become a quiet oasis in the middle of the city.

From Savignyplatz two narrow pedestrian streets lead past the **S-Bahn Arches**, towards **Bleibtreustrasse** and also towards **Uhlandstrasse**. The two thoroughfares now house cafes, art galleries and exclusive stores.

A little further is the imposing structure which houses the **Theater des Westens** (Theater of the West), designed in 1896 by Bernhard Sehring and elaborately restored in 1984. Since 1987 artistic director Helmut Baumann has managed to transform the theater into one of the best stages for musicals in Europe, with such productions as *Cabaret* and *La*

Above: Berliner Weisse with a shot – something every visitor to Berlin should try.

Cage aux Folles, and Broadway guest performances like *Porgy and Bess*.

Right opposite a trademark of the new Berlin soars heavenwards, the **Kant Triangle** of the KapHag Group. The shining white metal sail on top of this office skyscraper is certainly a matter of taste. At least it does turn with the wind. A number of rundown stores were demolished as well, which once gave the Kantstrasse a rather shabby appearance.

The **Bahnhof (Station) Zoo**, located at the end of the Kantstrasse, has been thoroughly renovated in recent years, although with its gloomy passageways and generally seedy surroundings it is still rather repellant. Nonetheless, you should take a look around here, even though the days of the drug-scene at the Zoo – setting for the poignant *Christiane F., We the Children of Zoo Station* – are a thing of the past.

Nowadays this station is a gathering place for many of the city's poor and homeless. The crime in this area is basically limited to petty offences; it is not dangerous for tourists either. In addition, the plaza in front of the gold-colored wall clock is a thermometer of social change in Germany: Before the currency unification on July 1, 1990, money was exchanged here at black market rates and minor deals were also made. In the same year gypsies and other refugees from Romania begged here for the bare necessities of life. Today the city's stranded are again among their own kin.

The most unpleasant shopping arcade in Berlin is on the **Joachimstaler Strasse** which connects the Zoo to the Ku'damm. It is lined with cheap pubs, porno cinemas, shish-kebab booths and a 24-hour flower stand. After crossing the Kantstrasse, passing the cheap department store **Bilka**, one comes to the Ku'-damm. At this point, the ugly Ku'damm-Karree and a renovated turn-of-the-century corner house stand directly opposite one another: a typical Berlin mixture.

KURFÜRSTENDAMM
Transportation

U-Bahn (Underground): Lines 1 and 9 run to Berlin Zoo, lines 3 and 9 to Kurfürstendamm, lines 1, 2 and 3 (direction Uhlandstrasse) to Wittenbergplatz, line 7 to Adenauerplatz.

Traveling in and around Berlin on the yellow **buses**, although a much slower means of transportation, offers some interesting views of the city. Buses 119 and 129 run from Halensee to Wittenbergplatz, serving the whole Ku'damm.

Even at night a walk on the lively and crowded Ku'-damm is relatively safe. Don't be tempted to join the – apparently harmless – **Hütchenspiel** (hat-game) at the roadside: You can only lose your money in this con game. A marble, shuffled about at incredible speed, vanishes under one of three matchboxes (the "hats"); the idea of the game is to place a money bet on which "hat" is covering the marble. This illegal game is, of course, a scam: the delighted winners, raking in the money and tempting tourists to try their luck, are – what else – the hat-trick player's mates. Don't even stop to watch – this is an eldorado for **pickpockets**.

Cafés and Restaurants

On and around Ku'damm you can pick and choose between a large variety of cafés and restaurants, snack bars and steakhouses (also see pages 187 and 193). Here is a small selection to ease your choice:

Café Adlon, Kurfürstendamm 69, Tel. 883 76 82, from 8 a.m.-midnight daily.

Aschinger, Kurfürstendamm 26, Tel. 882 55 58, from 11 a.m.-1 a.m. daily.

Café Bristol, Kurfürstendamm 35, Tel. 881 41 80, from 11.30 a.m.-0.30 a.m. daily.

Café Kranzler, Kurfürstendamm 18/19, Tel. 882 69 11, from 8 a.m.-midnight daily.

Café Leysieffer, Kurfürstendamm 218, Tel. 882 78 20, from 9 a.m.-10 p.m. daily.

Café Wintergarten, Fasanenstr. 23, Tel 882 54 14, daily 10 a.m.-1 a.m., located in the Literaturhaus Berlin (see below).

I-Punkt-Café in the Europa-Center, Tel. 262 76 70, from 10 a.m.-11 p.m. daily.

Le Marché, Kurfürstendamm 14, Tel. 882 75 78, from 8 a.m.-midnight daily.

Mövenpick in the Europa-Center, Tel. 262 70 77, 8 a.m.–midnight, Fridays and Saturdays until 1 a.m.

Wintergarten in the Ka De We, Tauentzienstr. 21, Tel. 21 21 0, Mon - Sat from 9 a.m. - 6.30 p.m. New self service café with restaurant and panoramic views across the city.

Cinemas around the Ku'damm

Book your cinema tickets well in advance or join the queue at least one hour before the performance. Many cinema houses offer special rates on Tuesdays and Wednesdays where you can enjoy any film for DM 6-8 only; the usual ticket price is DM 9 to DM 15.

Arsenal, Schöneberg, Welserstr. 25, Tel. 24 68 48. **Astor**, Kurfürstendamm 217, Tel. 881 11 08. **Broadway**, Tauentzienstr. 8 (in the Minicity), Tel. 261 50 74. **Cinéma Paris**, Kurfürstendamm 211, Tel. 881 31 19. **Delphi**, Kantstr. 12a, Tel. 312 10 26. **Europa-Studio** (in the Europa-Center), Tel. 261 79 07. **Filmbühne Wien**, Kurfürstendamm 26, Tel. 881 48 88. **Film-Palast**, Kurfürstendamm 225, Tel. 883 85 51, the most beautiful and comfortable cinema in Berlin: Art-Deco style with excellent acoustics. **Gloria-Palast**, Kurfürstendamm 12, Tel. 261 15 57. **Hollywood**, Kurfürstendamm 65, Tel. 882 50 77. **Marmorhaus**, Kurfürstendamm 236, Tel. 881 15 22. **Royal-Palast** (in the Europa-Center), Tel. 261 17 75 (Berlin's largest screen). **Zoo-Palast**, Hardenbergstr. 29a, Tel. 261 15 55.

Sightseeing / Museums

Amerikahaus, Hardenbergstr. 21-24, Tel. 819 76 61; exhibitions, lectures.

Berliner Panoptikum, Kurfürstendamm 227/228 (Ku'damm-Eck), Tel. 883 90 00, daily 10 a.m.-11 p.m.

The British Council, Hardenbergstr. 20, Tel. 311 09 90, lectures, exhibitions.

Europa-Center with the tourist information office **Verkehrsamt Berlin** (entrance Budapester Str., Tel. 262 60 31), **Cabaret**, **Revue-Show** (see page 215) and the casino **Spielbank Berlin**: entrance Budapester Str., open 3 p.m.-3 a.m. daily, Tel. 250 08 90. **Observation Platform** daily from 9 a.m.

Jüdisches Gemeindehaus Berlin (Jewish Community Center), Charlottenburg, Fasanenstr. 79, Tel. 883 65 48. Lectures, readings and exhibitions.

Kaiser-Wilhelm-Gedächtniskirche (Emperor Wilhelm Memorial Church), Breitscheidplatz, Tel. 218 50 23, memorial hall in the old tower: open Tuesdays-Saturdays 10 a.m.-6 p.m.; Neue Kirche (New Church): open 9 a.m.-7.30 p.m. daily.

Käthe-Kollwitz-Museum, Fasanenstr. 24, Tel. 882 52 10, openWed-Mon 11 a.m.-6 p.m., closed Tue.

Königliche Porzellan-Manufaktur (Royal Porcelain Manufactory), Charlottenburg, Kurfürstendamm 26a, Tel. 881 18 02, open Mon–Fri 9.30 a.m.-6.30 p.m., Thur until 8.30 p.m., Sat 9.30 a.m.-2 p.m. Exhibition and sale of porcelain figurines.

Literaturhaus Berlin (House of Literature), Fasanenstr. 23, Tel. 882 65 52. Bookstore and Café Wintergarten, literature readings and exhibitions.

Maison de France, Kurfürstendamm 211, Tel. 881 87 02. Lectures and exhibitions.

Teddy Bear Museum, Kurfürstendamm 206/208 (Ku'damm-Karree), Tel. 881 41 71; open Wednesdays–Mondays 3-10 p.m.

**AROUND THE BRANDENBURG
GATE**

"When you come into Berlin, it's just to your right" – in his cocky Berlin manner, Max Liebermann gave these directions to his painting studio. As one of the leading representatives of Impressionism in Germany, this famous painter and honorary citizen of Berlin lived for nearly 40 years at the **Pariser Platz,** in house number seven, directly on the northern side of the Brandenburg Gate.

It is extremely hard to imagine that the barren square on the eastern side of the Brandenburg Gate was once among the most impressive addresses of the metropolis on the Spree. Historical pictures show it decked out in its finest attire, the stately palaces of the nobility, which bordered the square as a closed architectural ensemble from north to south. "Berlin's reception room" played a prominent role in international politics. The French, American and Dutch embassies stood here at the entrance to the government quarter. Palais Redern at the corner of the Wilhelmstrasse, which had been expanded by the architect Karl Friedrich Schinkel, was replaced by the legendary luxury hotel Adlon in 1905. However it will all shine again with its old glory in coming years: the Hotel Adlon is being transformed into a building of splendour and magnificence, and the embassies are indicating they wish to return to the Brandenburg Gate. The old architecture of Pariser Platz has already been restored, albeit timidly.

From 1907 on, the Royal, then the Prussian Academy of Arts, which Max Liebermann presided over from 1920 to 1932, resided in the former Arnim Palais. It was regarded as one of the most beautiful exhibition halls in Berlin. As a meager token of the original construc-

tion, a side wing remains at Pariser Platz number four. The East Berlin Academy still uses it as a workshop and gallery.

The Brandenburg Gate

Pariser Platz received its present name in 1814 to commemorate the return of the Prussian troops from Paris at the end of the war against Napoleon, and who staged a victory march here, casting a patriotic glow on the **Brandenburg Gate.** Prussia's glory was already long a thing of the past when, in the night from October 3 to 4, 1990, hundreds of thousands of people from east and west celebrated the unification of Germany around the illuminated monument. It was inaugurated without pomp or bathos on August 6, 1791, as one of Berlin's 14 city gates. The record states "that the same military guard took up watch at the newly built station at this gate."

At the end of the 18th century, Berlin numbered at least 150,000 inhabitants. As late as 1866/67, the so-called *Akzisemauer* (excise wall) ran all around the palace. Whoever wanted to enter or leave was required to pass through one of the designated customs gates for the purpose of a "visitation" by the state treasury. Some of these gates' names – for example Hallesches Tor, Oranienburger Tor or Schlesisches Tor – are still on the map of the city; but only the most splendid of these can still be seen in its traditional location.

Frederick the Great (1740-1786) had the Unter den Linden promenade expanded into an avenue. His nephew and successor, Friedrich Wilhelm II (1786-1797), added the Brandenburg Gate as a dignified conclusion to the western end of the street. A plain gate consisting of posts had stood at that spot from 1737 until it was torn down in 1788. Carl Gotthard Langhans (1732-1808) was responsible for the architectural renewal, and he no longer followed the rules of Baroque,

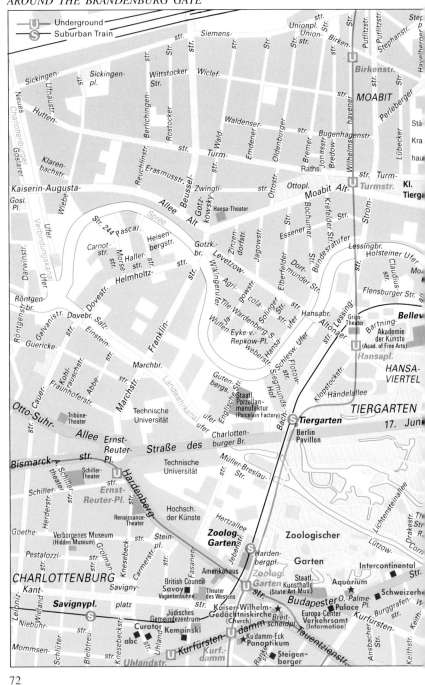

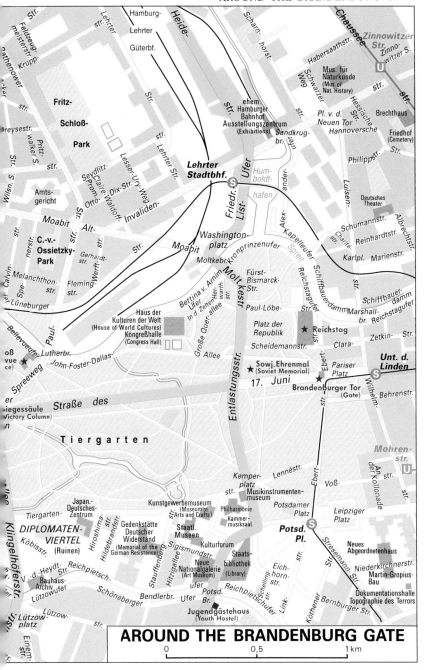

AROUND THE BRANDENBURG GATE

```
0               0,5              1 km
```

the prevailing style until then. In accordance with the new Bourgeois pulse of the times, the Chief Building Director, who had been invited to Berlin from Silesia, was inspired by the spirit and aesthetics of classical antiquity, specifically by the porticos of Greek temple courtyards.

Even if the design's general arrangement was based on the propylaea of the Acropolis in Athen, the Brandenburg Gate was "no mere imitation, but an intelligent new creation of significant monumental effect," as Richard Borrmann emphasized in 1893 in his seminal work on Berlin's architectural and artistic monuments.

Langhans crowned the portal with a victory chariot carrying as a symbolic figure the Goddess of Peace, Eirene. "The quadriga standing on the attic represents the triumph of peace," he wrote. The idea of a peace gate corresponded with the "owner's" intentions; "Fat Willy," as the Berliners called their corpulent

Above: An encounter between past and present at the Brandenburg Gate.

monarch, wasn't interested in military conquests. The state treasury's 110,000 talers for the Brandenburg Gate were a durable investment. Construction of the 20-meter-high gate of Saxon sandstone, (65.5 meters wide and 11 meters thick), lasted two years. Of the five openings, the middle one was reserved for the members of ruling house, who rode by coach back and forth along the bumpy avenue between the Berlin City Castle and Charlottenburg Palace.

To crown the monument, the sculptor Gottfried Schadow (1764-1850) created the copper **Quadriga.** The six-meter-high statue was put into place in the summer of 1793. The Potsdam coppersmith Emanuel Jury executed the design. His uncle in Berlin, Heinrich Jury, who operated a smithy at the Spittelmarkt, had twelve daughters. One of them, the well-shaped Rieke, modelled for the chariot rider, thus becoming anonymously famous throughout the country.

The Brandenburg Gate was conceived as the entryway to the capital. In contradiction to some apocryphal stories, the Quadriga was never turned around from West to East. "The good woman has also had her destiny...", mused German writer Heinrich Heine. In 1806 Emperor Napoleon had her kidnapped and took her to his capital. After his later defeat, Prussian soldiers brought the vehicle back from Paris. The transport to Berlin required six freight cars and 32 horses.

The insult had been repaired, and the Brandenburg Gate became a national symbol. Patriotic enthusiasm reached new heights when Friedrich Wilhelm III re-inaugurated the Quadriga at its accustomed place on August 7, 1814. To commemorate this victory, court architect Schinkel had the goddess modified to a Victoria. On her victory staff she now carried a military medal he designed himself, the Iron Cross. The Prussian eagle was enthroned on the oakleaf wreath.

The Prussian monarchy adopted "the most beautiful gate in all of Europe" – so the Berlin newspapers – as a backdrop for pompous parades. But the gate was also witness to the revolution of March 1848, when rebellious Berlin took to the streets to fight for democratic rights.

Since the founding of the Reich in 1871, Berlin, as Germany's most important metropolis, had grown far beyond the boundaries of the former Prussian seat of government. The Brandenburg Gate now sat at the middle of everything. There is hardly an event in the tides of recent history that is not reflected in the image of the heavily symbolic construction.

The Quadriga also gazed over the revolution of 1918, which paved the way for the election of a constitutional assembly; later it was misappropriated by the Nazis as a stage prop for their propaganda and self-glorifying choreographics. At the end of World War Two, it served as a tank barrier. In 1948, when the Cold War haunted the four-sector city, the portal became the symbol and site of the east-west conflict. Located on East Berlin ter-

ritory in the district Mitte, it marked the demarcation line between the Soviet and British sectors. "To beautify democratic Berlin," the city council in the east rebuilt it from 1956 to 1958. As owner of the only mold, the western Senate contributed a new quadriga. Before it was erected again in the east, Victoria again lost her Iron Cross to symbolize demilitarization. After fresh renovation in 1992 the cross returned to its old place – another act in this Berlin farce.

Traumatic memories are associated with the events of August 13, 1961; the order to close the border to West Berlin, signed by SED-party head Ulbricht, became effective an hour before midnight, and the Brandenburg Gate was the first crossing point to be sealed. A symbol of the divided capital and of a divided country, it dozed in the heavily-defended border strip for 28 years. Millions of tourists, as well as the high and mighty of the world, saw it there from one side or the other: John F. Kennedy and Ronald Reagan from the western side, Nikita S. Khrushchev and a thoughtful Mikhail Gorbatchev from the eastern side.

On November 9, 1989, the violent division of the nation came to a peaceful end. The incredible news of the opening of the Wall had hardly been announced, than the area around the Brandenburg Gate was crawling with people. Berliners from both parts of the city fraternized on the four-meter-wide concrete obstacle.

Unfortunately the damage to the Brandenburg Gate was expensive in the wake of the all-Berlin party-of-the-century that took place on the following New Year's Eve. A group of young climbers made it all the way up to the attic and, after plenty of champagne and beer, gave their vandalism free reign. The chariot was once again dismantled, lowered on ropes, and carried off to the Museum of Transportation and Technology for a thorough restoration. Since August 6, 1991, on the bicentennial of its opening,

the Brandenburg Gate, so charged with destiny once again basks in its old glory. Nevertheless it is also the subject of some controversy as Berlin's politicians have been unable to conclusively decide on how to open it to traffic, if at all. Regular private traffic is generously deviated around the gate, whereas taxis and public busses are allowed through. This ruling already irritates the cantankerous Berlin drivers and a new arrangement for the traffic is expected before the seat of government returns.

The Reichstag

The **Reichstag Building** is crowned with four corner towers and rises at the eastern edge of the Tiergarten. Built according to plans by Paul Wallot and dedicated in 1894, the magnificent building served as the German Empire's Parlia-

Above: The "Reichstag", soon to become seat of the German government. Right: Cycling in the Tiergarten.

ment for the first 24 years of its existence. On November 9, 1918, a new era began at today's **Platz der Republik,** when Philipp Scheidemann, leader of the Social Democratic Party, proclaimed the German Republic from the railing of the Reichstag balcony.

On the night of February 27, 1933, the glow of fire over the 35-meter-high iron-and-glass cupola signalled the growing grip of dictatorship. The Nazi rulers used the Reichstag fire as an excuse to neutralize their political opponents with emergency laws and police terror. The photo of a Red Army soldier raising the Soviet flag above the destroyed Reichstag on April 30, 1945, went and is still going around the world. About 20,000 Russian soldiers died in the battle for Berlin. In 1946 the Red Army erected the **Soviet Memorial** in their memory.

The Reichstag was rebuilt by resolution of the German Bundestag as a symbol of national unity on the political dividing line through Berlin, and the interior was designed as a modern parliament

building. A public exhibit in the western wing displays political ideas and decisions of the last 200 years of German history. On October 4, 1990, one day after the unification, a freely-elected representative assembly of all of Germany, this time consisting of delegates from the West German Bundestag and the last GDR Volkskammer, came together in the plenary hall. Ever since the Bundestag decided to make Berlin capital and seat of the federal government, discussions have been underway about how best to approach the restauration and modernizing of the Reichstag. The money issue, 150 million DM, is one problem; architectural changes are another. What is so far certain is that the glass dome destroyed in the 1933 fire will not be redone. The area in front of the Reichstag extending down to the river Spree has developed new significance since reunification. The new federal chancellery is now to be built beside the Reichstag, directly on the Spree. In additon an architectural competition has been opened for the entire area around the Reichstag. On the other side of the river the Bundesrat will get a new building. Offices for members of parliament and other federal agencies will complete the ensemble.

In 1937/38, as part of the monumental restructuring of the capital of the Third Reich, General Building Inspector Speer had today's **Strasse des 17. Juni** widened to a 51-meter-wide east-west artery, and the **Siegessäule** (Victory Column) and the **Bismarck Group** by court sculptor R. Begas, two typical symbols of imperial Germany of the 19th century, were transported from the Reichstag to the **Grosser Stern** (Great Star). The Victory Pillar was inaugurated with patriotic decorum in 1873 to celebrate the glorious campaigns against Denmark, Austria and France. Thanks to the "golden Else," as Berliners call the eight-meter-high **Victoria** at the top of the column, the Victory Pillar has become a popular "trademark" of the Tiergarten. A 285-step climb to the viewing platform at 67 meters is recommended for the panoramic view.

The Tiergarten

The area over which the bronze lady now gazes, the **Grosser Tiergarten**, was originally graced by a jewel of the Baroque era. The 225 hectare common stretches from the Brandenburg Gate to Charlottenburg. It served originally as a game preserve for the electoral princes. In the past century, Peter Joseph Lenné transformed the Tiergarten into a landscaped park. Information plaques point out the way to quiet areas and historical sights.

The way northward ends at the **Spreebogen**, a bend in the Spree. The **Kongresshalle** (Congress Hall) which is standing there, an American contribution to the international architectural exhibit of 1957, bears the nickname "pregnant oyster", due to its daringly sweeping, shell-like roof; in fact too daring: it already collapsed once. Artists from non-European countries come regularly to

Above: The Congress building – known as the "pregnant oyster" in Berlin dialect.

discuss north-south issues in the **House of the Cultures of the World.** A former princely palace on the Spreeweg has been used by the federal presidents as an official residence in Berlin since 1959. Ex-President Richard von Weizsäcker pointed out the future of things when he made the Berlin residence into the real official residence in 1993. Flags on the roof signal the president's presence in the **Schloss Bellevue**. A side-trip leads to the Hanseatenweg, where the **Academy of Arts** offers exhibits and other events.

In the middle of the 19th century, westward migration began with the transformation of **Tiergarten-Süd** into an affluent residential neighborhood. This noble quarter was destroyed in World War Two. Half-ruins of some embassies lead a shadowy existence in the former **Diplomatic Quarter**. Since the decision to make Berlin once more the capital of Germany, several nations have declared their willingness to re-open their old embassies. That is the case, for example, with the **German-Japanese Center,** an exact copy of the former Japanese embassy, which houses economic and cultural exchange programs with the Far East.

At Stauffenbergstrasse 13-14, once the seat of the German Army High Command (OKH), the officers' Putsch against Hitler failed on July 20, 1944. Four main conspirators were put before a firing squad on the very evening of the failed assassination attempt. In the historical offices of the former Bendler-Block, the **Gedenkstätte Deutscher Widerstand** (Memorial to German Resistance) has an exhibit on the topic, with over 5000 photos and documents.

Kulturforum and Potsdamer Platz

At the **Landwehrkanal,** on the southern edge of the Tiergarten near the **Herkules-Brücke**, one can spot projects from the international architectural exhibit of 1987, such as the **IBA-City Villas** on Stülerstrasse. The **Bauhaus Archives** building, opened in 1979, is a late work of Bauhaus founder Walter Gropius. Hans Scharoun bequeathed a document of contemporary architecture in the **Philharmonie.** This concert house was built 1960-62 as an overture to the **Kulturforum**, now housed on the eastern edge of the Tiergarten, which unites the most important new museum buildings of the Foundation for the Prussian Cultural Heritage. There is still no convincing and comprehensive concept for the area between Potsdamer Bridge and Kemperplatz. All construction restrictions and directives for the area around the Brandenburg Gate have to be reconsidered, now that the western world no longer ends at the **Potsdamer Platz.**

"The old heart of Berlin is beginning to beat again", rejoiced the then governing mayor of the time, Walter Momper, when the first border crossing point in the middle of the city was opened on November 12, 1989. It was initially a needle's eye for the traffic between the two Berlins, but today the deserted area is among the strategic seams on which the German capital will grow together. There is no lack of funds for this prominent downtown location. The service center planned by Mercedes Benz could form the basis of a new highrise city. The foundation stone for this gigantic project of debis, the Mercedes-Benz subsidiary, was laid in October 1994. Before the turn of the century a cool three billion DM will have been spent on the building. This includes – spread over 67,000 square meters – shops, apartments, restaurants, a musical theater, a cinema complex and a five-star hotel of the Hyatt group. The building promoters and the state fathers thus intend preventing the Potsdamer Platz ending up as a lifeless office and dormitory city. At any rate these modern 100-foot high buildings cluster around a piazza.

Next door Sony intends to build its European headquarters, and towards the south Asea Brown Boveri will have their central offices. Planners and engineers are still struggling with the traffic problem: traffic is to be routed on a north-south axis through a new Tiergarten tunnel. This structure will be a technical masterpiece as the concrete foundations must be built right on the water table. In this largest building site in Europe around 5 million tons of concrete will be erected and around 100,000 freight cars of earth transported out of the city.

Located at the intersection of five busy streets, in the 1920s and '30s the Potsdamer Platz was awash in the traffic of a metropolis. After the war it was a gold mine for black marketeers, since the Soviet, American and British sectors met here. In the years of the division, Potsdamer Platz "enjoyed" a dubious fame as a viewing platform for pilgrims to the Wall. Nowhere was the Wall so photogenically spray painted, nowhere was the view into the "far East" more depressing. Now this elegy is nothing but a part of history.

FROM UNTER DEN LINDEN TO ALEXANDERPLATZ

Once upon a time Marlene Dietrich sang: "*Solang noch untern Linden die alten Bäume blühn, bleibt Berlin Berlin.*" ("As long as the old trees on Unter den Linden bloom, Berlin remains Berlin.") The song is quite right of course: **Unter den Linden** has exerted a powerful attraction on people, even today when it is slowly turning into a genuine boulevard once more.

The history of Unter den Linden is the history of the Hohenzollern dynasty. In 1573 a riding path for the electorate was laid out so that the upper ranks of the nobility could ride to the hunt in the Tiergarten. In 1647, Elector Friedrich Wilhelm had this promenade planted with walnut and linden trees. Friedrich II enlarged the *Lindenallee* to a showpiece boulevard. The architectonic history of this avenue began when he gave Wenzeslaus von Knobelsdorff initial instructions to make plans for its expansion.

After twelve years under National Socialism and the destruction wrought by World War Two, much of the Linden's flair was lost. After the war, the government of the GDR expanded it into a lifeless parade route that came to a dead end at the Brandenburg Gate.

The 1390 meters of Unter den Linden are fascinating from the aspect of the German past and present they illustrate. Just beyond the **Pariser Platz**, which is overflowing with souvenir and snackstands, Unter den Linden is flanked by numerous embassies. These are still only branch offices, so to speak, as the ambassadors are still located in Bonn.

Albert Speer, Hitler's chief architect, considered this area very significant when, in 1939, he built the New Chancellery at the corner of **Otto-Grotewohl-** and **Voss-**

Left: History in a nutshell, the cathedral, the arsenal and the TV tower.

strasse – in 1945 the building was reduced to ashes and rubble by the Allies.

The Old Gendarmenmarkt

Having arrived at the Friedrichstrasse, it's worth making a detour via the **Gendarmenmarkt**. Friedrichstrasse, once a haunt of elegant strollers, will remain one vast construction site until 1998. Some billions of marks are being invested here in projects which include the **Lindencorso** and the **Hofgarten** right on the corner of the Linden and the gigantic new **Friedrichstadtpassagen** into which the up-market French store, the **Galeries Lafayette**, will move. At the end of Friedrichstrasse, almost in Kreuzberg, the **American Business Center** is also being built. Whether all of these business will make any money is debatable, considering the enduring lack of the right caliber of purchasers in Berlin.

The **Grand Hotel** stands in counterpoint – so to speak – to the **Haus der Demokratie**, once the meeting place for various political movements that formed the basis of the political parties in the east after the revolution of 1989. At this point take a look at the **Komische Oper** (Comic Opera) where Walter Felsenstein acted his way to supra-regional renown. Another emporium of music is located on the Gendarmenmarkt: The old **Schauspielhaus** (Playhouse), now called the Konzerthaus, constructed by Schinkel in classical style and restored in 1984. The **German** and **French Cathedrals** border the Gendarmenmarkt. The French Cathedral houses the **Huguenot Museum** on the ground floor, and an exclusive wine tavern in its cupola. The German Cathedral is still being restored after the fire in 1994.

Around Bebelplatz

If you walk along **Behrenstrasse** you will eventually arrive at the Linden again, specifically **Bebelplatz**, which is usually

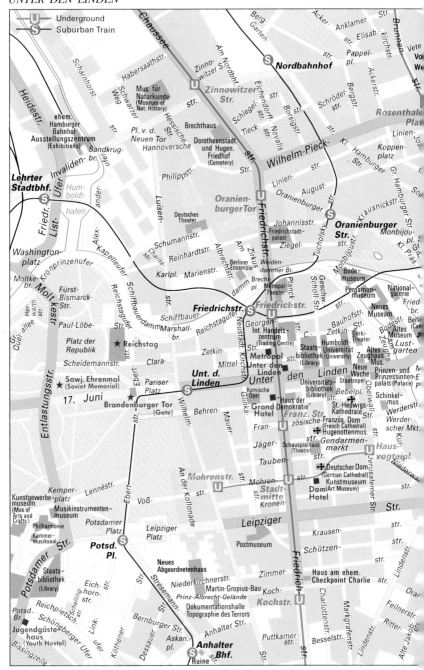

U — Underground
S — Suburban Train

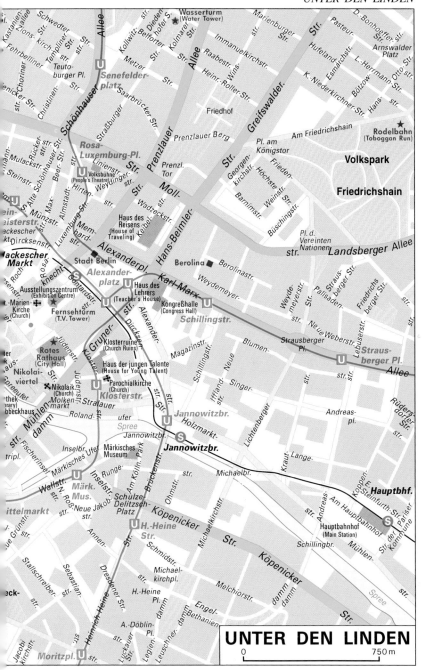

UNTER DEN LINDEN

0   750 m

full of parked cars. As so frequently happens in Berlin, it also recalls some of Germany's less savory past. On May 10th, 1933 Joseph Goebbels ceremoniously had 20,000 books publically burned that had been declared un-German. These included the works of Heinrich Heine, Kurt Tucholsky, Heinrich and Thomas Mann, and Bertolt Brecht. It's a striking bit of cynicism that Goebbels should have sought out the plaza in front of the state opera, a glorification of the mind and the muse. When the state opera was reconstructed in the fifties, the architects went to great lengths to imitate the original style of Knobelsdorff, who completed the first building in 1743 as the first free-standing theater. Knobelsdorff's special design is best reflected today in the six-columned gabled portico.

Towering over the southeast end of the Bebelplatz is the dome of the **Cathedral**

Above: Equestrian statue of Friedrich the Great. Right: The Gendarmenmarkt with the theater and the French cathedral.

of St Hedwig, modelled after the Pantheon in Rome. Friedrich II had this church – a cathedral since 1929 – built for the approximately 10,000 Catholics who lived in Berlin at the time. Philantropy can certainly be ruled out on the part of the king; with the construction of the church, Friedrich II was attempting to pacify the Catholics in his own country after his annexation of Catholic Silesia.

You can see an **equestrian statue of Friedrich II** just before the Bebelplatz on the Linden: On May 31st, 1851, the wraps were taken off this work. Sculptures portraying his contemporaries decorate the monument's pedestal. The former GDR had problems with this part of its national heritage and banished "Old Fritz" to Sanssouci. Not until 1980 was the equestrian statue restored to its old spot. From here, the statue has a view of the **Lindenforum**, the set of buildings surrounding the Bebelplatz. St. Hedwigs Cathedral, the Palace and the Opera are all portions of the *Forum Fridericianum*, which Friedrich had constructed as the ostentatious core of the Prussian royal seat. To this day it has lost but little of its splendor.

There are two additional sculptures diagonally across the street, albeit not on horseback, rather sitting in a pose of deep thought: **Wilhelm** and **Alexander von Humboldt**. In 1810, on the initiative of the older of the scholarly brothers (Wilhelm), a university was founded in the former palace of Prince Heinrich. It has consistently attracted and produced scientists of world repute. Over the course of time, the **Humboldt University** has employed 27 Nobel Prize winners alone. Directly opposite stands the **Alte Bibliothek** (Old Library) which today houses seminar rooms for the university. Because of its convex façade the Berliners refer to it simply as the *Kommode* (a chest of drawers). Right next to the college, the former **Deutsche Staatsbibliothek** der DDR (State Li-

brary of the GDR) contributes to the atmosphere of science and learning. Since merging with the State Library in the west the library houses over 6 million books, 600,000 manuscripts, maps and incunabula.

Standing further to the east up the Linden is the **Neue Wache** (New Guard) designed by Karl Friedrich Schinkel. It was employed by the former GDR as a monument dedicated to the victims of fascism and militarism. A change of the guard – marching in Prussian goosestep no less – took place hourly; every week there was a full-blown military parade. This spectacle continued until reunification and the demise of the GDR people's army.

A sculpture by Käthe Kollwitz, *Mourning Mother with a dead Son*, was placed as a memorial in the Neue Wache in November 1993. The 800-pound bronze statue bears the following controversial inscription: "To the victims of war and tyranny." Two bronze plates at the right and left of the entrance carry the names of the various groups who suffered from these plagues. The Jewish community in Berlin criticized the concept of the Neue Wache, complaining in particular that the memorial fails to properly differentiate between the criminals and their victims.

The **Altes Zeughaus** (Old Armory) adjacent to the Neue Wache previously served as a war museum and was converted in 1952 into a museum of German history, displaying the history of humanity from primitive man up to the latest "socialist achievements," with everything seen from a Marxist viewpoint of course. After the Wall fell, there was an exhibition here of the great variety of vehicles used in escapes from East to West Germany. After reunification the **Deutsches Historisches Museum** relocated here and soon the building is to be renovated and enlarged.

Close by is the **Kronprinzenpalais** (Palace of the Crown Prince), a pompous construction originally built for Crown Prince Friedrich, later used by the Berlin city authorities to accommodate important guests.

Marx-Engels-Platz

Coming over Castle Bridge, you arrive at **Marx-Engels-Platz**, which is delineated by the **Palace of the Republic**, the former **Council of State** (Staatsrat) building and the former **Foreign Ministry** of the GDR. The square will one day become part of the entire government complex.

The Palace of the Republic, from whose façade the SED party emblem was removed in March 1990, served as the seat of the then-elected parliament until the day before its dissolution. Shortly before reunification, the "Palazzo del Prozzo" was closed because of its high asbestos levels. (This nickname is a play on the meaningless Italian word *prozzo,* which sounds like the verb *protzen* in German, meaning to show off). What will happen to the building is unclear. Some argue for tearing it down, others would like to see it protected.

Gate IV, the last remnant of the **Berliner Stadtschloss** (City Castle), was integrated into the façade of the Council of State building. This certainly wasn't done to honor the Hohenzollerns, but rather in memory of Karl Liebknecht, who proclaimed the Socialist Republic from the balcony of the castle in November 1918. The castle was heavily damaged in the Second World War, and the remnants were dynamited in 1950, when it still could have been saved. Wilhelm von Boddien, a businessman from Hamburg, had the castle façade rebuilt in 1993 as a structure of steel and plastic sheeting. Although most Berliners were enthusiastic about it, a real rebuilding of the castle still seems unrealistic, on financial and city planning grounds.

Today the **Rathausstraßw** extends along where the Hohenzollerns once resided. Since 1986, the "victorious

Right: The Red City Hall. Far Right: The global clock on Alexanderplatz.

battle of the proletariat against exploitation" has been displayed between the Spree and Spandauer Strasse. In the center stands a bronze sculpture by Ludwig Engelhardt which depicts Marx and Engels in their usual brooding poses.

It took the work and skill of many masterbuilders before the **Berlin Cathedral** achieved its current appearance. The original Dominican church, dating from 1297, was torn down in 1747 and replaced three years later by the cathedral, conceived by Knobelsdorff and Boumann. Between 1817 and 1822, Schinkel gave the building its Classical grandeur, before a new building replaced the old. This one was realized by Julius Karl Raschendorf between 1894 and 1905. Heavy damage during the bombings of World War Two made extensive restoration necessary. This work has been for the most part finished. The main room, the **Predigtkirche**, is now accessible, and that is where the six sarcophagi of the Hohenzollern are located, representing one of Germany's most important historical treasures. The restoration of the crypt, with further sarcophagi being added, still depends on financing but is expected to be completed in 1995.

Museum Island

Adjacent to the castle, a triumphal arch leads into the **Lustgarten** (Pleasure Garden), which is bordered on its north side by the **Old Museum**. This building, completed in 1830 by Schinkel, is considered to be Germany's oldest museum. Today it has exhibitions of modern art, copperplate engravings, and houses the **New Berlin Gallery**. The Old Museum is part of the **Museum Island**, which is surrounded by the Spree and one of its tributaries, the Kupfergraben. I n addition to the New Museum and the National Gallery, the **Pergamon-** and **Bode-Museum** are part of this renowned complex.Practically everything is repre-

sented on this island – an immensly valuable treasure of art history – from the **antique collection** with the famous **Pergamon Altar** to the **Egyptian Museum** and the collection of the National Gallery.

The Television Tower

The "little GDR" derived a lot of pride from its huge **television tower**. At a height of 365 meters it looms over the entire city center and is visible from a great distance in good weather. The 26,000-ton colossus, with a diameter of 42 meters attracts some 1.3 million visitors annually. From the tower's dome, at 203 meters in height, visibility extends over a radius of about 40 kilometers covering the entire area of Greater Berlin.

Built between 1965 and 1969, at the same time as the television tower, were the enclosing two-storied pavilions with restaurants, cafés and the **Alexanderplatz Exhibition Center**. Next door, the **Marienkirche** today is the only remaining stone witness to the time of the city's

foundation. The **Neptune Fountain** is another point of interest for passers-by on the plaza between the Marienkirche and the **Rotes Rathaus** (Red Town Hall). The fountain, designed in 1886 by Reinhold Begas, portrays the god of the sea with his royal retinue, putti and marine beasts. The acting mayor of Berlin has already moved back into the Rotes Rathaus. The building received its name from the red brick used in the building, which was completed in 1869, and not from its administrative role during the Communist years.

Excursion into the Past

All that is left of the medieval town hall of Berlin is the **Gerichtslaube**, a yard where the court adjourned, that was reconstructed in the Nikolaiviertel, using the original one as a model. It is just one of several historical re-discoveries that were built up around the **Nikolai Church** from 1981 to 1987. The church itself, dedicated to the patron saint of seafarers

and merchants, was Berlin's first stone church (1264). It was destroyed many times, and was finally completed in the 19th century.

A little haven of traditional Berlin exists in the surrounding **Nikolai Quarter** between the Spree river and Spandauer Strasse. Love of detail however stopped with the style of construction. The standard Communist concrete slabs were used in the eighties to build old-fashioned Berlin cafés, bars and museums. In additions to the Gerichtslaube (the Court Arcade), also worth seeing in the pedestrian zone of the Nikolai Quarter is the relief by Gerhard Thieme depicting Berlin's history, the **Foundation Fountain**, the **Museum of Crafts** and the **Taubennest** (dove's nest) **Inn**. The **Ephraim-Palais**, built in 1764, was literally removed in 1935. The blocks of stone were all numbered and have been

Above: In the restored Nikolai Quarter.
Right: High-rise buildings and the massive television tower on Alexanderplatz.

stored, which meant that it was possible to rebuild the "palais" (mansion).

Alexanderplatz

The passages under the town hall lead, in westerly direction, to the **Alexanderplatz**. During the Socialist era something undefinably stuffy seemed to pervade the Alexanderplatz due to the sterility of its buildings and its vast emptiness. The impression of deadness is something that may disappear before the end of the century, as it is planned to build eleven skyscrapers here, including a department store, a luxury hotel and also a publishing house (Gruner & Jahr). Today it is hard to believe that in the 1920s the Berlin writer Alfred Döblin, author of the novel *Berlin Alexanderplatz* (filmed by Fassbinder) which immortalized the square could have felt it to be "the pulsating heart of a world city."

A lot has changed since reunification: At the latest after crossing the underpass of the Alexanderplatz S-Bahn station,

you will find life on the Alex coming alive with colorful street peddlers. The stalls have already smothered two artistic remnants of the GDR era: the **Weltzeituhr** (World Time Clock) by Erich John, a symbol of the internationalism of the former GDR, and the Brunnen der Völkerfreundschaft (People's Friendship Fountain), by Walter Womacka, both dating to 1969. The 39-storey **Forumhotel Berlin** dominates the entire square. Its exclusive restaurant on the top floor boasts a spectacular view of the city center.

The rebuilding of the Alexanderplatz, which ultimately led it to becoming a pedestrian zone, began in 1961 with the construction of the **Haus des Lehrers** (Teacher's House) and the neighboring **Kongresshalle**. In the following years the **Haus des Reisens** (House of Travel) appeared, a cynical title considering the draconian restrictions placed on traveling for East German citizens. Furthermore, the headquarters of the Stasi, East Germany's much-feared secret police, in the **Keibelstrasse** abutted onto the back of

the building. A police station has made its home in what the Stasi used to use as a jail. A surviving section of the 13th-century town wall graces the Klosterstrasse not far from the Alex. The impressive ruin of the **Klosterkirche** (monastery church) is followed by the former **Haus der jungen Talente** (house of young talent). The house is a favorite meeting place for the younger generation. It was originally built in 1700 by Jean de Bodt and restored in 1954.

This little nook of traditional Berlin architectonic design around the Klosterkirche is rounded off by the Parochial Church and the **Traufenhäuser**. One of the latter houses the *Kneipe* "Zur letzten Instanz" (Court of Last Appeal).

Friedrichstrasse and Scheunenviertel

Diagonally opposite the church when looking towards the Alex is a bus stop. From here, you can walk to Friedrichstrasse. On the way there you pass by the **Molkenmarkt** (once the main market-

place in Berlin), cross the Spree river and turn onto the Breite Strasse. Continue to the **City Library** (*Stadtbibliothek*) and the **Ribbeckhaus**, ending up at the old Gendarmenmarkt. A stroll along Friedrichstrasse on the other side of Unter den Linden makes sense at this point. The **International Trade Center,** opened in 1978, towers a short distance before the Friedrichstrasse S-bahn station. Service industries and restaurants, trade associations and representatives of various firms have set up shop in this skyscraper, which was constructed by a Japanese firm.

On the other side of Friedrichstrasse station, the entertainment district of downtown Berlin's 300 year-old north-south axis begins. On one side are the **Metropol Theater**, the cabaret **Distel** and the **Friedrichstadtpalast**; on the other side is Brecht's **Berliner Ensemble** and Max Reinhardt's renowned **Deutsches Theater**. The area around the **Oranienburg Gate**

Above: On Alexanderplatz, showing little respect for the Marx-Engels Monument.

was once the so-called Scheunenviertel (literally "barns quarter" or slums), Berlin's Jewish residential neighborhood. The Nazis extended the name of this quarter to the entire **Spandauer Vorstadt** (Spandau suburb), as this part of the city should still be called, in order to defame the Jews. The remains of the **Synagogue** on the **Oranienburger Strasse,** destroyed in 1938 on the so-called "Reichskristallnacht" (Night of Broken Glass), recalls the 150,000 Berlin Jews who were exterminated during the Second World War. At the present time, Berlin's Jewish community is having the synagogue reconstructed.

The **Scheunenviertel** was once one of Berlin's poorest precincts, though full of liveliness and crazy bars. Today there's not a trace left of the old atmosphere, although the new look of the Oranienburger Strasse may remind one of days gone-by. In the meantime, efforts are being made to salvage the old buildings. The entire quarter was declared a national monument in 1990.

BRANDENBURG GATE
BERLIN-MITTE

Transportation
The zoo and Berlin's historical center are best visited by bus; bus 100 connects most of the important sights. The area between the Reichstag and the Alex can easily be explored by foot.

Cafés and Restaurants
Café Bauer im Grand Hotel, Unter den Linden, Tel. 232 32 03, daily 8 a.m.-1 a.m. **Café Hardenberg**, Charlottenburg, Hardenbergstr. 10, Tel. 312 26 44, open 10 a.m.–midnight, frequented mainly by students. **Opernpalais**, Unter den Linden 5, Tel. 200 22 69, 11 a.m.–midnight daily, arguably the most beautiful coffee house in Berlin, with several cafés and restaurants. **Spreeblick**, Mitte, Probststr. 9, Tel. 242 52 47, daily from 11 a.m. **Turmstuben im Französischen Dom**, Mitte, Französische Str. 5, Tel. 229 93 13, 12 noon–1 a.m. daily. Elegant wine tavern.

In the **Nikolai-Quarter** you'll find most cafés and *Kneipen* around the church square: **Gasthaus zur Rippe**, Poststr. 17, Tel. 243 13 235, 11 a.m.–midnight daily. **Georgbräu**, Spreeufer 4, Tel. 242 42 44, daily from 10 a.m. **Mutter Hoppe**, Rathausstr. 21, Tel. 241 56 25, daily from 11.30 a.m.

Sightseeing
Berliner Antik- und Flohmarkt (antiques and flea market), S-Bahn arches, Friedrichstrasse, open daily 11 a.m.–6 p.m. In addition, a number of exclusive antique shops have opened up under the arches. **Berliner Dom**, Mitte, Strasse am Dom, Tel. 246 91 35, Predigtkirche with Hohenzollern sarcophagi, popular for marriages and baptisms; Mon–Sat 10 a.m.-6 p.m., Sun 11.30 a.m.-5 p.m. **Berliner Rathaus** (town hall), Mitte, Jüdenstrasse/Rathausstrasse, Tel. 240 10. **Brecht-Haus**, Mitte, Chausseestr. 125, Tel. 282 99 16, Tue-Fri 10 a.m.-12 noon, Thur 5-7 p.m., Sat 9.30 a.m.-12 noon, 12.30-2 p.m., closed Sun and public holidays. Visit the studies of Brecht and Helene Weigel and try Weigel's recipes in the cellar restaurant. **Dorotheenstädtischer Friedhof** (Cemetery, Mitte), Chausseestr. 126, open 8 a.m–7 p.m. daily, with the **Hugenotten-Friedhof** next door. On these cemeteries are the last resting places of celebrities like Bert Brecht, Johann Gottlieb Fichte, Karl Friedrich Schinkel, Heinrich Mann and Arnold Zweig. **Deutscher Dom**, Mitte, Gendarmenmarkt, expected to reopen in 1995. **Ephraimpalais**, Mitte, Poststr. 16, Tel. 238 09 20, Tue–Fri, 9 a.m.–5 p.m., Sat 9 a.m.–7 p.m., Sun 10 a.m.-5 p.m. Exhibition of Berlin art from the Baroque to the Biedermeier period. In the palace is a very elegant restaurant, Tel. 242 51 08; 242 51 53. **Fernsehturm am Alex** (TV-Tower, Mitte), Alexanderplatz, Tel. 242 33 33, observation floor, daily 9 a.m.–midnight. **Französischer Dom** (French Cathedral, Mitte), Platz der Akademie 5, Tel. 229 13 07, open for visitors Tue-Sat 12 noon-5 p.m., Sun 1-5 p.m.; glockenspiel daily at noon, 3 and 7 p.m; concerts every first Tuesday of the month at 7.30 p.m. **Gedenkstätte Deutscher Widerstand**, Tiergarten, Stauffenbergstr. 13/14, Tel. 26 54 22 02, exhibition commemorating German resistance, Mon–Fri 9 a.m.–6 p.m., Sat/Sun 9 a.m.–1 p.m. **Haus der Kulturen der Welt**, (House of World Cultures), former Congress Hall, Tiergarten, John-Foster-Dulles-Allee 10, Tel. 39 78 70. **Hugenottenmuseum im Französischen Dom** (Huguenot Museum in the French Cathedral), Tel. 229 17 60, Wed-Sat 12 noon-5 p.m., Sun 1-5 p.m. **Marstall** (Royal Stables), **Berliner Stadtbibliothek** (City Library) and **Akademiegalerie** in the Neuer Marstall, Marx-Engels-Platz, Tel. 244 23 39. **Alter Marstall**, Breite Str. 36. **Nikolaikirche**, Nikolai-Kirchplatz, Tel. 238 09 00, Exhibition on Berlin history, open to the public Tue-So 10 a.m.-6 p.m. Glockenspiel daily 9 and 11 a.m., 2 and 5 p.m., concerts Sat 11 a.m. **Parochialkirche**, Mitte, Klosterstr. 67, Tel. 242 41 90, daily 11 a.m.-7 p.m., guided tours of the Baroque church daily at 11.30 a.m. **Reichstag**, Tiergarten, Platz der Republik, Tel. 397 70, exhibition of German history, open Tue-Sun 10 a.m.-5 p.m. **Schinkelmuseum** in the church Friedrichswerdersche Kirche, Mitte, Werderstr., Tel. 208 13 23, Wed-Sun 10 a.m.-6 p.m. **Siegessäule** (Victory Column), Tiergarten, Strasse des 17. Juni, Tel. 391 29 61, Mon 1-6 p.m., Tue-Sun and public holidays 9 a.m.-6 p.m. **Deutsche Staatsbibliothek**, (State Library), location 1: Mitte, Unter den Linden 8, Tel. 2015-0, Mon-Fri 9 a.m.-9 p.m., Sat until 5 p.m. Location 2: Potsdamer Str. 33, Tel. 2 661, Mon–Fri 9 a.m.–9 p.m., Sat until 5 p.m., phone for times of guided tours **St.Hedwigs-Kathedrale**, Mitte, Bebelplatz, Tel. 203 48 10, Mon–Sat 10 a.m.–5 p.m., Sun 1–5 p.m. **St. Marien-Kirche**, Mitte, Karl-Liebknecht-Str. 8, Tel. 242 44 67, Mon–Sat 10 a.m.-12 noon, 1–4 p.m., guided tours 1 p.m., Sat 12 noon–4 p.m. **Zeughaus / Deutsches Historisches Museum** (German history), Unter den Linden 2, Tel. 21 50 20, Thur-Tue 10 a.m.–6 p.m., Sat, Sun 10 a.m.–5 p.m., guided tours Sat, Sun, Mon 3 p.m. **Additional museums** see page 167, **restaurants** see page 187.

BERLIN DISTRICTS

KREUZBERG
PRENZLAUER BERG
THE NORTH
THE WEST
THE SOUTH
THE EAST
SPANDAU

KREUZBERG

Every big city has its anti-city district, a mark of shame lovingly cultivated by friends, subjected to the abusive tirades of self-professed arbitrators of law and order, proudly trotted out as being so very different from the run-of-the-mill, yet at the same time so typical. Where else but in the middle of Berlin could Kreuzberg ever be found?

The Kreuzbergers have a lot more ideas than money. Today Kreuzberg means poetry, music and painting in some dismal courtyard in a romantically dilapidated ambience. The loud cry of myth seems to ring in our ears and myths are not so fond of having their feet put back on the ground: But that's what Kreuzberg can expect now that Berlin itself has rejoined the world at large.

Kreuzberg Mixture

Modern Kreuzberg is a social ghetto in an overcrowded space: A total of 151,540 Kreuzbergers live together in a space of only 10.4 square kilometers, a greater density than anywhere else in all of Ber-

Preceding pages: Ornate façades recall Kreuzberg's once prosperous past. Left: An artist bearing the typical Kreuzberg look.

lin. The inhabitants' average age is 30 years, making it by far the youngest district of Berlin, and the greatest number of singles lives there too; half of all the residents live alone. But Kreuzberg is also poor – 17 percent of all people of working age are on welfare.

Through the tinted windows of tour buses, visitors can study punks and bums from a safe distance and can experience society's contradictions in full collision, live and in color.

Particularly the *Wessis*, as nonlocals from West Germany are called, glorify Kreuzberg as a Mecca and El Dorado for drop-outs, as a promised district for the so-called scene, which sometimes behaves like a Gallic village, continuously squabbling with itself, but united against the "enemy:" the inhabitants of Zehlendorf's villas, Ku'damm's chi-chi crowd and Christian Democratic senators.

Kreuzberg has a unique atmosphere, a colorful blend of opposites. Originally, the term conjured up the vision of working in the back courtyard and living in the front building. Today it means cohabitation with pensioners who have lived here for decades, West German Kreuzbergers-by-choice and Turkish families: the beer-drinking Berliner in the same boat as the social outsider and the Kreuzberg yuppie. The Kreuzberg mixture is also a feeling

for life, for letting the imagination soar to utopian heights, in spite of the district's unfavorable living conditions.

But almost everything that has been written about Kreuzberg up until now is no longer true: Kreuzberg was roughly pushed from the edge back into the middle in both geographic and socio-economic terms. The Wall had pressed the district onto the margin, so that in some corners the world seemed to have come to an end. Suddenly the district is in the middle of Berlin and has become attractive for real estate companies. Business rents have in some cases increased tenfold. Many a *döner kebab* stand has had to close its business overnight. And artists' studios, alternative businesses and off-theaters are also being threatened by the fall of the Wall. Of the 46 kilometers of Wall between East and West Berlin, nearly nine kilometers were lo-

Right: The ruins of the Anhalter Railway Station. Above: Punk with a Huron-cut in front of a Wall painting.

cated in Kreuzberg. "Thorn in the flesh of the city and time-barrier between two velocities," is what GDR dramatist Heiner Müller called the Wall.

Kreuzberg is a product of the administrative reform of 1920, when Greater Berlin was created. At the time, the district was patched together from the historical districts Südliche Friedrichstadt, Tempelhofer Vorstadt and Luisenstadt. These were mostly poor suburbs for workers toiling in Berlin's factories. Thus, Kreuzberg was long the classical Berlin working class quarter. Today, inofficially, there are even two Kreuzbergs: Kreuzberg 61 and SO 36, the latter being an old, prewar postal designation standing for southeast.

The wounds the Wall inflicted on the city are nowhere more visible than in the former **Südliche Friedrichstadt,** the part of Kreuzberg that today borders on the old, once elegant center of the city, which was destroyed in World War Two and later split down the middle by the Wall. Today it is a sad sight, a concrete desert

with shoddy suburban character, disrupted and lifeless.

At the **Hallesches Tor** subway station, an exit leads directly onto **Mehringplatz.** The former Belle-Alliance-Platz was a public marketplace in the era of the Kaisers. Today it is a concrete circle of apartments standing in closed ranks. **Friedrichstrasse,** the only street in the axis of the square, has been preserved here as a pedestrian zone. The western segment of the street is an ugly site today, though once upon a time it was the heart of the business and entertainment quarter. Running almost at a right angle to it is **Stresemannstrasse,** whose name has been changed to conform to new political situations at least six times. Once it boasted the residence of such famous literary figures as Theodor Fontane, Günther Eich and Joachim Ringelnatz. But, above all, it was an important access street to the **Anhalter** train station. Only three arches of the latter's entry portal still stand, seemingly lost in the middle of **Askanischer Platz.** These are remnants

of the grandiose terminal station which was built in 1874 in imitation Renaissance style: After all, the still-young German capital needed an impressive train station! It was called the "gate to the great blue." From here, trains left for Anhalt, Dresden, Halle, Munich and Frankfurt. In 1936 at the zenith of the travel boom, 1000 taxis waited here for the approximately 180 trains arriving and departing daily, whose cars carried more than two million travelers throughout Europe annually.

Terror and the Wall

Where Stresemannstrasse crosses the Anhalterstrasse, stands the **Martin Gropius Building,** the former Berlin Museum of Handicrafts, built in 1877 in the style of a bombastic Italian palazzo. The building was destroyed in World War Two, rebuilt in fits and starts in 1978 and since then houses changing exhibits. The Wall used to run along Niederkirchnerstraße, but today on the east side of the street, opposite the Gropius building, you can see the former Prussian Members of Parliament Building. After a costly and therefore controversial renovation, this has been the home since 1993 to the Berlin Members of Parliament House, whose former location, in the old Schöneberg city hall, had become to small for them.

In front of the Gropius building is a large, empty, uneven piece of land, such as are found here and there in Berlin. This piece of land between **Niederkirchnerstrasse** (named after Katja Niederkirchner, who was a member of the antiNazi resistance), **Stresemannstrasse, Wilhelmstrasse** and **Anhalterstrasse** is called **Prinz-Albert-Grounds.** After the Second World War, the city planners forgot it – perhaps intentionally. For during the National Socialist period, the Gestapo, the SS and the Secret Service terrorized the country from this seemingly harmless lot.

On a hill in the middle of the grounds is an overview map tracing the course of the old streets and the buildings lining them. The hill is all that remains of the Gestapo cellar, where prisoners from the so-called "house prison" were interrogated and tortured. In 1987 the remnants of this cellar were discovered and excavated. Just in time for Berlin's 750th anniversary, the Senate decided to erect a monument for the victims of the Nazi regime. Today, visitors to the documentation hall **Topography of Terror**, and to the now accessible cellars can get a very strong sense of what happened back then in the middle of Berlin.

Nothing at the intersection of **Zimmerstrasse** and **Kochstrasse** recalls the once famous Checkpoint Charlie, the old border crossing for allied personnel, diplomats and foreigners. That capitalism has been victorious is clearer here than anywhere else: a major American investor is having an **American Business Center** built here at a cost of DM 600 million.

Zimmerstrasse, together with **Jerusalemerstrasse** and **Kochstrasse** belong to the old Berlin newspaper quarter. At the end of the twenties, the newspaper boom reached its height with 114 newspapers published daily; in 1945 the quarter was bombed out. Nothing is left of that former variety. Axel **Springer,** whose publishing house still dominates Berlin's media landscape, built his company highrise as a "bulwark against Socialism" directly in front of the Wall and on the exact spot where the right-wing Scherl publishing company, bought out from Hugenberg, had had its seat before World War Two. Springer, for many years a solitary figure in this deserted landscape, received company in 1989 when the al-

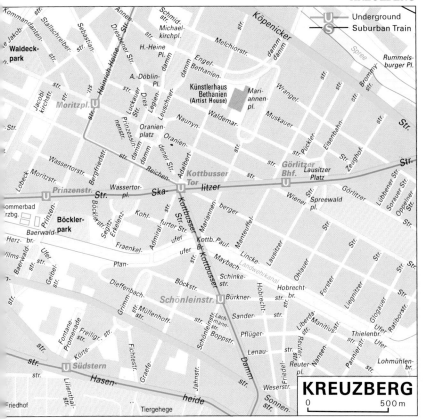

KREUZBERG

0   500 m

ternative **Tageszeitung** moved from the Wedding district to Kochstrasse, where it now sits right in the middle of everything.

The Ullstein publishing house, a subsiduary of Springer, is located on **Lindenstrasse,** which marks the border between the Südliche Friedrichstadt and Luisenstadt. Here stands the **Berlin Museum,** the only construction in western Berlin still remaining from the time of Friedrich Wilhelm I. The Prussian Court held sessions within its walls as late as the 19th century; in 1969 a citizens' initiative gathered enough interest and support to found this city museum. Today, a piece of the Wall with original graffiti graces its entrance.

During the first decades of the 19th century, **Luisenstadt** was a prime business address. Some of today's industrial moguls, Siemens for example, started out as a mini-business in one of its interior courtyards.

The End of the World?

Behind Moritzplatz begins the section of **Oranienstrasse,** which is SO 36's main boulevard. Here are more than the average number of black leather jackets, bandanas, Turkish vegetable shops and *döner kebab* stands. Oranienstrasse is the street where the most leaflets and posters have been posted in the display windows and with the most slogans on the walls of

99

buildings, as for example: "Make rent sharks into fish sticks." It is a street that, despite its colorfulness, always wears a veil of gray. In the snack bar "Brooklyn" – its name is its agenda – on the corner of **Adalbertstrasse** one can sometimes hear "*We gotta get out of this place*", and everyone nods in time to the music. Or, between coffee and Mick Jagger, someone may scream out his or her nightmares. This may be the street with the greatest number of social outcasts. The punks at **Kottbusser Tor** around the corner make no bones about their no-future attitude. The multi-storey concrete complex in whose shadow they sit or lie seems to be the petrified confirmation that, in this spot, one can only feel awful.

Bethanlendamm, which ends at **Mariannenplatz,** leads to one of Kreuzberg's idyllic spots: the first square in Berlin that was planned to be decorative, and it has remained quite a jewel, if hard-

won. Originally, the Senate wanted to tear down the buildings in the Bethanien quarter, but the residents raised a ruckus and were just able to prevent a radical "renewal" of the area. Instead it was modernized and restored: Interior courtyards and annexes were torn down to make way for green areas, and, with them, all the backyard factories disappeared. The center of Mariannenplatz is the **Künstlerhaus Bethanien,** a former deaconesses' hospital. 21 studios for Turkish and German artists are located here, as well as the Turkish district library, workshops and rooms for exhibits and theatrical and musical performances. While there are a few German-Turkish meeting places in Kreuzberg, everyday life goes on mostly in benign indifference to each others' culture at best, even though one-third of all Kreuzbergers have Turkish passports. Unluckily the German inhabitants' contact is usually restricted to shopping at the Turkish vegetable vendors' or to eating a *döner kebab*. One minor exception is the *Ham-*

Above: Demonstrations on the Kottbusser Damm – almost a daily event in Berlin.

mam, a Turkish steam bath in the women's center **Schokofabrik** (Chocolate Factory), where young Turkish and German women enjoy relaxation and body care together.

Only one stop with the elevated subway separates the **Görlitzer Bahnhof** station at the end of the Oranienstrasse from the **Schlesisches Tor** station. Until November 1989, this was the terminal station in every sense of the word. Hardly anyone strayed onto the **Oberbaumbrücke,** the bridge over the Spree leading to the Friedrichshain district. Before the Wall was built, two lanes of traffic thundered over the red brick bridge built in the style of a castle. Now pedestrians stream in both directions again.

The **Landwehrkanal** was built in the middle of the 19th century to connect the Upper Spree at Schlesisches Tor with the Lower Spree in Charlottenburg. Freight barges transported coal, gravel, limestone, fruit and potatoes. Today, only excursion steamers chug past.

Savoir-vivre in Kreuzberg

Regal buildings, some of them with ivy-covered Art Nouveau façades and small front gardens, line the **Paul-Lincke-Ufer.** It is a chic place even label-conscious yuppies need not be ashamed of. In the summer it's a gorgeous spot to enjoy the sunshine in one of the cafés on the bank of the river, or to cast a glance across to the **Maybachufer** with its colorful Turkish open-air market.

Distinguished buildings from the age of the Industrial Revolution can also be seen diagonally across the canal on the **Planufer** and around the **Südstern**, an exclusive area of Kreuzberg. The Südstern also marks the beginning of the **Bergmannstrasse.** In good weather, the stretch on the other side of the cemeteries can always pass as a strolling boulevard. The quarter's "shopping center" is the

Marheineke-Markthalle, one of three market halls remaining from the 14 that the Magistrate had built in the last century to improve hygienic conditions of the weekly markets.

Although the slope is quite steep behind the Bergmannstrasse, this part of Kreuzberg is completely built-up, so that there is not a single free spot. In the middle of the concrete wilderness is the **Chamissoplatz,** a beautiful, quiet, nostalgic little square. A piece of Kreuzberg as it once was: dignified, but not genteel. Straight ahead on the Bergmannstrasse, here named Kreuzbergstrasse, is the **Viktoriapark,** in which the **Kreuzberg mountain**, indeed the "Cross Mountain", rises. This hill also used to be called Goetzscher Vineyard, for wine was in fact cultivated here. It is worth climbing the mere 66 meters – after all, the district adopted the mountain's name, though only after long disputes.

From the top, one sees almost all of Kreuzberg and, of course, the little waterfall, which seems to babble off to the **Grossbeerenstrasse.** On this street, a mighty gateway leads into **Riehmers Hofgarten**, a small idyllic garden courtyard with 24 apartment buildings of upper-crust lineage. The master mason and building contractor Wilhelm Riehmer built this unusual complex in 1881. Buying the grounds at a bargain price he showed true speculator's sense, for the Hofgarten became the address of the upper class. Officers from the nearby dragoons' barracks and important treasury officials rented the 5-6 room apartments, which are divided into smaller ones today. As ever, illustrious tenants still live here: doctors, a gallerist and the obligatory Kreuzberger artists, such as Ter Hell or Walter Störer, whose pictures can be seen regularly in the **Café Mora.** A hotel, Riehmers Hofgarten, also belongs to the complex.

If one continues along the end of the Grossbeerenstrasse, the Hallesches Tor soon comes into sight again.

PRENZLAUER BERG:
SCENE AND KIEZ IN THE EAST

Long before the Wall came down and the city was reunified, **Prenzlauer Berg** was one of the liveliest districts in East Berlin. Not because it became a showcase community while the Socialists were in power – quite the contrary. Except for one little area where new apartment buildings went up alongside narrow streets, Prenzlauer Berg has been seedy for four decades.

It was the GDR's avantgard scene that chose the grey, dilapidated buildings for their residences: artists, dissidents, citizens pressure groups and squatters moved in. Since reunification in 1989, this mixture has become flashier and received new stimuli from the now much larger outside world. Yet this district is still counted among those parts of the city with the lo-

Above: Kiez tranquility in the recently restored Husemannstrasse. Right: Children at play in a secluded backyard.

west real incomes. Gradually the houses are being repainted and stuccoed, but well over half of them qualify as "encumbered by restitution" – which means, following the agreement which sealed German reunification, that the house-owners from before the socialist period will have their property returned to them.

Until this predicament has been resolved, nothing permanent can be done with the area. The district is thus granted a kind of interim period which can be used for experimentation and trying out. This means attitudes will remain somewhere between Kiez and scene, on the one hand typically Berlin and on the other hand experimental and extremely vivacious. Nowhere else in the East are there so many small shops where one can buy anything from stamps to cookies – sometimes even real health food.

The Tenement-Block District

Anyone who has heard of Berlin being the biggest tenement-block city in the

world, will find this prejudice confirmed: five and six-story buildings that extend over up to five tiny courtyards. These complexes were built at the end of the 19th century in accordance with a particular architectural concept: James Hobrecht at that time defended the idea of having poor and rich families jammed together in the front and rear buildings of these complexes as constituting a social revolution. The child from a basement apartment in the fourth building back would pass out, on his way to school, through the same front gate as the child who lived in the luxurious second floor of the first building. His critics thought his idea was social quackery.

But the small apartments with their common toilet in the hallway have attracted young people in recent decades. They moved into those apartments that had been cleared by socialist housing policies. Their predecessors were usually families with small children who had moved – not always happily – to the huge ghetto-like new housing projects on the

north-eastern edge of Berlin. The elderly were the only ones who stayed. The people who move in now are from France, the United States and often from West Germany. Some squatters have even managed to legalize their status, as they once did in the west part of the city. They receive grants from the Federal Government and renovate the houses.

Schönhauser Allee

If you would like to get an idea of what this district with its many small neighborhoods is like, start at the Schönhauser Tor. You might notice that most of the lime-trees are gone. They have been dying off since the 80s and had to be felled due to permanently overdosing on car exhaust fumes or defective gas lines. This is an evil which has cost this thickly populated area more than 400 trees, many of which were a hundred years old or more. Still, this street with its typical Berlin charm its a good place for a stroll. Right behind the Senefelderplatz the sub-

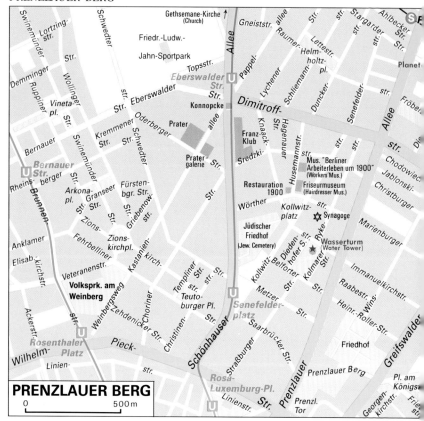

PRENZLAUER BERG

0   500m

way appears above ground and continues until just before Pankow. The elevated subway viaduct, nicknamed "the city council's umbrella", is quite a sight. In 1990, the **Schönhauser Allee** became an urban renewal project, with renovation, digging, closing of gaps and restoration of the beautiful buildings from the promoterist period are being renovated. The color grey, formerly the characteristic color of the East, is disappearing.

The **Senefelderplatz** is typical of this rapidly built district – but it will hardly be possible to guess its original appearance once the garden architects have implemented their plans over the next few years. A monument was erected here in 1892 to commemorate the inventor of li-

thography, Alois Senefelder. A few steps further along the allee is number 22, a large brick building which is today a police station.

This **police station** was built in 1880 by the Jewish financiers Manheimer as an additional old people's home for the then large Jewish community of Berlin. In 1944, the community was removed as owner from the land register and the building became one of the notorious "assembly points" for the Nazi death camps. Until recently, there was not even a plaque to commemorate the fact that Jewish citizens were sent from here on their last journey to the death camps. Adjoining the former old people's home is the **Jewish Cemetery**, with its 5000 graves

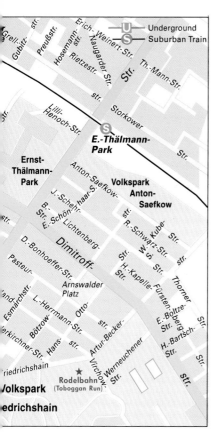

the largest cemetery in Berlin. It was consecrated in 1827. The Manheimers are buried here, as are famous Berliners such as the painters Max Liebermann, David Friedländer and the composer Giacomo Meyerbeer. Along the main paths monumental family memorials reflect the rise of many Jewish families in the years after 1850.

Kollwitzplatz and its Surroundings

The Wörther Straße turns right off the Schönhauser Allee and continues to **Kollwitzplatz**, so named after the artist Käthe Kollwitz, who lived here and portrayed the social misery of her neighborhood. Two monuments on the Kollwitzplatz

commemorate her work. The square, surrounded by high residential buildings, is one of the centers of the district. Here and in the side streets there is a plethora of restaurants, bars and trendy cafés.

The **Husemannstraße** begins at Kollwitzplatz. During the GDR regime it looked like the backdrop for a movie about the turn of the century. It then was the only restored part of the district amongst all that melancholic grey, but now other streets are catching up and it is slowly losing this originality. However, it does remain a mile for strollers, with its old-fashioned stores, craftsmen's shops, cafés and bars which bring back to life the late years of the 19th century.

Not far from here is another biotope of the Prenzlauer Berg: the area around the waterworks, between three streets: Kolmarer, Diedenhofer and Rykestrasse. The graceful watertower at Knaackstrasse 23 was the first one in Berlin, built in 1856. The second, fat tower dates back to 1876 and has been lived in since the 50s.

Debates have raged over this strange piece of property, whether it should become a public facility or be renovated for expensive apartments. Around the fat tower, bars and numerous little restaurants have clustered, including a Russian one. At Rykstrasse 53 a small **synagogue** is hidden, which was one of the few Jewish temple buildings in Berlin to survive the twelve years of Nazi terror. Since its restoration at the end of the late 70s it has once again become a meeting-place for the the Jewish community.

Gethsemane Church

We continue on to Stargader Strasse, which leads to **Gethsemane Church**. This building is more than 100 years old and since 1989 has symbolized passive resistance in the GDR. When the regime started its slow decline in the autumn of that year, Gethsemane Church and its silent vigils of admonishment suddenly became the center of opposition. On the night of October 7, the predominantly young people who had gathered here were faced by police forces who went berserk. Equipped as if for a civil war they unleashed a brutality on the demonstrators unprecedented in the Honecker state. There were random arrests of those holding candles and calling for political change. It took six months to quash the judgments that were passed out that night.

From Stargader Strasse we continue on to **Schliemannstrasse 23** which houses not only the publishing house of the citizen action groups and Basis Druck, but also the Robert Havemann Foundation and its archives. In addition to the writings of the dissident Havemann, who is generally considered the intellectual mentor of the East German opposition movement, documents pertaining to the Wende are kept here too.

Right next door are the Matthias Domaschk Archives – named after a young civil rights activist who died while being detained by the Stasi and whose death still has not been cleared up even today – and the Environment Library, another nucleus of East German opposition. Until 1990, it was part of the Zion Temple located at the square of the same name and which, during the GDR period, was the only library in East Berline holding Western publications – under the roof of the temple.

The cemetery on Lychener Strasse – you won't miss it as it is surrounded by a red wall – is called the **cemetery of free thinkers**. Heinrich Roller, the inventor of stenography, is buried here, as is Wilhelm Hasenclever, a publisher and the first chairman of the SPD. The cemetery has now been restored and is a kind of a green oasis in the midst of this district of stone, concrete and brick.

Right: The old water tower in Prenzlauer Berg, a local hallmark.

Kastanienallee

If you continue on through the Pappelallee and cross the Schönhauser Allee, you will hit Kastanienallee ("Chestnut Avenue"). The chestnut trees used to cover the street like a green cathedral, but unfortunately most of them have succumbed to leaks from the city gas pipes. The street isn't very appealing at first glance, but in a way it still represents the character of Prenzlauer Berg best: if you pass through the front courtyards, you end up in a maze of back courtyards.

A lot of the traditional workshops are still located in these courtyards – the old Berlin mixture: people live in front and work in back; sometimes this arrangement gets a little mixed up too. As well as all kinds of restaurants and cafés you will find a slew of little groceries.

At the beginning of the street is the famous **Pratergarten**, one of the oldest beer-gardens in Berlin. Unfortunately as yet they haven't been able to come up with financial backing to carry out the urgently needed restoration. Number 77 is the oldest building in the district.

The **Oderberger Strasse** turns off right and left from the Kastanienallee and this is where you will find avant-garde galleries. Worth seeing is a **public swimming pool**, designed by Ludwig Hoffmann and built in 1902, which unfortunately was closed ten years ago. You can try to talk the custodian into letting you have a look at the pool hall: reminiscent of a cathedral, several stories high promenade floors enclose the old public swimming baths.

The Thälmann Monument

Behind the Prenzlauer Alllee, near the S-Bahn station, is the new residential area, **Thälmannpark**, which extends as far as Greifswalder Strasse. It was one of the last prestigious projects of the old GDR, built in extreme haste to commemorate an anniversary of the birth of Thäl-

mann, the murdered leader of the worker's party. The residential area went up on a piece of land where the gasworks used to be, without cleaning up the contaminated ground first. Beneath the residential high-rises, environmental protectionists fear the worst. The old gasometers, a precious industrial monument, unfortunately were blown up in 1984. The **Zeiss Planetarium** is right next door, with interesting exhibitions and a cinema in addition to the astronomy.

Between Fröbelstrasse and Dimitroffstrasse is the present district authority, which used to be a hospital for the poor. It starts at Prenzlauer Allee No. 75 and has a little chapel where once the dead were laid out in. Today this is where the **Prenzlauer Berg District Museum** puts on exhibitions of contemporary history. In 1945, the first Soviet Commandant lived here; the basement was used as a prison, which the Stasi later took over.

Dimitroffstrasse 100 houses the little museum; the Cultural Center, which has a small gallery, is right in front of it.

At the end of a wretched little park lies the district's number one bone of contention: the massive **Thälmann Monument**. Some people are fighting bitterly to have this 40 foot colossus torn down, while others who want it to remain oppose this with gentle obstinacy. For a long time there has been a generous new plan for an unusual park that would distance the observer from the gigantic statue, without destroying it. It would be hidden behind a maze of green poplars – but yet again, there are no funds. This giant heroic statue with its raised fist could serve as illustrative material for those who want to find out what the GDR was like.

The square in front of the statue used to be the site for parades. It was built – in the teeth of stiff resistance from the East Berlin artists – by Lev Kerbel, a Soviet artist who specialized in this kind of monument, and therefore resembles Lenin. The local genius came up with the portmanteau name of Le-Mann for the monument, summarizing the situation in a word.

THE NORTH

In the North of Berlin lie the districts of Reinickendorf, Wedding and Pankow. In contrast to Wedding, which is a densely built-up district, the outlying districts of Reinickendorf and Pankow boast extensive natural landscapes.

Reinickendorf

Reinickendorf's district coat-of-arms shows a fox next to six ears of wheat, symbolic of the six villages that once lay among forests and fields and which, together with two manors and a garden city, were incorporated into Greater Berlin's 20th administrative district in the municipal reform of 1920. With an area of about 89 square kilometers, Reinickendorf is, after Köpenick, the second largest district in Berlin, with over 250,000 inhabitants. This northernmost district in the Greater Berlin area is still marked today by an extensive forest landscape and a great deal of water. Reinickendorf's nickname, the "Green North," is certainly deserved. The old villages and settlements have, for the most part, managed to maintain their individuality, since the separate communities never really grew together.

The old village of **Tegel** has always been popular with Berliners as a goal for outings. Architecturally interesting here is the modern residential settlement **Am Tegeler Hafen**, which was built in 1987 under the aegis of the **Internationale Bauausstellung**, the architectural exhibition. The most imposing building is by far the **Humboldt Library** on the **Karolinenstrasse**. The carefully planned combination of living, culture and leisure has been achieved only partially so far. The architectural exhibit also spawned another project, namely construction of a

Right: The oppresisve skyline of the highrise settlement in the Märkisches Viertel.

special plant to remove phosphates from the **Tegeler Lake**. Right next to the old harbor basin, the **Tegeler Fliess** flows into the lake. Hiking paths lead through charming natural surroundings, a unique swamp landscape of the March, that stretches from Tegel to **Lübars**.

The **Tegeler Forest** separates the village of **Heiligensee** from the other Reinickendorf communities. Far afield of the highrise quarters and industry complexes, Heiligensee lies on a narrow spit of land between the River Havel and Heiligensee (lake). In this fishing village, first documented in 1308, time seems to have stood still. Fishermen smoke their own fish as they have been doing for ages. The old village green is among the largest and prettiest in Berlin. Farmhouses, smithies, a village pub and a government- and schoolhouse from the last century are grouped around the village church.

Nearly as idyllic, but more modern, is the garden city **Frohnau,** located all the way in the north of Reinickendorf. An affluent neighborhood with villas and country houses clustered around the **Zeltinger Platz** and neighboring Ludolfinger Platz at the beginning of the century. Evidence of this posh past is the polo field on **Gollanczstrasse**, opened in 1913, where tournaments are still held.

The **Edelhoffdamm** is the site of a Far Eastern curiosity. In 1920, the Berlin doctor and language specialist Paul Dahlke, a convert to Buddhism, built a **Buddhist House** in Frohnau. One enters the grounds through a portal in the shape of an elephant. One must then climb 73 steps to reach the temple, which stands on an elevation. This institution in Frohnau is, in the meantime, open to the general public, and serves as the center of the Buddhist community in Berlin, which is permanently supervised and instructed by three monks from Sri Lanka.

A true jewel on the edge of the metropolis is the former village of **Lübars**. The

old village core is tucked away in the fields and moor meadows of the Tegeler Fliess valley.

Within eyeshot of this idyll towers the silhouette of the **Märkisches Viertel**, which was the most famous satellite city of the sixties. The high-rise buildings were considered repulsive tenements, and even caused a controversy in expert circles. The approximately 17,000 newly built apartments house a crowd of about 50,000. In the meantime, however, people have taken a liking to the settlement, partly because of various improvements that were made on the façades of the houses, giving them a brand new look, and because of the increased park space that makes life more pleasant in the Märkisches Viertel. One of the best illustrations of this new attitude is the change in the nickname of the longest building on the **Wilhelmsruher Damm**, which was designed by the architects René Gagés and Volker Theissen: It used to be called *Long Misery,* but made its way up to *Champagne Building.*

Wedding: Industry and Kiez

Around the turn of the century, **Wedding** developed into the most important industrial district in the north of Berlin, and soon gained notoriety as a "red" workers' district. Schering, Schwarzkopf, AEG and other major companies were founded here. Today, a population of 160,000 crowds together in the relatively small district. Wedding lost its character as a purely working-class district a long time ago; a colorful mixture of nationalities now lives here and the off-off cultural scene knows how to make good use of old factory halls.

The district's history traces back to the year 1251. The name derives from the nobleman Rudolf de Weddinge, who had an estate established here around 1200. The district's second historic root lies in the **Gesundbrunnen** section. The name means "healthy source", and according to an old legend, the Prussian King Friedrich I discovered a spring whose water is rich in iron. This later became a spa

109

named "Friedrich-Gesundbrunnen". In the last century, the surrounding area developed into an entertainment quarter. On the Art Nouveau façade of the building at **Badstrasse 38/39**, a relief of the former well house still recalls the old spring. This quarter has retained the name Gesundbrunnen, but the Berlin dialect simply refers to it as the "Plumpe". Wedding's diverse life best reveals itself in the old buildings of the **Arnheim'sche Safe Factory** in the Badstrasse, which house the largest sculptors' atelier in Europe, and by the **Innovation Centers BIG** and **TIP** in the **AEG Building**, where small companies test out new technologies. Another symbol of modern transformations is the juxtaposition of the historic gate to the AEG grounds and the contemporary glass and steel construction of the Nixdorf computer company on **Brunnenstrasse**.

Above: The simple village church of Lübars in a poetic sunset lightning.

Since 1961 the dreary apartment buildings, erected on both sides of the street at the turn of the century, have been demolished to improve living quality. **"Meyers Hof"** in the Ackerstrasse, torn down in 1972, was examplary for of the poor living conditions endemic in these mass residential sections. The complex consisted of a front house and annexes in which up to 2000 people lived. This ambitious urban renewal project, the most extensive in Germany, affected 14,700 apartments and 1760 businesses. New housing with greenery, schools, kindergartens and retirement homes replaced the old buildings.

The most famous street in Wedding is without doubt the **Bernauer Strasse.** In 1961, when the Wall was being built, tragic scenes took place here when the entire length of the street was divided down the middle. In desperation, East Berliners jumped from windows onto West Berlin territory. Until November 1989, the street attracted plenty of visitors wanting to have a look at the Communist border facilities. On November 9, 1989, the first crossing for East Berliners was set up here. Since then there has been vehement discussion as to whether a **Berlin Wall Memorial** should be set up here. Many local residents who had been forced to live cheek by jowl with the concrete border for so many years do not want any reminder of the horrors of the Cold War. But the city fathers are having their way. However, the open competition for a concept for this memorial received no first prize, but rather three second prizes. The winner will be chosen at some as yet unspecified time by the Department of the Interior in Bonn.

One of Berlin's best-known hospitals, the **Rudolf-Virchow-Krankenhaus**, still stands on the **Amrumer Strasse**, where it was built between 1889 and 1906 according to plans by the famous Berlin architect, Ludwig Hoffmann. Unfortunately, some of the buildings had to make way for the modern clinic, which is being expanded to a university clinic. The **Berlin Heart Center,** a world-famous institute, also stands on the clinic grounds.

Historic buildings are rare in Wedding. Between 1832 and 1835, Berlin's most famous architect, Karl Friedrich Schinkel, built the **Alte Nazarethkirche** on **Leopoldplatz** in the style of a basilica. In the future, the church will provide room for cultural projects.

Schinkel also designed a second church in Wedding, the **St. Pauls Church** at the corner of Pankestrasse and Badstrasse. The **Wedding District Court** on the **Brunnenplatz** was designed in quite a strange way. Erected at the beginning of the century, this court building with its decorative portal and pompous vaulted ceilings is a reproduction of the Albrechtsburg in Meissen.

Pankow: Functionaries' Idyll

The little stream **Panke,** whose source is north of Bernau, gave this district its name. Today, about 116,000 people live in Pankow, which, together with Köpenick, is considered by and large one of the better residential areas in Berlin's eastern section. During the Cold War, the district achieved dubious fame in the expression "Pankow regime."

Schloss Niederschönhausen, in the heart of Pankow, was the office of Wilhelm Pieck, the first and only president of the former GDR, and later became the temporary seat of the State Council. A wall now separates the inconspicuous construction and its auxiliary buildings from the public **Schlosspark**, which was designed by architect Peter Joseph Lenné.

Nearby **Majakowskiring,** colloquially known as "the town," was off-limits until the seventies. Residents of this former government quarter included Otto Grotewohl (Nr. 46), Wilhelm Pieck (Nr. 29) and Johannes R. Becher, poet and first GDR Minister of Culture (Nr. 34). Pankow also attracted a considerable number of artists: writer Arnold Zweig, brother of the better known Stefan Zweig, lived at Hehmeyerstrasse 13, singer Ernst Busch at Leonhard-Frank-Strasse 11 and Ossietzky's family at what is now Ossietzkystrasse 24-26.

Two of a total of 69 Pankow buildings declared national monuments are located in **Johannes-R.-Becher-Strasse**: the **Altes Rathaus** (old city hall), with its impressive tower, and the old **Parish Church** on the old **Village Green**. The church, built of fieldstone, is the district's oldest building, probably dating back to the 15th century. For over 130 years, the **Pankower Wochenmarkt** (a weekly open-air market) has thrived behind it.

The tiny communities of **Rosenthal, Buchholz, Buch** and **Karow,** which are surrounded by forest and meadows, exude a pastoral atmosphere more typical of the March of Brandenburg than of the city of Berlin. It is just another bit of evidence that Berlin's northern area has many faces.

THE WEST

Once upon a time **Schöneberg**, **Charlottenburg** and **Wilmersdorf** were independant communities outside the gates of Berlin. The three districts, that were incorporated into Greater Berlin in the reform of 1920, developed into residential districts for well-to-do citizens.

The Schöneberger Kiez

Schöneberg, a relatively small district with 154,000 residents in an area of 12.3 square kilometers, is known primarily for its **town hall**. Between 1949 and 1990, West Berlin's politicial decisions were made here. This stately edifice was built between 1911 and 1914 at a cost of 8 million gold Marks, a visible demonstration of the wealth of the city of Schöneberg. High above the town hall stands the 70-

Above: An angel – symbol of peace in a Schöneberg yard. Right: An almost rural scene – the Grunewald hunting lodge.

meter-high tower, where the **liberty bell**, a copy of the famous Liberty Bell in Philadelphia, has been rung every day since 1950. In June 1963 hundreds of thousands of Berliners cheered the American President Kennedy on the plaza when he proclaimed, "Ich bin ein Berliner"("I am a Berliner"), a rhetorical statement of solidarity with the beleaguered city. In the course of the same year, the Berliners renamed the square **John-F.-Kennedy-Platz**.

The original town hall was on **Kaiser-Wilhelm-Platz**, the former center of Schöneberg. This square crowns a small elevation, called "Schöner Berg" (beautiful mountain), which gave the district its name. Few traces remain of the village that once was here. The **Landkirche** rising above the **Hauptstrasse** was built in 1766, in the time of Frederick the Great. Its façade was renovated in 1955.

Next to it, an old cemetery harbors the mausoleums of Schöneberg's *Millionenbauern* – the 19th century millionaire real estate sharks. These Berlin citizens made fortunes by speculating on the land. Their former

villas on the Hauptstrasse recall the district's past splendor.

The **Heinrich-von-Kleist-Park**, situated on the **Potsdamer Strasse**, is the successor of the botanical garden, which was located in Schöneberg until 1908. The **Königskolonnaden**, or royal colonnades, designed in 1780 by Carl von Gontard, line the Potsdamer Strasse. They originally adorned the Königsbrücke at Alexanderplatz, but the expansion of the inner city displaced them in 1910. The **Superior Court of Justice** of Prussia, built between 1909 and 1913, is located in the rear of the park. During the Nazi period, the notorious "Volksgerichtshof," the People's Court, under infamous Roland Freisler held its sessions in the building. After the war, the Allied Control Council took up quarters in it for three years, and in 1972 the Four Power Treaty for Berlin was signed here. Until 1991, the Center for Allied Air Security worked here. A year later, the Allies gave the building back to the city, and the Superior Court moved back into its old

quarters. Not far from the Kleistpark, on the corner of **Pallasstrasse** and **Potsdamer Strasse**, the Berliners once cheered the six-day races in the Sportpalast. But they also cheered in the same building when, in 1943, Joseph Goebbels held forth on the notion of a "total war".

In the course of its turbulent history, the **Potsdamer Strasse** has been completely transformed. During the days of the Kaiser and the Weimar Republic, it was one of Berlin's best business addresses, but after the construction of the Wall it deteriorated into a seamy and "sinful" district, with gambling halls and prostitution accounting for much of its financial turnover. In the meantime the street has become more attractive again, numerous publishers and public relations departments have opened offices here.

Schöneberg Island between **Torgauer Strasse** and the **Sachsendamm** is a densely built-up part of the city, a typical workers' *Kiez*. Today it is completely surrounded by railroad tracks. Berlin's oldest **gasometer** towers over the roofs, visible far and wide; it is still in operation. The "island" also contains the historic **St Matthäus Cemetery** at Grossgorschenstrasse 12/14 where the Grimm brothers and Berlin's famous doctor, Rudolf Virchow, rest in peace.

The town of **Friedenau** developed very differently: Well-heeled officials and retirees preferred the quiet of this settlement of country houses on the **Bundesallee** to the noise of the big city. Later, numerous artists followed them, including the writers Max Frisch, Erich Kästner, Günter Grass, Hans Magnus Enzensberger and Uwe Johnson. Children in Berlin captured the area's atmosphere in a little ditty that goes: "In Friedenau, the sky is blue, the goat and his wife are dancing, too." The Berlin scene meets evenings on the **Winterfeldplatz** and during the day it comes to buy fresh fruit at its open-air market. *Kneipen,* cafés, small stores and rows of antique stores line the street as far as **Nollendorfplatz**.

Charlottenburg Beyond the Ku'damm

This district's traditional *Kiez* lies around **Gierkeplatz** with the **Luisen-Kirche**, built in 1716. *Kneipen,* small shops and old apartment buildings embody traditional Berlin *Gemütlichkeit.* The oldest buildings are the former **Ackerbürgerhaus** at Schustehrusstrasse 13 and the former **schoolhouse** in the Gierkezeile, built in 1786.

Charlottenburg's highest building provides Berlin with one of its great symbols: the **radio tower** on the trade fair grounds. The 138-meter-high construction was dedicated in 1926 on the occasion of the third German Radio Exhibit.

The buildings of the trade fair now standing are of later date, built in 1936. Between 1973 and 1979, when they were

no longer big enough to serve the exhibitors properly, the **Internationales Congress Centrum (ICC)** was added to the complex. A special bridge crosses the *Autobahn,* joining the two complexes. Over 20,000 people fit into the colossal building reminiscent of a spaceship.

The **Gedenkstätte Plötzensee** was established in 1952 by the Senate of Berlin in the prison where 1800 members of the resistance against the Nazi regime were executed between 1933 and 1945.

Wilmersdorf: Churches and Government Offices

Wilmersdorf exhibits two diverging faces. The district consists of densely built-up metropolitan areas as well as the nearly rural exclusive settlement of Grunewald. Most of its 146,000 residents are government officials or white-collar workers. The famous and infamous "Wilmersdorfer widows," beneficiary heirs of the afore-mentioned, live here as well.

Little remains of the old farming community of Wilmersdorf. The core of the village made way for the **Wilhelmsaue** and, parallel to it, the **Berliner Strasse**, today a lively business street. A granite block near Mehlitzstrasse recalls the old village green. The **Schoeler-Schlösschen**, Wilmersdorf's oldest residential building, stands as a last relic of times past. Built in 1752, it was later converted into a Rococo palace and, at the end of the 19th century, was purchased by a Berlin doctor named Heinrich Schoeler. It now houses a day-care center. Behind it lie the **Schoelerpark** and the Neo-Gothic **Auenkirche**.

Berlin's largest administrative center, with over 30,000 employees, sprawls all around the **Fehrbelliner Platz**. The buildings on the square exemplify the National Socialist style of monumental construction. The Wilmersdorf town hall, the local gallery, the Berlin Senate's administration for Interior Affairs and for

Right: The TV tower. Far right: Celebrating summer in a Kreuzberg yard.

Housing and Construction, have offices here, and also house the Federal Insurance Agency.

In contrast to Wilmersdorf's densely laid-out inner city, the section called **Schmargendorf** seems like a small town. The old village church on the **Breite Strasse**, Berlin's smallest, makes it plain that Schmargendorf once lived from farming. The fieldstone foundations and bell date back to the 14th century. Schmargendorf's most beautiful building is certainly the town hall on **Berkaer Platz**, built of brick between 1900 and 1902 in the Neo-Gothic style typical of the March. Architect Otto Kerwien designed the façade imaginatively with crenelations, small towers and decorative coats-of-arms.

Koenigsstrasse in the Grunewald quarter took its name from banker Felix Koenigs, who participated in the laying out of the surrounding garden suburb. Established in 1889, it forms the genteel conclusion of the Kurfürstendamm, which had just been expanded to a boule-vard celebrating imperial pomp. 234 hectares of forest fell victim to the elegant quarter, and the swamp had to be drained. During the Weimar Republic, well-known artists and politicians moved into the magnificent villas.

On the corner of **Koenigsstrasse** and **Wallotstrasse**, a stone memorializes Walter Rathenau, the Weimar Republic's statesman who was murdered on this spot by right-wing radicals in 1922. Rathenau lived at Koenigsstrasse 65.

Wilmersdorf enjoys a reputation for religious tolerance. The houses of worship of the most varied religions coexist peacefully here. The architecture of the **mosque** on the corner of **Berliner Strasse** and **Brienner Strasse** lends the area an exotic flair. This Muslim prayer center with its round cupola and minarets, constructed between 1924 and 1927, took exotic Indian chapels as its models. Not far away, light green onion domes indicate the path to the Russian-Orthodox **Christi-Auferstehungs-Kathedrale** on Konstanzer Strasse. It was built in 1938.

THE SOUTH

Berlin's south exhibits a heterogenous appearance, to say the very least. **Zehlendorf** is a popular goal for excursions and it boasts an expensive residential quarter. **Steglitz** and **Tempelhof** are similarly quiet, but more middle-class, whereas **Neukölln** and **Treptow** still bear the typical characteristics of a genuine working-class district.

Green Zehlendorf

Zehlendorf is one of Berlin's most exclusive residential quarters and a paradise for affluent retirees. And this is little wonder, since the district is a true haven from Berlin's hectic big-city bustle. The Zehlendorfers live among greenery. Forest, water and green areas cover more than half of the dictrict's total area. Al-

Above: The Glienicke Bridge spans the Havel. Right: The tower restaurant in Steglitz, nicknamed the "Beer Brush".

though Zehlendorf witħ its 70.6 square kilometers is more spacious than most of Berlin's districts, only 100,800 people live here. That makes Zehlendorf a favorite destination for outings for the rest of the city's inhabitants. In the summer months, when Berlin's inner city becomes intolerably hot, they like to swim or sun at the **Strandbad Wannsee** (Wannsee beach), which is within comfortable walking distance from the S-Bahn station Nikolasee. In 1928 Martin Wagner and Richard Ermisch greatly expanded this beach on the Grosser Wannsee, originally opened in 1907. Every season, over 500,000 day-trippers stream to the 1275-meter-long sandy beach, Europe's largest artficial swimming area.

Alexander von Humboldt praised the magnificent view of the Havel from the **Glienicker Bridge** in the south of Zehlendorf when it was only a wooden bridge. The present iron construction, built between 1908 and 1909, made the headlines several times while Germany was divided. East and west used to make spectacular trades of captured spies on this bridge, whose middle constituted the border to the GDR. Now, the most beautiful route from Berlin to Potsdam once again runs across the bridge, which had been close to normal traffic since 1961.

Not far from the Glienicker Bridge, **Blockhaus Nikolskoe** lies on an elevation in the middle of the forest. The Prussian King Friedrich Wilhelm III had this Russian-style log cabin built in 1819 for his daughter Charlotte, who had been married to the later Czar of Russia, Nikolaus I. The caretaker of the log cabin operated a tavern, a side line that became a tradition handed down to the present. Arson almost completely destroyed the restaurant in 1984, but the building has been reconstructed to match the original perfectly. Next to it, a nice onion-shaped Russian cupola crowns the **Church of St. Peter and St. Paul**. Couples wanting to marry like to use this house of worship as a wedding chapel, and Berliners, in general, love to attend Christmas Mass in the midst of its romantic surroundings.

Steglitz – the Downtown of the south

In contrast to Zehlendorf, Steglitz is an inner-city district with an above average population density. 187,000 inhabitants live here in an area of only 32 square kilometers. More than half of all Steglitzers now live in newer housing complexes, but the neighborhoods of **Lichterfelde** and **Lankwitz** have managed to retain their suburban character and their old 19th-century villas, and by extension, their human dimensions.

Schlossstrasse makes a good side-trip into the district. In the postwar years it developed into one of the most popular shopping streets in Berlin's south. A six-storey shopping center, the **Forum Steglitz**, grew on **Walther-Schreiber-Platz**. The inconspicuous building next door cherishes memories of a glorious past. In 1928, the **Titania-Palast** opened as Ber-

lin's largest cinema house, with 1900 seats. After the war, the Berlin Philharmonic gave its first concert here, somewhat raising the spirits of the bombed out Berliners and, in 1951, the Titania-Palast hosted the first Berlin Film Festival.

The **Tower Restaurant**, opened in 1976 beside the *Autobahn* overpass, is the modern landmark on Schlossstrasse. Berliners nicknamed it the "Beer Brush" *(Bierpinsel)*. Old and new Steglitz meets at **Hermann-Ehlers-Platz**. On one side of the square, the 130-meter-high **Steglitzer Kreisel** stretches into the sky. This highest of Berlin's highrises became a write-off ruin in the seventies. Today it houses a hotel and part of Steglitz' district administration.

Diagonally across from the Steglitzer Kreisel stands the **old town hall**, built between 1896 and 1898 in the Gothic style characteristic of the March. In 1901, young people founded the "Wandervögel" (wandering birds) youth movement in the building's cellar restaurant, which today no longer exists.

The popular field marshall, Graf von Wrangel, once lived in the **Wrangel-Schlösschen** on the corner of Schlossstrasse and Wrangelstrasse, in the heart of the former village of Steglitz. The quaint building has since become a restaurant. In the manor's former annex, the world famous **Schlosspark-Theater** has found a permanent home.

The pioneer aviator Otto Lilienthal also lived and carried out flying experiments in Steglitz. In 1932 a monument to him was erected in the **Lilienthal-Park** on Lichterfelde's **Schütte-Lanz-Strasse**, where he conducted his experiments.

One little curiosity in Berlin is the animal cemetery next to the Lankwitz home for abandoned animals on the Dessauer Strasse. It is the final resting place for over 2000 animals, and a touching testimony to the love people have for their two, four or more-legged pets – or no-legged, as in the case of snakes of course.

Above: The Wrangel Manor in Schöneberg, an inviting place for a visit and a meal.

Tempelhof

185,000 Tempelhofers live in near isolation in their residential district and enjoy a reputation for being quiet, law-abiding citizens. The quarter is primarily known for its airport, but, with its areas of **Mariendorf**, **Marienfelde** and **Lichtenrade**, it has more to offer than the sound of jet engines and the smell of kerosene. Horse racing aficionados gather on Wednesdays and Saturdays at the **Mariendorf Trotting Track**. The racetrack, built in 1913, attracts half a million visitors annually.

Activity is much calmer on the former **UFA Studio Grounds** on Oberlandstrasse, the second-largest UFA studio complex. Today Germany's second television channel, ZDF, produces films here. Another "dream factory" of the past has its offices on **Viktoriastrasse,** where the **UFA-Fabrik** now operates a movie theater, a stage for performances and other events and a café. The former **Ullsteinhaus** at the Stubenrauch Bridge,

with its 72-meter-high tower, is by far
Tempelhof's most conspicuous building.
Professor Eugen Schmohl erected this
publishing house between 1925 and
1926. It was Berlin's first reinforced concrete highrise.

Neukölln

300,000 people live in **Neukölln** in
Berlin's southwest, making it the city's
most populous district. Formed in 1920
from the city of Neukölln and the villages
of **Britz, Buckow** and **Rudow**, Neukölln
is still a typical Berlin workers' *Kiez,* but
it also has some pleasant green areas. **Richardplatz** shows traces of Neukölln's
village past. It served as the core of the
ancient Richardsdorp, first mentioned in
a document in 1360. A 14th-century village church on the edge of the former village green merits a visit. The village
smithy on Richardplatz dates from the
18th century and has been considered a
national monument since 1949. Its fires
still burn for the traditional craft.

Not far from the Richardplatz, the
Bohemian Village stretches along the
Kirchgasse. The monument for Friedrich
Wilhelm I, dedicated in 1912, reminds us
that the king granted asylum to religious
refugees from Bohemia in 1737.

Directly behind the monument is the
former schoolhouse of the **Bohemian
Brothers Community**, one of Neukölln's oldest buildings. Workers felled
the first tree for its construction on March
2, 1753. A chalice is visible in the gable,
which is also reminiscent of the Bohemian immigrants. To this day, the Bohemian Village's old colonists' farmsteads
still exhibit a rural flair and a touch of
Bohemian tradition in the middle of the
big city.

The **Hufeisensiedlung** (horseshoe settlement) in Neukölln's Britz neighborhood is considered one of the most beautiful settlements to emerge from the wave
of urban construction in the twenties in
Germany. This settlement, completed in
1927, initiated a new phase in apartment
construction: Along the street an uninter-
rupted facade, and on the inside spacious
garden courtyards. The settlement was
built around a focusing center and was of
uniform design. It was built by architect
Bruno Taut and Berlin's urban construction councillor Martin Wagner. During the
Weimar Republic, Wagner was one of the
leading proponents of a public policy for
residential building. Taut came up with the
design which surrounds a small pond dating
back to the Ice Age which was re-designed
into a pleasant lake with a shore laid out in
terraces. Also in Britz, a short distance from
the place where in 1985 the Federal Garden
Exhibition was held, stands the restored **Ste-
chan'sche Mühle**. The **Holländermühle**, a
Dutch mill built in 1865, is the second of two
remaining mills in Neukölln.

Nature and Industry in Treptow

Originally a fishing village and now an
odd mixture of expansive parks and large
industrial complexes, Treptow stretches
along the banks of the Spree. Its 102,000
residents live in the areas of **Adlershof**,
Baumschulenweg and **Niederschön-
weide**. **Bohnsdorf** and **Alt-Glienicke**, on
the other hand, have preserved a largely
rural character.

Treptow's garden and country taverns
once attracted flocks of visitors especially from the city, but their former flair
has all but vanished today. Workers in
particular sought recreation in Treptow.
Many restaurants advertised with the slo-
gan: "Families can brew their own coffee
here." The tradition of bringing ones own
food and drink remains alive to this day.
Only the largest and best-known of the
restaurants from the old days still exists,
the **"Haus Zenner,"** which offers a direct view of the Spree river. The neoclassical building was designed in 1822
by the architect Carl Ferdinand Langhans
the Younger.

THE EAST

The color gray still dominates Berlin's eastern half and the streets still lack the dizzying dazzle of the western half. The streets in the center of this part of the city are often dilapidated and deserted, but the outlying areas are worst of all.

Marzahn, Hohenschönhausen, Hellersdorf

In these districts anonymous, uniform, pre-fabricated houses weigh heavily upon residents and visitors alike. The buildings and the neighboring playgrounds are equally devoid of imaginative design. The shops here couldn't lure anyone to a shopping spree, nor do the restaurants or *Kneipen*, so much a part of Berlin life, seem to place any value on attract-

Above: Berlin's East is dotted with anonymous highrises. Right: The renovated Schloss Friedrichsfelde shines with new splendor.

ing guests. In 1986 Marzahn and Hellersdorf were created by appropriating acreage from Lichtenberg.

Lichtenberg

Lichtenberg renounced two-thirds of its area, but its remaining 26 square kilometers show greater contrasts than any other district in the eastern part of Berlin. Its remaining 172,000 inhabitants live mostly in "rental barracks" built during the second half of the 19th century. These stand next to ostentatiously expensive villas from the turn of the century. Lichtenberg may not have the most, but it does have the highest chimneys in East Berlin. They belong to the **Rummelsburg Heating Plant** on the Hauptstrasse, formerly called Klingenburg power plant, which was constructed between 1926 and 1927. The first European attempt to fire a power plant with coal dust was made here. But the black clouds of smoke badly polluted the environment – only now are filters being installed in the smokestacks.

Lichtenberg's treasures are the **Tierpark** (zoo) in **Friedrichsfelde** and the **Schloss Friedrichsfelde**. This palace, built at the end of the 17th century and completely renovated in 1981, hosts excellent concerts. **Karlshorst,** which became known for its **Trotting Racetrack** (Trabrennbahn), also belongs to Lichtenberg. As early as 1893, horse races have been held on the grounds, which extend over about 80 hectares of land.

One of Lichtenberg's landmarks is the **town hall**. The foundation stone for the March-style brick building with its three little towers was laid in 1897. Now exiled to the western edge of the district, it is still an essential Berlin sight, although its fame is not as great as that of the Red, Köpenicker or Pankower town halls.

Friedrichshain

Friedrichshain is one of the smallest districts in Berlin's east, with 109,000 residents. It seems repellent at first glance, dominated as it is by ugly apartment buildings, factories, the central stockyard and the **Ostbahnhof** (eastern train station). The **Karl-Marx-Allee** is the axis of the district. The street was originally named Frankfurter Allee, but dubbed Stalinallee in 1950, and has borne its current name since 1961. During World War Two, bombs flattened the buildings along this avenue, which is why pompous buildings in the elaborate Stalinist style flank this great east-west thoroughfare.

Most tourists see nothing of **Friedrichshain** but the Karl-Marx-Allee, yet the district has more to offer. Another well-known and frequented site is the **Volkspark** (People's Park) **Friedrichshain.** The Friedrichshainers built it in 1840 in answer to the expansion of the Tiergarten behind the Brandenburg Gate.

Everyone turns up in the Volkspark for some air. In winter, people seeking solitude, in summer, sun-worshippers; lovers and those in need of inspiration come year-round. The peaks of the two **Hainberge** can be climbed. The larger rises about 78 meters. Berliners call it simply **Mont Klamott**. This "mountain" and its 30-meter-high smaller brother are artificial elevations, constructed after 1945 from Berlin's rubble. In the meantime, stately trees and tangled bushes have grown on Mont Klamott. The plateau topping the bunker mountain offers a view of Berlin's east.

Directly below the hill is the former **Leninplatz** which until early 1992 was dominated by a monumental sculpture of Lenin. The controversy over whether to leave it or tear it down raged for weeks, until finally the prevailed and had the stone monstrosity demolished. At present entries are invited in an architectural competition to redesign the square.

The path from the smaller rubble mountain toward the western tip of the park leads to the **Fairy Tale Fountain** (Märchenbrunnen). In 1913, the city architect, Ludwig Hoffmann, designed the fanciful sculptures for this Neo-Baroque fountain. In summer, water rolls down terrace by terrace to the **Königstor** (kings' gate). Near the swan pond, the curved roof of a **Japanese pavilion** rests on lathe-turned beams of bright vermilion. A bell hangs from the eaves as a symbol of peace, donated for this purpose by the World Peace Bell Association. Over 50 hectares in size, the park grounds also contain sports facilities, exciting playgrounds and an open-air stage seating 3000.

At the intersection of Dimitroffstrasse and Landsberger Allee, the **Sports and Recreation Center** offers something for everyone: swimming pool, sauna, open-air pool, an ice-skating and roller-skating rink, a restaurant, an ice cream parlor and a café. The **Hauptbahnhof** (main train station) is the only one of the four Berlin long-distance train stations that is located in the core of the city. In its 145-year history, it was remodelled and expanded

Right: A bird's eye view of the Jewish cemetery in Weissensee.

several times. The name, too, has changed. First it was called Frankfurter Bahnhof, then Schlesischer Bahnhof, and, until 1985, Ostbahnhof.

Weissensee

Originally only a quiet village on the March, **Weissensee** first awoke from its age-long slumber during Berlin's 19th century industrial boom. The "prince" who kissed this Sleeping Beauty awake was a Hamburg businessman. He bought the Weissensee estates, and in gratitude, the people of Weissensee named two streets after him, Schönstrasse and **Gustav-Adolf-Strasse**.

Like Lichtenberg, this district was truncated in 1986 – today, 52,000 people live here on a mere 1.5 square kilometers, making Weissensee the smallest of all Berlin districts. It has managed to preserve its nearly pristine suburban character in the midst of the big city: The district is replete with single-family houses, gardens and plenty of idyllic verdant spots.

Weissensee owes its reputation as a site for relaxation primarily to four connected lakes: **Obersee**, **Orankesee, Fauler See** and **Weisser See**. Fauler See and its surroundings are a nature reserve. 30 different species of birds have been spotted here, in the middle of the metropolis. On a hot day, people go for a swim in the Orankesee or the Weisser See. Rowboats also ply the Weisser See, which is relatively sheltered from the noise of the **Klement-Gottwald-Allee**. The latter leads cityward to **Antonplatz**.

There, directly across from the movie house **"Toni"** the sculpture of a mischievously smiling gardener greets the passers-by who commemorates the *Schusterjungen*, Berlin's shoemaker apprentices of the 19th century.

Weissensee's fame for its rural character extends far beyond Berlin's borders; it owes this wider fame to the **Jewish Ce-**

metery, whose gate opens onto the **Herbert-Baum-Strasse**. This largest of all European Jewish cemeteries contains 150,000 grave sites. Before World War Two, a high percentage of Jewish Germans lived in Weissensee and many kept small stores here.

Inaugurated in 1880, the cemetery grounds seem almost consoling, with their abandoned, wild vegetation bursting with life. But the inscription "Auschwitz" on many of the more recent gravestones serves as a reminder of the terrors of National Socialism. Simple and elaborate graves lie close to each other; the graveyard contains the remains of unknown people as well as famous personalities from the cultural and political spheres.

Rudolf Mosse (1843-1920), one of Berlin's great publishers, once owner of the newspaper *Berliner Tageblatt,* lies here, as does his chief editor, Theodor Wolff (1866-1907). The founder of the publishing house *S.-Fischer Verlag,* Samuel Fischer (1859-1934), has found his final resting place here beside Hermann Tietz (1837-1907), one of Berlin's most famous businessmen and founder of the

Hertie chain of department stores. And finally, the parents of writer Kurt Tucholsky, Alex (1855-1905) and Doris (1869-1943) Tucholsky, are buried in this cemetery.

The Weissensee Jewish Cemetery not only silently witnessed the violence of Germany's past, but also people's efforts to save themselves: During the period of Nazi rule, Jews repeatedly hid in the mausoleum of the singer Josef Schwarz (1881-1926).

Köpenick: Suburb on Müggelsee

With 127 square kilometers and only 111,000 people, **Köpenick** is the largest and least densely populated district of Berlin. Köpenick is most famous as a recreation area for Berliners, as one of the city's great green areas: In summer, cruises with the **Weisse Flotte** (white fleet) on the **Grosser Müggelsee**, and visiting the **Köpenicker Schloss** are especially popular. (More on these in the Chapter "Green Oases: Palaces, Parks and Lakes" on page 168).

SPANDAU

The Spandauers probably display the strongest degree of local patriotism of any Berliners. In the eyes of the 212,300 people who live here, their district is still located *next to* Berlin. When they go shopping "in the city," they mean in Spandau's old town, but if they drive to the Kurfürstendamm, they say that they are going "to Berlin."

This city on the Havel was first mentioned in a document in 1197, and by 1232 it had already been granted civic rights – five years earlier than Berlin. In the 16th century, Spandau became a garrison town; in 1873 it was made into a fortress to protect the rising munitions businesses. The defensive walls enclosed the entire old town until 1903.

Spandau's old town is the only one in Berlin proper that still has a genuinely

Above: The Spandau lock. Right: Enjoying food and drink in the cosy atmosphere of the Spandau Citadel's cellar.

original look. Its oval form recalls the shape of the erstwhile fortress.

The Old Town of Spandau

Rathaus Spandau, the town hall at the U-Bahn station of the same name, is a good starting place for a stroll through the old town. Architects Reinhardt and Süssengruth drew up the plans for this stately town hall, which was built between 1910 and 1913. Due to the ground's poor suitability for building, the 72-meter-high tower stands in the courtyard instead of crowning the main construction, as would have been customary. This government building, which cost nearly 3.5 million gold marks, proudly expressed the independence of a city not assigned to any county at the time. In 1920, the citizens lost their independence – by law, not by attitude – when Spandau, together with five other rural communities and three large estates was integrated into Greater Berlin as the eighth administrative district.

Carl-Schurz-Strasse and the **Breite Strasse** run straight through the old town. Car traffic is prohibited from these two main business streets, making them very attractive for a leisurely shopping stroll. Restoration work has been carried out on the **Gothic House** at Breite Strasse 32, built around 1500, and thus Berlin's oldest existing residential building. Part of the **Spandau Museum** and a lecture hall will then move into what will be a cultural center.

The rectangular **marketplace** (Markt) where the Spandau open-air market was held until the turn of the century, connects the two shopping streets. Today, only the traditional Christmas market – Germany's largest – is still held on the square and in the pedestrian zones. All the houses here date from the postwar years, since an aerial bombardment in 1944 destroyed the buildings between the Mönchstrasse and the Charlottenstrasse. The "modernization" fever of the fifties finished the job. But the **Marktstrasse** and the nearby alleys still emanate true old town atmosphere, even if some of the façades' restoration lacks authenticity.

The **St. Nicolai Church** on the **Reformationsplatz** dominates the skyline in the center of the old town. It was built in the middle of the 15th century and is among the oldest Gothic city churches in the March of Brandenburg. But it did have a precursor: A market church in Spandau is mentioned in a document dating to 1240. Among its most valuable furnishings are a bronze baptismal font from the year 1398, a Baroque wooden pulpit and a Renaissance altar, donated in 1582 by the master builder of the Spandau fortress, Count Lynar. In front of the main portal of the St. Nicolai Church stands the monument to **Elector Joachim II**, which was dedicated in 1889. It commemorates the Elector's 1539 conversion to Lutheranism, which took place in this church. This event made Spandau the starting point for the Reformation in the March of Brandenburg. That's why long-time residents call this church the Spandau Cathedral.

The cellar of the house on Reformationsplatz 3/4 contains another historical remnant: The left-over wall of a 13th-century Dominican monastery, kept behind a protective glass pane.

No part of Spandau's old city is more romantic than the **Behnitz**. Picturesque wealthy burgher's houses and more modest half-timbered houses define the appearance of the streets in the quarter's narrow, cobbled alleys. Behnitz No. 3 was built in 1868 and once housed the Spandau Office for Military Construction and the arsenal. Nowadays it contains the St. Nicolai Church's congregational daycare center. Behnitz No. 4 is a restored half-timbered house from the 18th century. Next to it stands the **Heinemann-sches Haus**, named for composer Wilhelm Heinemann. The stately home was built between 1770 and 1780 in late-Baroque style.

The Church of St Mary, dedicated as a basilica in 1848, was the first Catholic church built in the March of Brandenburg after the tumultuous tides of Reformation. It served as a garrison church on occasion. Excavations uncovered a well shaft from the 14th century in front of the church's northern wall.

The Behnitz, the oldest part of the old town to be settled, has furnished archaeologists with an abundance of valuable finds, some going back as far as the stone age. People often refer to the part of town just behind the busy Strasse Am Juliusturm as **Kolk**, but the Kolk is only a street in Behnitz.

A 50-meter-long section of the old city wall rises to its original height on the **Hoher Steinweg**. On its rear side, the remaining sections of an old defensive tower from the 14th-century have come to light. What is nowadays called the **Möllentordamm**, was once upon a time a little fishing village known as Damm, consisting of merely six plots of land. The inhabitants, however, have maintained their fishing rights to this very day.

The **Spandau Locks** are clearly visible from the intersection of the Möllentordamm and the Behnitz. Opened in 1910, they connect the Upper Havel with the Lower Havel; evidence of a lock on this spot goes back to 1723.

The Spandau Citadel

At the point where the Havel and Spree rivers meet, only a few steps away from the old town, the **Spandau Citadel** guards against non-existent enemies. It is an outstanding monument of Italian Renaissance fortress-building skill, and proved quite redoubtable in its day. No other construction of this magnitude has been so well preserved in Europe. Four

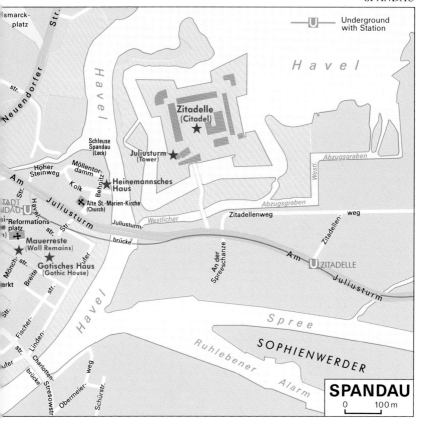

SPANDAU

0   100 m

powerful bastions extend from the corners of the rectangular foundation. The entire citadel is surrounded by a moat. The Slavs had already built a wooden fortress on this strategically important spot. Later, the Ascanians erected a solid defensive complex in the 13th century to secure the Havel crossing for the trade route that passed this spot on its way from Magdeburg to Poland.

Construction of the present citadel began in 1560, most probably according to the plans of the Italian master builder Franziskus Chiaramella de Gandino. The work was completed in 1594 by master builder Rochus Guerrini, Count of Lynar, who was also responsible for the fortresses in Dresden and Kassel.

The citadel not only served for centuries as a fortress, but also as a prison, sometimes for rather eminent people. Robber baron Dietrich von Quitzow, Benjamin Raulé (the Great Elector's admiral), "Turnvater" (father of gymnastics) Jahn and hundreds of Berlin's 1848 revolutionaries were incarcerated here.

The Spandau fortress prison once stood on Wilhelmstrasse and, in 1946, was put to use as a prison for war criminals. Seven major war criminals sentenced at the Nuremberg trials were incarcerated here. In 1987, the last prisoner, Hitler's former deputy Rudolf Hess, committed suicide here and a short time later the prison was torn down. The citadel served military purposes until the

end of World War Two. The Wehrmacht developed extremely poisonous combat substances in secret laboratories here – leaving a heritage of environmental contamination that is only now being cleaned up.

The fortress facilities have been in the process of restoration since 1977. The **Kommandantenhaus**, where an exhibition on the Citadel can be seen, and the **Palas**, originally a Gothic construction from the middle of the 14th century, have already been restored. Changing exhibits are shown in the Palas' authentic Gothic Hall. A museum of Spandau's history is now open shows not only documents and objects from the town's past but also skeletons of mammoths.

Spandau's hallmark – and oldest section – of the citadel, however, is the **Julius Tower**. It was probably built during the first half of the 13th century and served as a watchtower and place of re-

Above: Forestry workers in Spandau Forest, using old-fashioned methods.

fuge. It is 30 meters high and measures more than 12 meters in diameter. Its masonry is 3.60 meters thick at the ground floor level. 145 steps lead to a viewing platform with a magnificent panorama of the town and its surroundings. Karl Friedrich Schinkel designed the turret that was added to the tower in 1838.

Spandau's Precincts

For centuries, the fortress reigned in Spandau's development. Not until its "de-fortressing" in 1903 did the city expand into the surrounding countryside. **Neustadt** or "new city," formerly called Oranienburger Vorstadt (suburb), grew to the north of the old town on **Falkenseer Platz**. On the Feldstrasse and Blumenstrasse, town houses and wealthy farmers' houses still radiate a suburban impression.

In a few years, a further Spandau precinct may extend west of the Neustadt: The Senate intends to build about 18,000 apartments around the **Eiswerder** island in a mammoth project called "Watertown Berlin – Upper Havel." Together with shops, small companies and offices, a settlement could emerge in which 50,000 people would live and work. But up to now, only industrial facilities, environmentally contaminated fallow land and junkyards line the shores of the Havel and of Eiswerder itself.

These eyesores also blight the area around the **Hakenfelde** precinct, accessible through the Neuendorfer Strasse. But even here there are still idyllic spots: A forest settlement, built between 1914 and 1917 according to plans by architects Steil and Wolf, is a veritable garden city. In the middle of the Spandauer forest, on **Schönwalder Allee,** is the Lutheran **Johannesstift**. This foundation, which moved to Spandau in 1910, devotes itself to caring for the aged, the sick and handicapped people, and to the training of qualified nurses.

In the sixties, a new settlement grew to the north of the old town on the **Falkenhagener Feld** on both sides of the **Falkensee Chaussee**. About 11,500 loosely arranged apartments grew up on a surface of 132 hectares.

Wilhelmstadt, formerly known as the Potsdamer Vorstadt (suburb), lies to the south of Spandau's old town. Several buildings from the late 19th century line the **Pichelsdorfer Strasse**.

Architect Paul Schmitthenner designed the **Staaken garden city** on the **Heidebergplan** as a counter-model to inner city tenements. In this settlement, based on English models and built between 1914 and 1917, every apartment has its own more or less lovely garden.

In Spandau's south lie the former villages of Pichelsdorf, Gatow and Kladow. They were not incorporated into Spandau until 1920, and even today farmers still raise crops and livestock in what could be considered rural communities – indeed, Spandau includes a total of 1125 hectares of agricultural land.

The earliest record of the fishing village of **Pichelsdorf** is in a document from the year 1375. In 1816, the first German steamship, the *Prinzessin Charlotte von Preussen,* was built here. The construction of the Heerstrasse split the village in two. The oldest building is the **historic wine cellar** at Alt-Pichelsdorf 32.

The center of old Gatow, first documented in 1258, is its 14th-century village church, built of fieldstones. An American **loggers' house**, built in the twenties, stands at Alt-Gatow 36. **Gatow Airport**, established in 1935 and used by the British military as an airfield since 1945, is on the **Ritterfelddamm**.

The earliest document mentioning **Kladow** dates back to 1267: The village church in **Alt-Kladow** dates from the year 1818, but it had a predecessor. Next to the churchyard, a 300-year-old linden tree casts its shadow on the plaque recounting its history. Several old farmhouses surround the village green.

The industrial and residential buildings of the Siemens AG dominate the **Siemensstadt** in Spandau's east. Siemens, with about 20,000 employees, is the largest company located in Spandau. As early as 1897, the electric company Siemens & Halske bought its first plot of land on the **Nonnendammallee** and erected a cable and dynamo plant.

In the following years, more production plants and the first apartments for employees were built. Architect Hans Hertlein created the Siemensstadt's typical architecture using red brick. He also designed the landmark of this part of Spandau, the **Siemensturm**, which still towers over the part of the factory complex on the **Wernerwerkdamm**.

This 70-meter-high edifice, with its mighty tower clock, dominates the skyline of the "electropolis." Aside from Siemens, over 6500 businesses have made a home here, making Spandau one of the largest industrial districts in Berlin and Germany.

BERLIN DISTRICTS

Kreuzberg

The best way to reach to Kreuzberg is by **U-Bahn** (Underground train) **line 1**, which runs across the whole length of the district on an elevated rail. A slower alternative is bus 129, leaving from Ku'-damm and traversing the Kreuzberg quarter.

Don't forget to pay a visit to the colorful **Kreuzberg Markets**. A weekly market is held at Kottbusser Tor, the **"Turkish Market"** takes place on Maybachufer (Tue and Fri 12 noon-6.30 p.m.), and the **Krempelmarkt**, a flea market on Reichpietschufer, tempts visitors and locals alike to hunt for hidden treasures (Sat, Sun 8 a.m.-3 p.m.). Two Berlin market halls, with splendid architecture, have survived in Kreuzberg (Eisenbahnstrasse and Marheinekeplatz).

In this quarter you can find a variety of small alternative and scene shops selling fashionable accessories, jewelry and second-hand clothes, especially on **Oranien-** and **Bergmannstrasse**.

For a look at the latest art trends and exhibitions, for buying an unusual work of art or just listening to lectures, visit the **Elefanten Press Galerie** (Oranienstr. 25), the **Galerie am Chamissoplatz** (Chamissoplatz 6) or the **Galerie Grober Unfug** (Zossener Str. 32/33) with one of the largest comic-book shops in Berlin.

No visit to Kreuzberg is complete without a Turkish meal; try delicious food in one of the Turkish snackbars **(Imbiss)** around the Kottbusser Tor or in one of the following, reasonably priced restaurants: **Altin Köse**, Dresdener Str. 126, daily from 10 a.m.; **Beyti**, Adalbertstr. 10, daily from 11 a.m., or **Imbiss Bagdad**, Schlesische Str. 2, open for delicious turkish meals until late at night.

Take a break from sightseeing in one of Kreuzberg's **Cafés**, for instance in **Anton**, Oranienstr. 170, daily 9 a.m.-2 p.m.; **Café Jenseits**, Oranienstr. 16, daily 8 a.m.-2 a.m.; **Marylin**, Muskauer Str. 23, daily 11 a.m.-3 a.m.; or **Café Mora**, Grossbeerenstrasse 57a, Tel. 785 05 85, daily 11 a.m.-1 a.m. These cafés usually serve a good, hearty breakfast at all hours of the day.

A large number of cafés and cultural centers stage regular cultural events, i.e. the **Künstlerhaus Bethanien**, Mariannenplatz, Tel. 614 80 10, open Tue -Sun 2-7 p.m.; **Mehringhof**, Gneisenaustr. 2, Tel. 691 50 99 and **Schokofabrik** (cultural center for women only, with Turkish bath), Naunynstr. 72, Tel. 615 29 99.

Topography of Terror, Stresemannstr. 110, Tel. 25 48 67 03, open Tue–Sun 10 a.m.-6 p.m. Here, an exhibition gives detailed information on the infamous years of Nazi regime in Berlin.

Prenzlauer Berg

Starting from Schönhauser Allee, all sights in this quarter can be reached by foot: the **Jewish Cemetery** is at Schönhauser Allee 23-25, Mon–Thur 9 a.m.-4 p.m., Fri 8 a.m.-1 p.m., closed Sat.; men are requested to cover their heads when entering the cemetery.

Further points of interest: the **Friseurmuseum** (Barbers' Museum) on Husemannstrasse 8, Tel. 449 53 80, Mon, Sat 10 a.m.-6 p.m., Tue-Thur, 10 a.m.-5 p.m., Sun until 4 p.m., guided tours Mon and Thur by appointment only.

Museum Berliner Arbeiterleben um 1900 (Museum of Workers' Life in Berlin around 1900), Husemannstrasse 12, Tel. 448 56 75, Tue, Thur, Sat 10 a.m.-6 p.m., Fri until 3 p.m.

For a well-deserved rest try one of the lovingly restored cafés and *Kneipen* on Husemannstrasse: **Budike** (Nr. 15, warm meals until 9 p.m.), **Kaffeestube** (Nr.6) or **Restauration 1900** (Nr. 1, closed on Sundays).

The first address for cultural events in Prenzlauer Berg is the **Franz-Klub**, Schönhauser Allee 36-37, Tel. 448 55 67; those in the know don't turn up before late evening.

It's also worth visiting the **Prater**, Kastanienallee 7-9, Tel. 448 56 88, which is, at the moment, still undergoing extensive restauration. The **Prater-Garten**, Berlin's oldest beer garden, still evokes the leisurely atmosphere of days gone by.

Since the fall of the Wall two large, alternative cultural centers have come into existence: The **Kulturbrauerei**, Knaackstr./corner Dimitroffstr., Tel. 440 92 43, offers rock concerts, exhibitions and various other cultural events. In the gigantic storage halls **Pfefferberg**, Schönhauser Allee 176, Tel. 282 72 73, the scene from Berlin East meets for pop concerts and performance art.

And for those wishing to study a faithful replica of Berlin's starry sky, the **ZEISS-Grossplanetarium** is a must; Prenzlauer Allee 80, Tel. 420 09 16.

Reinickendorf, Wedding and Pankow

Detailed information about the history of **Reinickendorf** can be obtained at the **Heimatmuseum**, Alt-Hermsdorf 35, Wed–Sat 10 a.m.-6 p.m., closed on public holidays.

During an excursion to **Lübars**, don't miss the two country inns **Lustiger Finke** (Alt- Lübars 20, Tel. 402 78 45) and **Alter Dorfkrug** (Alt-Lübars 8, Tel. 402 71 74), for a coffee and hearty Berlin fare.

A visit to **Frohnau** should include the **Borsig-Werke**, the **Russian Cemetery** and the **Buddhist House**.

In **Tegel**, a circular walk starting from the underground station Alt-Tegel continues across Berlin's oldest pedestrian zone, the **Tegel-Center**, to the former village green, the **Greenwich-Promenade** and the lake **Tegeler See**.

Visitors wanting to explore **Wedding** should take the U-Bahn line 9 to Leopoldplatz or Nauener Platz: the *Kiez* (the locals' expression for the heart of a colourful, lively and mostly proletarian quarter) is situated in this area. Wedding's interesting past is documented in the **Heimatmuseum**, Pankestr. 47, Tue-Thur 12 noon-6 p.m., Sun 11 a.m.-5 p.m.

The sights of **Pankow** can be explored on a circular tour starting at the S-Bahn (suburban train) station Pankow (train line 9). Continue to the nearby old village center and the **Schlosspark** next to the **Majakoswkiring** with the literature museum **Johannes-R.-Becher-Haus**, Tel. 482 61 62, Tue 2-6 p.m., Wed, Thur 9 a.m.-12 noon, 2-5 p.m.; Fri 9 a.m.-12 noon. The **Heimatmuseum**, Henstr. 8, Tel. 489 40 47, Tue 9 a.m.-6 p.m., Sun 10 a.m.-5 p.m., is worth a visit too.

Finish your day's sightseeing with a hearty dinner at the **Pankower Ratskeller**, Breite Str. 24a/26, Tel. 482 83 97, daily 11 a.m.-midnight.

The West
From Spandau to Schöneberg

Spandau and downtown Berlin are connected by the **Heerstrasse** and U-Bahn line 7. Starting from **Carl-Schurz-Strasse**, buses run to all parts of Spandau. The **Spandauer Zitadelle** is open to the public Tue-Fri 9 a.m.-5 p.m., Sat, Sun 10 a.m.-5 p.m., guided tours Sat 2-4.30 p.m., Sun 10 a.m.-4.30 p.m. The **Zitadellenschänke** in the vaults of the **Torhaus** offers substantial food without frills. Tel. 334 21 06, daily from 6 p.m.

The exhibition rooms in the **Gotisches Haus** have recently been opened to the public again; Breite Str. 32, Tel. 330 326 20, Tue-Fri 10 a.m.-5 p.m., Sat 10 a.m. until 1 p.m.

Charlottenburg's *Kiez*, a fair distance from the Ku'damm, spreads around the streets north of Kaiserdamm and Bismarckstrasse. You can still discover parts of old Charlottenburg on both sides of the **Schlosstrasse**. The **Funkturm** (radio tower, 10 a.m.- 8 p.m. daily), guarantees a marvellous view over the city. Try the restaurant (at a height of 55 m) for best views – but don't expect the menu to bowl you over. Tel. 303 829 96, daily 12 noon-3 p.m. and 6-11 p.m.. **Gedenkstätte Plötzensee**, a memorial for the victims of the Nazi regime (Hüttingpfad, 8.30 a.m.-5.30 p.m. daily, Tel. 344 32 26) is situated in the former prison where about 1800 Nazi opponents found their death by execution.

Points of interest in **Wilmersdorf** are the **Communal Museum** and **Gallery** with permanent and changing exhibitions, Hohenzollerndamm 174-177, Mon, Wed, Fri 10 a.m.-2 p.m., Tue, Thur 2-6 p.m., closed on public holidays, Tel. 868 95 39).

The city hall **Schöneberger Rathaus** is open to the public. (Entrance Freiherr-vom-Stein-Strasse, guided tours by appointment, Tel. 783 80 47). A weekly market is held on the city hall square Tue, Fri 8 a.m.-1 p.m. For a touch of genuine local color, take a stroll around the *Kiez* at **Nollendorfplatz** and **Winterfeldplatz** (market Wed, Sat 8 a.m.-1 p.m.) and the area around **Potsdamer Strasse.**

Districts in the Green South and in the East

Zehlendorf and **Steglitz** are best explored by bus Nr. 148. From the terminal of U-Bahn 2 (**Krumme Lanke**), take a walk via **Mexikoplatz** to the **Potsdamer Chaussee**. The S-Bahn (suburban train) station Mexikoplatz is the only Art Deco station to have survived the war.

The observatory **Wilhelm-Foerster-Sternwarte** and the **Planetarium** are situated on top of the artificial hill **Insulaner**; Munsterdamm 90, Tel. 790 09 30, demonstrations Tue, Thur 6 and 8 p.m., Fri, Sat 8 p.m., Sun 5 and 8 p.m.; telescope observations Tue, Thur-Sat 7 and 9 p.m., Sun 3, 4 and 9 p.m.

In **Tempelhof**, a visit to the "alternative culture" **UFA-Fabrik** (Viktoriastr. 13, Tel. 752 80 85) on the grounds of the former film studios, is a must.

The center of **Neukölln** (U-Bahn line 7) spreads around **Hermannplatz**; genuine Berlin atmosphere can be sampled on a walk along the **Sonnenallee**. **Schloss Britz**, in the south of Neukölln, is open to the public (Alt-Britz 73, Tel. 606 60 51, guided tours Wed 2-6 p.m.).

Treptow's two lovely avenues, **Stralauer Allee** and **Treptower Park**, run along the park of the same name. Inside the park is the observatory **Archenhold-Sternwarte** (Alt-Treptow 1, telescope observations Wed 6 p.m., Sat, Sun 4 p.m., Tel. 272 88 71). The nearby restaurant **Haus Zenner** (Alt-Treptow 14-17, Tel. 272 72 11) offers good meals.

Lichtenberg and **Friedrichshain**, spreading along both sides of the **Karl-Marx/Frankfurter Allee**, are served by the S-Bahn line 3.

The genuine flavor of the Friedrichshain *Kiez* is best experienced in the **Petersburger** and **Boxhagener** streets and in the area around **Bersarinplatz**.

In **Weissensee**, the **Jewish Cemetery**, Herbert-Baum-Str. 45, is open Mon-Thur 8 a.m.-4 p.m., Fri, Sun and before Jewish holy days 8 a.m.-3 p.m., closed on Jewish holy days; Tel. 965 33 30. Male visitors are requested to cover their heads.

AROUND BERLIN

POTSDAM

LANDSCAPES OF THE MARCH

POTSDAM

Potsdam lies immediately to the southwest of Berlin, surrounded by a string of Marchland lakes. "Prussia was built up from Potsdam and illuminated from Sanssouci. The Havel river can assume its place among German cultural waterways," wrote Theodor Fontane in his *Wanderings Through the March of Brandenburg*. Thanks to its palaces and historical buildings, the city has indeed become one of Europe's most important cultural sites. About 25,000 buildings and parks in Potsdam have been declared national monuments. Some of the greatest minds of Europe created in Potsdam: Voltaire lived here between 1750 and 1753, and Lessing completed his *Miss Sara Sampson* in 1755 in Potsdam. Heinrich Heine, Ludwig Tieck and Theodor Fontane found a favorable climate for their work in this city as well.

The City of Potsdam

In the year 993, the written history of Potsdam began in a document signed by Otto III granting the town civic rights.

Preceding pages: Adolph von Menzel's "Friedrich the Great's Flute Concerto." Left: The terraces of Sanssouci Palace.

But the community remained insignificant until the 17th century, when Elector Friedrich Wilhelm had the Stadtschloss (City Castle) built by his architect Memhardt from 1664 to 1670, and made it his official residence. In the 18th century, Friedrich Wilhelm I, the austere "Soldier King," turned Potsdam into a kind of garrison town, bequeathing it the strict architectural lines that it still bears today to a certain extent. His son, Friedrich II, later began to reconstruct Potsdam as a showcase for visiting dignitaries. The city also owes him **Sanssouci Palace**, the "Prussian Versailles" as it became known. After World War Two, the city of Potsdam was rebuilt, albeit in rather slipshod fashion in its shadow. Now that Potsdam has regained its status as capital of the state of Brandenburg, which it had lost in 1952, it will most probably regain some of its former glamor.

Potsdam's 140,000 residents will be faced with a great deal of work in the next years. The architectural wounds inflicted during the Second World War and during the subsequent decades of neglect will heal only gradually. The city itself and the state of Brandenburg lack the financial means for rapid restoration of the historic buildings. A foundation for the preservation of the palaces and parks has meanwhile been formed and will be fin-

anced primarily by the federal government. The city's millenial celebrations in 1993 was a powerful incentive for Brandenburg and a great chance for the capital to regain some of its old lustre.

The inner city area is framed on the west by Potsdam's own **Brandenburg Gate**, in the north by the **Jägertor** (hunters' gate) and the **Nauener Tor** and in the east by the **Bassinplatz** with the **French Church**, built in 1752-1752. Architect Knobelsdorff designed this round Baroque church, built in 1753; Schinkel planned the 1833 refurnishing of the church's interior. The noteworthy ensemble around the Nikolai Church (1830-1837), with the **Altes Rathaus** (old city hall, 1753) and the **Marstall** at the **Alter Markt** (old market), forms the southern edge of the Bassinplatz.

The cupola of the neoclassical **Nikolai Church** presides over the center of Pots-

*Above: Potsdam's pleasant pedestrian zone.
Right: The Dutch Quarter, where Friedrich the Great's Dutch craftsmen resided.*

dam. Schinkel designed it and supervised its construction from 1830 to 1837, adopting the ideas of then Crown Prince Friedrich Wilhelm.

Potsdam's Stadtschloss, the city palace, which the Great Elector ordered built in the 17th century, used to stand on the old market. His successor transformed the modest building into a splendid piece of architectural extravaganza. Unfortunately, bombardments during World War Two caused irreperable damage to the palace and the garrison church, and what was left standing was finally torn down in the sixties, a purely political decision, and rather a painful mistake that destroyed the harmony of the Baroque inner city. From a technical point of view it would have been possible to repair and maintain these two buildings.

The **Hans-Otto-Theater**, an unsightly heap of concrete, was irreverently erected in front of the Nikolaikirche. It was the former GDR's first new theatrical building; the old SED leadership was intending to redesign the inner city for

Potsdam's millenium in 1993. After unification, the building increasingly became a tough bone of contention in community politics. Finally, the city council decided to tear down this 17 million DM nightmare on this square's generally harmonious architectural lines.

A pedestrian zone leads from Potsdam's Brandenburg Gate to the **Church of Peter and Paul**. Schinkel's pupil W. Salzenberg built this church between 1867 and 1870, imitating Istanbul's Hagia Sophia. The cross streets leading to the shopping avenue are the site of intense construction work now. The mainly two-story Baroque houses had been abandoned to their own fate for decades. Today the ticklish issue of ownership often prevents swift restoration, however. The same applies to the **Holländisches Viertel** (Dutch Quarter), north of the Church of Peter and Paul. Special efforts are now being made to rescue the 134 brick buildings of this 18th century settlement. The houses were built in typical Dutch style under the direction of Johann Boumann to accomodate the Dutch craftsmen Frederick the Great had invited to Potsdam to work on Sanssouci. The expected influx did not materialize and it was predominantly local soldiers and their families who moved in.

An architectural history of Potsdam should also include the **Russian colony Alexandrowska** in front of the **Nauener Tor**. In 1812, 62 Russian prisoners-of-war arrived in Potsdam. King Friedrich Wilhelm III enlisted them in his men's choir. After Czar Alexander I allied himself with the King of Prussia, he didn't demand their return but gave them to the Prussian monarch as a present instead. In 1826 the King built 14 log cabins for them as well as the **Alexander Newski Church**, modelled on Kiev's Desiatin Church. West of the Russian colony, the **Neuer Garten** (new garden) spreads on the western banks of the Heiligensee.

Schloss Cecilienhof stands in the midst of this park. Here, in 1945, the victorious powers of World War Two negotiated the Potsdam Treaty, which divided Germany into four zones of occupation.

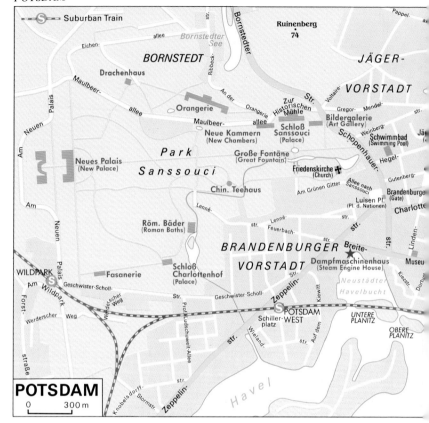

POTSDAM

0   300 m

The famous round table and the rooms where the delegates did their work can be visited. The remaining rooms of the palace serve as a luxury hotel with an elegant restaurant.

An unusual monument to technology graces the Neustadt's Havel cove, an old-fashioned **waterworks**. From the outside, the building looks like a Moorish mosque with a minaret. Inside, the steam engine driving the water works is still functional. The facility, built between 1841 and 1842 according to plans by L. Pesius, pumped water from the Havel up to the **Ruinenberg** (ruin mountain), an artificial collection of Roman and Greek ruins above Sanssouci palace, and supplied all of the park's fountains.

Potsdam-Babelsberg

Northeast of the inner city, in **Pots-dam-Babelsberg,** Schinkel built the Neo-Gothic **Schloss Babelsberg** in the shape of a fort. Prince von Pückler-Muskau had the park laid out according to designs by Lenné. Babelsberg is a film city. Bioscop was already making movies here between 1912 and 1924, until UFA-Films was founded in 1945. Between 1946 and 1990, DEFA made some films that were so controversial, the public only saw them after 1990. Today the studios belong to a French media corporation which is trying – with Volker Schlöndorff as managing director – to revive the old legend. Visits can attend rehearsals,

see the backdrops, enjoy stunt shows, watch costume-makers or inspect the world's largest prop collection. The School for Film and Television, where some of Germany's finest actors and directors trained, is next door. It is a relatively new institution with a fine reputation. Students from German-speaking countries compete fiercely for a place to study acting, camera, cutting or screenplay-writing.

Left and right to **Karl-Marx-Strasse**, the former villas of once famous movie stars Marika Rökk, Brigitte Horney, Heinrich George and many other film stars recall the old UFA period. Some of the buildings where prominent personalities lived, once belonged to Jewish owners who had to sell them at absurdly

low prices during the Nazi era. In the southern part of Babelsberg, behind the Heinrich-Mann-Allee, the cupolas of the **Sternwarte Babelsberg** rise from the **Telegrafenberg**. Astronomers have used this observatory since 1876. The architect Mendelssohn drew up the unusual plans for the **Einsteinturm** at one end of the park. Built in 1920, it now serves as a solar observatory.

Sanssouci

Friedrich II, who was later called "Old Fritz," provided his own plans for **Schloss Sanssouci**, which was constructed in Rococo style between 1745 and 1747 above terraced vineyards near Potsdam. The palace's name means "without worry," a fact which is reflected in the entire complex – most of the buildings and the gardens, with their pleasant symmetry and overgrown trellises, seem light and carefree. But many of the buildings have lost their charm due to the inevitable dilapidation brought about by lack of care. In 1990 the park administration provided 14 million DM for restoration work – the sum proved not nearly enough for all the buildings. The UNESCO put the Sanssouci complex and other Potsdam monuments on the list of the world's cultural heirlooms, so hope is growing that financial support will be forthcoming.

Sanssouci Park is best explored along the **Hauptallee**. This path traverses the grounds from west to east, connecting the main entrance, the **Obelisk Portal**, with the **Great Fountain** directly at the foot of the palace terraces, and with the **New Palace** at the western end of the park. The **Art Gallery** standing to the right of the palace has gone down in museum history as the first building expressly built to exhibit paintings (1755-1757). On the left-hand side rise the **New Chambers**, built in 1747. Originally built as an orangery between 1771 and 1774, they were converted into a guest house and so received

over 300-meter-long, monumental building. The panoramic view of the entire park and Potsdam from the Orangerie's towers is magnificent. Friedrich Wilhelm IV's unusual collection of copies of Raffael paintings hangs in a gallery that has been arranged in several of the rooms. The central building also contains five magnificent guest rooms, which were furnished for Friedrich Wilhelm IV's sister, Czarina Charlotte of Russia, and her husband, Czar Nicholas I.

Villages around Potsdam

The **Heilandskirche**, built between 1841 and 1844, stands a few kilometers north of Potsdam in **Sacrow**, on a spit of land between the Havel river and the **Jungfernsee** (virgin's lake). Only since the opening of the GDR borders has it been possible to visit the church.

their present name. At the beginning of the 19th century, King Friedrich Wilhelm IV sketched ideas for a park and palace. The result, executed by Schinkel and Lenné, lies further to the south: **Charlottenhof**. The palace, the **Fasanerie** and the **Roman Baths** exhibit neoclassical and Florentine styles.

The Hauptallee leads to the **New Palace**, an elaborate showcase built between 1763 and 1769 as the home of the royal family after the end of the Seven Years' War. The palace is in the process of intensive restoration; 55 rooms, some of them authentically reproduced, a theater, reopened in May 1991, and an enchanting café, set up in original rooms, all await visitors here. Another grandiose building stands in the north of the park: the **Orangerie**, which Friedrich Wilhelm IV ordered built in 1840. Italian Renaissance palaces provided the models for this

In May and June, the blossoms of orchards and strawberry fields lay a beautiful blanket of "snow" on the **Havelland**, the region surrounding Potsdam as far as Werder. Early summer lures campers and water sports fans into the woodlands along the Havel river. The area between Potsdam, Rathenau and Genthin used to be a large flood plain. The incline of the Havel's bed was too gentle, causing backwash whenever there was high water in the Elbe river. During the middle ages, fishermen and farmers instituted flood control measures by building levies around the water-driven mills. They diked the Havel, allowing lakes and bogs to form around *Werders,* the name given to the settlements. The **Havelland-Hauptkanal** (main canal) has drained the area between **Fehrbellin** and **Nauen** (Nauener Luch) since 1718.

The **Ketziner Wetlands** conservation area offers a particularly romantic hike. Today grebes and swans breed here, water lilies blossom and colonies of herons nest in the lakes northwest of the city of **Kienitz**; just over 100 years ago,

Above: Gold-plated sun symbol in the park of Sanssouci palace. Right: Between Pfaueninsel and Nikolskoe.

140

these bodies of water were clay quarries for the brick industry booming with the rapid construction of apartment buildings for workers in Berlin. Ships on the Havel canals transported the bricks into the city. Ironically, after World War Two, many of the clay quarries were filled back up again with the rubble and debris of the demolished city. The **Ketzin Refuse** dump continued receiving West Berlin's garbage for many years after.

If you take a boat southwest from Potsdam you will pass through the **Templin Lake** and arrive in **Caputh**, a town on a spit of land between Templin and Schwielow lakes. A Baroque palace, built in 1662, with unusual stucco decoration, graces Caputh. A room in the cellar has been decorated with original Delft tiles. Friedrich I loved to have himself rowed out here from the city palace on a magnificent gondola. Another illustrious resident, Albert Einstein, had a country house in Caputh at Waldstrasse Nr. 7 until 1933, when the Nazis forced him to emigrate to the United States.

From here, it's a short trip overland or with the car-ferry to **Werder**, the center of the Havelland's fruit-growing region. The little city developed from an old-Slav castle mound on a Havel islet, the *Werder*. Until the 18th century, no bridge connected it with the western shore of the Havel, which is as wide as a lake at this point. Werder's favorable climate has enabled the cultivation of fruit and grapes since the Middle Ages, and by the 19th century fruit-growing had become the most important source of income. Most of the orchards are no longer competitive and were forced to close at the beginning of 1991. So far, the trees have been cleared from nearly half of the 1600 hectares of cultivated area around Werder.

Werder, with its old fishermen's houses and the **Church of the Holy Spirit** which houses the painting *Christ as Pharmacist*, is worth a visit. The **Hoher Weg** looks out over the city and the Havel landscape, where sailing regattas enliven the river in the summertime. On clear days the view stretches all the way to Potsdam.

AROUND BERLIN: IN THE MARCH LANDSCAPES

Oranienburg and Sachsenhausen

The approximately 650-year-old city of **Oranienburg** before Berlin's northern gates is one of the major intersections on land and water routes. The Ascanian princes kept a castle here, that stood guard over the Havel. The old Slavic village of Bötzow was renamed Oranienburg in 1651. The **Baroque palace** dates to that period, as does the general Dutch design of the city, all done in honor of the Dutch Electress Luise Henriette, who was by birth the Princess of Orange.

In 1814 a chemical factory was established in the palace, where chemist Friedlieb F. Runge isolated aniline, caffeine, atropine and carbolic acid. The palace is still closed to the public. The former **Baroque pleasure garden** with its garden portal (I. A. Nerung, 1690) and orangery (G. C. Berger, 1759) rewards the effort of a walk.

The northeastern part of the town, **Sachsenhausen**, earned itself a rather dubious fame. In 1933, on the grounds of a bankrupt brewery, the first concentration camp on German soil was established. It held more than 7000 permanent prisoners. From 1936 onwards, the concentration camp served the Nazis as a full-fledged extermination camp and subsequently claimed the lives of more than 100,000 people.

In the period between 1945 and 1950, the Soviet Army turned the existing camp into their own "Special Camp Nr. 7." Without rhyme, reason, or due process of law, they condemned young people, women and men to forced labor or sentenced them to deportation to the Soviet Union. Mass graves were unearthed in the spring of 1990 in a forest area near

Right: Wall surrounding the concentration camp at Sachsenhausen, north of Berlin.

Schmachtenhagen. More than 10,000 people had died of disease or hunger in the Soviet camp and been buried there. Today, survivors and relatives are helping to investigate this gloomy chapter of Germany's postwar history.

Hiking Trails around Oranienburg

The diversity of the surrounding landscape makes Oranienburg a favorite recreation area for Berliners. Starting from the **Lehnitzsee**, some excursion steamers cruise as far as Niederfinow. A hike around Lehnitzsee beginning at the S-Bahn station Lehnitz, especially enjoyable in the summer, offers broad views over the lake.

A good hiker with a whole day at his or her disposal can set off from the S-Bahn station **Birkenwerder**. This trail extends for a good 13 kilometers, leading from Birkenwerder through the very charming **Briesetal** and **Oranienburger Heide** as far as Lehnitzsee. The Briese, a small stream, leaves the Wandlitzsee to feed into the Havel at Hohenneuendorf. The trail follows the stream through the valley past the **Elsenquelle** and the **Helenenquellen** springs, and then crosses over the **Hubertusbrücke** (bridge).

On the **Schlagbrücke,** a left turn onto the **Mühlenbecker Gestell** puts you on a nearly empty road connecting Summt and Lehnitz and leading directly to the S-Bahn station Lehnitz.

From the eastern shore of Lehnitzsee, a round-trip hike wends past the locks on the northern tip of the lake. From here it is only a few meters to the Sachsenhausen concentration camp memorial.

Bernau

20,000 people live in the city of **Bernau**, about 30 kilometers away from downtown Berlin in the direction of Stralsund. About 100 meters from the S-Bahn station connecting the town with

Berlin, a city wall surrounds Bernau's old town core. This quaint little district town so typical of the March merits a comfortable stroll. The path to follow runs parallel to the old town wall, which has been completely preserved and is gradually being restored.

The imposing stone gate surmounted by the **Hunger Tower** is the only one of formerly three gates to the city still in good condition. The five-storey brick construction houses a good part of the **Bernauer Heimatmuseum** (museum of local history), which, however, is open only in the warmer part of the year.

The city proudly shows off such old, restored buildings as the **Kantorhaus**, the **Adler pharmacy**, the hotel **Schwarzer Adler** and the **town hall** at the market, as well as its modern apartment buildings, none of which is over five storeys high and whose open inner courtyards fit in well with the small-town ambience.

A beautiful, four-aisled, late-Gothic hall church dating to 1519 is one of the main attractions on the **Bernauer Market Square**. The Bernauer parish **Church of St Mary** displays a rich interior, especially the chorus. Art historians attribute the six-winged main altar, which can be transformed twice by opening flaps, to the workshop of Lukas Cranach the Elder (around 1520). Experts have restored the *Madonna under the Canopy,* the nearly life-sized *Triumphal Cross Ensemble,* the *Sacramental Tabernacle* and other artworks. Traditional concerts on the 29-stop organ are among the cultural highlights of Bernau.

On the market between the church and the town hall, a relief on a cast iron column illustrates the history of the town. According to a legend about the founding of Bernau, around the year 1140, Margrave Albrecht the Bear got lost while on a bear hunt in the marshy river area. By chance he came upon a lonely forest inn. The beer tapped here pleased the Margrave's palate so much that he immediately decided to found a city on the spot: the subsequent Bernau. Indeed, for centuries,

143

AROUND BERLIN

0   15 km

Bernau has brewed the best beer in the March of Brandenburg; at some point, other breweries in the area usurped Bernau's beery reputation. Ever since then, the Bernauers import their beer.

Hikes around Bernau

Hiking out of the city to the northeast, you pass through the former city gate at the **Pulverturm** (powder magazine). Directly to the left, right up against the city wall, the **hangman's house** displays some of the Bernau executioners' instruments of torture.

A special hiking area beckons beyond the city's cobblestones: the **Liepnitzsee**, a lake with perhaps the purest water in Germany. The water of the Liepnitzsee is of drinking quality, for its only feeder is a vigorous, cold, deep spring. To keep the lake and its shore clean, motorboats have

Left: Shipbuilding, the only game in town in Eberswalde-Finow. Right: Musicians in front of the Strausberg town hall.

been forbidden and cars prohibited from parking near the lake. Only fishermen are permitted to sometimes try their luck.

Another charming hike, and one particularly rewarding for amateur botanists, leads from Bernau through **Ladeburg**, whose marketplace boasts two ancient trees, to **Lobetal**. Many different species of conifers from various climatic zones thrive in the forest park set up in 1930, one kilometer south of the village.

The path leads further, first to **Biesental**, then to **Lanke**. More than ten lakes still provide swimmers and nature lovers with water clean enough to pass the most fastidious muster. In Lanke, people also swim in the **"Krumme Lanke,"** the lake that perhaps best illustrates the Berlin expression "j.w.d. – janz weit draussen" (out in the boondocks). Old, shadowy forests with pure beech groves frame the crystalline lake. The idyllic landscape conservation area between **Barnim** and the **Eberswalder glacial valley** displays rich contrasts. To fully enjoy and explore it, one should bring along a bicycle and perhaps a few days' time. The truly primordial landscape deserves it.

Hikers in the **Prenden lake area** will be rewarded with unbuttoned, romantic beauty. A longer tour by car or bike (about 40 kilometers) leads from Bernau through Briesetal to Eberswalde-Finow and to the ship elevator in Niederfinow. Like so many other towns of the March, neighboring Eberswalde also has a local museum with plenty of historical and local information.

The itinerary then proceeds to **Niederfinow** (nine kilometers on the F 167, and then north for another two kilometers). The **ship elevator** is located here. This imposing technical construction received its present form between 1927 and 1934. A 157-meter-long canal bridge connects it with the Oder-Havel Canal. The lifting apparatus raises the ships in a huge, water-filled trough, achieving differences in height of up to 36 meters.

Strausberg

Berlin's easternmost advance guard, the county seat of **Strausberg**, lies on the southern edge of the recreational area known as the **Märkische Schweiz** (best translated as the "Switzerland of the March," at the end of the S-Bahn line Strausberg.

As early as 1200, the margraves of Brandenburg entertained estates here, later developing them into a town. The name "Strutzberch" appears for the first time in the 1240 chronicle that was written by the bishop of Magdeburg. The name derives from the ancient Sorbian and originally meant "pod" or "hull," referring to the form of the **Straussee**, on whose eastern shore the city spread. Originally, the city's name had nothing to do with the *Strauss* (ostrich), depicted on Strausberg's coat-of-arms.

The ferry crossing the Straussee every thirty minutes is unique in the whole of Europe: it moves on electrical overhead wires supplying the energy.

Strausberg has preserved remnants of the medieval fieldstone city walls, including a few guard houses and the remains of the two gates to the city.

The parish church of St Mary, an early Gothic fieldstone church, underwent a number of changes but still exhibits late-Gothic characteristics, particularly in the interior. Figure paintings from the 15th century, including a *Christ as Judge of the World* and a *Coronation of Mary* decorate the vaults, and the precious late Gothic winged altar with Mary on the moon's crescent and the carved altar depicting the Madonna with a radiant halo are treats for art-lovers.

Strausberg is a gold mine of military history. During the Weimar Republic, German army leadership maintained its headquarters in Strausberg. The severe officers' quarters near the garrison grounds have seen several army generations since then, including the Soviet military commands in the GDR.

After the National People's Army of the GDR was disbanded, the top brass of the Bundeswehr command occupied the apartments and staff buildings.

In the Switzerland of the March

Strausberg marks the edge of the **Barnim**, an extensive ground moraine plate. Idyllic forest lakes have formed in deep-cut watercourses which provide wonderful places for swimming or fishing. This "Switzerland of the March" is a prime hiking area, especially in autumn or winter. In the fall, extensive deciduous and mixed forests adorn its beautiful hills and dales in colorful dress.

The rugged relief of the **Naturpark Märkische Schweiz** also enchants hikers and casual visitors. Mixed forests and lakes, the largest of which is the **Scharmützelsee**, provide the backdrop for the town of **Buckow**, famous for having been the home of Bertolt Brecht and the actress Helene Weigel. The bus runs about 15 kilometers from Strausberg to Buckow. Brecht's and Weigel's former home, where such plays as *Coriolan* and *Turandot* were written after 1952, is now open to the public.

Beech groves abound in the forests around Buckow, and the city's name derives directly from the Slavic word for beech, *bukov*.

There are further natural wonders on the **Wildbach Sophienfliess**. A small parking lot is accessible about 100 meters beyond the turnoff from the Strausberger Chaussee toward Buckow. If you come by bus, ask for the **Wurzelfichte** stop, starting point for a 1.5 kilometer stroll to the town. A few steps lead down into a small valley. A 20-meter-high, about 150-year-old fir tree grows on the other bank of the stream. 20 people can crowd into the confusion of its washed out roots. The hiking trail, called **Poetensteig** (poets' path) for good reason, enchants

Right: Sorbish women in Spreewald still weave flax the way they used to.

every hiker with the romance of its wild, natural beauty.

The Poetensteig climbs steeply past the **Gasthaus Tirol** (Tyrolean restaurant) up to the stately **Jenas-Höhe** (111 meters). From here, the path leads through the **Finkenherd** and the **Wolfsschlucht**, around the small **Tornowsee**, past the **Günterquelle**, a spring with high iron-content, and finally back to the town. The path ends near the city park, which was designed by landscape architect J. P. Lenné.

Königs-Wusterhausen

Southeast of Berlin, directly where the Dahme and the Notte canals flow together, is **Königs-Wusterhausen** – or **"KW,"** as Berliners call this recreational area. Here, at the end of the S-Bahn line, an extensive system of bus lines and passenger trains offers connections to the near and more distant surroundings of KW all the way to the Spreewald. The *Autobahn* will also take you to the city, but if you're going by car, the country roads through the posh suburbs of **Grünau**, **Schmöckwitz**, **Eichwalde** and **Zeuthen** might be worth your while. **Wildau**, an industrial park, was built according to an exceptional architectural plan. In 1898 the locomotive factory Wildau and the workers' housing project were both constructed in the same style.

Königs-Wusterhausen itself is a fairly small town. The consumer attractions offered along the pedestrian zone in its center are modest. For the last 40 years, most residents of this satellite city have worked and done their shopping in Berlin. Königs-Wusterhausen was important and well-known not only as a Prussian garrison town, but also for its coal harbor and the radio broadcasting facilities on the **Funkerberg** (broadcaster's mountain). In 1913 the army erected its radio station on the hill and broadcast the first German radio program on December 22, 1920. In-

terestingly, the broadcasting towers also figure in the town's coat-of-arms.

The story of KW's founding is quickly told. In 1690 the two-year-old son of the King of Prussia was made owner of "palace and people." Then, after he was enthroned as Friedrich Wilhelm I in 1713, he ordered the hunting palace built as we know it today. For 20 years, the "Soldier King" regularly used the palace as his lodge during the autumn hunting season. He made Wusterhausen into Königs-Wusterhausen. A particular attraction is the weekly market held each Saturday. KW has been trying to rid itself of the suburban image and achieve greater independence as a local capital. In this way it will become a center of business where new industrial and commercial zones will be set up.

16 campsites, most with facilities for trailers, provide accommodation for visitors to the lakes of the region.

The **Schlosshotel** in the little town (2000 residents) of **Teupitz** makes a good vacation home for those preferring more comfort. Located on a peninsula extending into the **Teupitzsee** (accessible from the marketplace), the medieval water castle of the Schenken von Landsberg dynasty was converted into a hotel. Its private beach provides a magnificent panoramic view of the lake. Parts of Teupitz are still vaguely reminiscent of its past as a fishing village.

From Teupitz to Bad Saarow

Hikers starting out from Teupitz to explore the lakes of the March encounter hardly any limits to their *Wanderlust.* From Teupitz, waterways lead into the **Spreewald** or, by way of Storkow, to the **Scharmützelsee**.

Of course, you don't have to paddle the whole way. The suburban train to Beeskow from KW arrives in **Wendisch-Rietz** on the southern shore of the March's "sea" in about 20 minutes. At the train station, one can first gaze at the lake stretching northward for 11 kilometers. It's one kilometer to the dock of the pas-

senger steamer to **Bad Saarow,** and about two kilometers to the vacation village in **Wendisch-Rietz**. Sails spangle the huge lake, especially in the summer months and on weekends. Besides swimming, the waters also provide anglers with ample opportunity for fishing. Waterfront property owners have purposely left long stretches of the shore free for a path, so visitors can take leisurely strolls around the lake. Only the occasional tree or un-cooperative owner obstructs the view or the path.

Theodor Fontane, who hiked over all the trails in the March of Brandenburg, walked around this lake in the spring of 1870: "It was a wonderful path; the blue skies arched over the blue water, and the sparse reeds lining the shore were hung with equally sparse shreds of foam, which constantly swayed back and forth in the sharp east wind," he later remembered.

Above: A relaxing summer weekend in the natural surroundings of the Spreewald.

Bad Saarow has been an exclusive health spa ever since 1910, when healing mud and the **Solequelle** spring were discovered. In past years, the military, particularly the upper echelons of the former GDR National People's Army, used it as a spa and sanatorium; the political bigwigs of the time also held the lake in high esteem – the SED Central Committee maintained a group of bungalows here for its own private use.

But Bad Saarow has its best years behind it: In the twenties, many celebrities of Berlin society spent time here relaxing from their busy lives, among them Max Schmeling, the actress Käthe Dorsch and Harry Liedtke, whose request to be buried in Bad Saarow was finally fulfilled. And in 1922-1923, the Russian writer Maxim Gorky came here to take the waters. A little museum has been set up recalling his visit. Many famous people met in the **Weinstube Peters** on the Moorstrasse; autographed photos and witty phrases decorate the walls and guest book.

In the summer, if you look out from the deck of the passenger steamer cruising from Wendisch-Rietz to Bad Saarow, you will see that enchanting water lilies have joined the reeds, which are still as sparse as in Fontane's days.

The **Rauen Mountains** rise in the north. Miners dug lignite here from the forties of the last century until about 1905. One of the few remaining witnesses to this mining history, the **Steigerhaus**, stands under monument protection at Chausseestr. 35 in the small community of **Rauen**. A massive 13th century fortified church built of fieldstone dominates the village green.

Rauen first became known for its **giant boulders** brought down from Sweden by ice age glaciers. Architect Schinkel commissioned the sculpting of the larger of the two stones into a huge **granite bowl** nearly 30 meters in circumference. In 1834, the Berlin Pleasure Garden exhibited it in front of the old museum. The smaller stone and what remains of the larger one still attract admirers to the Rauen Mountains.

In the fall, when the summer guests gradually depart, mushroom pickers take over the huge forest area between Königs-Wusterhausen and **Halbe**. Armed with pocketknifes and baskets, they roam the woods hunting for edible mushrooms of all kinds, sometimes selling their harvest on Sundays at the highway rest stops.

To the Spreewald

The marshy Spree river region, which in parts almost resembles a dense jungle, attains a width of up to 11 kilometers in the **Spreewald**. The nature here is unique in Europe.

Several hundred canals, arms of the Spree and a variety of smaller streams intertwine to form the extensive network of what the local inhabitants, the *Spreewäldler,* use as their main transportation sys-tem. As in Venice, most local traffic and transportation is carried out on the water and every house has its own little dock. The "capital" of the Spreewald, **Lübbenau**, where the majority of boats dock, boasts the largest harbor,

The *Spreewäldler* have lived from fishing and vegetable cultivation for ages and they now supply Berlin households with horseradishes, cucumbers and onions. Since 1908, tourism between Pentecost and October has also been a fairly important source of income. Spreewald towns have adapted to the streams of tourists. Seemingly every visitor to the Spreewald wants to be punted through the confusion of canals by a Spreewald girl in traditional costume.

The enchanting **Lehde open-air museum** provides a wealth of information on the history of the Spreewald region. The uniquely romantic charms of a canoe or paddling tour captivate almost everyone. The train leaving from Lübbenau's main train station arrives at the Lehde station in just under one hour.

But you can also explore the Spreewald villages along the shore. Narrow paths lead over arched bridges, while underneath the region's characteristic long boats glide past. A conversation with the locals will acquaint you with the Spreewald quickly.

The ancient, over one-meter-thick oaks and the dark log cabins with garlands of onions create an almost timeless atmosphere. But inevitably the inhabitants of the Spreewald will soon have to readjust themselves to the new economic times. Much of the agriculture in this region is no longer competitive.

The government of the state of Brandenburg will be hard pressed to effectively protect this unique culture. Whether the *Spreewäldler* manage to maintain the balance between their traditional way of life and tourism – combined with the effects of German reunification – remains to be seen.

POTSDAM

Transportation

CAR: From Berlin Central, the district of Potsdam can be reached by car via one of the exits from the city peripheral road, via the Glienicker Bridge or via the AVUS (A 115, road section used for car races) taking the exit Wannsee or Babelsberg.

S-BAHN: From the S-Bahn station Wannsee suburban trains leave for Potsdam.

BUS: Bus Nr. 199 runs to Bassinplatz in Potsdam.

SHIP: During the summer, a cruise with the ships of the *Weisse Flotte* (White Fleet) to Potsdam is a charming alternative to rail and road. The ships run every hour and berth next to the S-Bahn station Wannsee.

Tourist-Information

Potsdam-Information, Touristenzentrale, Am Alten Markt, 14467 Potsdam, Tel. 29 11 00 / 29 33 85; Mondays-Fridays 9 a.m.-8 p.m., Sat, Sun, holidays from 9 a.m.-6 p.m. **Branch office**: Brandenburger Str. 18, Tel. 29 30 38, Mon-Fri 10 a.m.-6 p.m., Sat 10 a.m.-2 p.m. Tourist service includes admission tickets, city tours and a list of private quarters.

Accommodation

Residenz-Hotel Potsdam, Saarmunder Str. 60, Tel. 883 00. **Hotel Schloss Cecilienhof**, Im Neuen Garten, Tel. 370 50. **Travel Charm Hotel am Jägertor**, Hegelallee 1, Tel. 29 18 34 / 29 23 90. **Hotelschiff "Friedrich der Grosse"** (hotel ship), at the berth of the Weisse Flotte, Tel. 61 90 04.

Post / Telephone / Lost and Found

Telephone: The **area code** for Potsdam is 0331. **Main Post Office**: Heinrich-Rau-Allee 16/18, Tel. 380. **Lost and Found**: office at the City Council, Friedrich-Ebert-Str. 79/81, Tel. 2890.

Rental Cars
Breakdown Service / Taxi

Rental Cars: Interent, Rudolf-Breitscheid-Strasse 15, Tel. 748 14 28-31. **Breakdown Service**: ADAC, Tel. 291 770. **Taxi**: Tel. 876 555.

Museums / Parks / Cemeteries

Altes Rathaus and **Kulturhaus Potsdam** (Old City Hall and House of Culture), Am Alten Markt, Tel. 29 31 75, Tue-Sun 10 a.m.-6 p.m.

Dampfmaschinenhaus, (Steam Engine House), Breite Strasse, Tel. 969 42 48. Open Wednesdays - Sundays 9 a.m.-12 noon, 1-5 p.m.

Babelsberg Studios (film studios, with adventure park and tours), Grossbeeren-/Grünstr., Tel. 965 27 55, daily 10 a.m.-6 p.m.

Einsteinturm, Telegrafenberg, Tel. 29 17 41.

Film Museum Potsdam, Marstall, Schlossstr. 1, Tel. 29 36 75 / 280 10 59. Tue-Fri 10 a.m.-5 p.m.; Sat, Sun, holidays 10 a.m.-6 p.m.

Friedenskirche, Marylgarten, Am Grünen Gitter, Tel. 29 31 56.

Memorial of the Potsdam Treaty, Schloss Cecilienhof, Neuer Garten, Tel. 96 94 244, daily 9 a.m.-12 noon and 12.30-5 p.m., closed every 2nd and 4th Monday in the month.

The church **Heilandskirche Sacrow**, located ca. 14 km north of Potsdam, can be reached by car via the road to Falkensee.

The church **Kirche St. Peter und Paul**, Bassinplatz, Tel. 280 49 42, is currently undergoing restauration and open during service only.

Potsdam-Museum im Ständehaus, Breite Str. 13, Tel. 289 67 00, Tue-Sun 9 a.m.-5 p.m.

Schloss and **Park Babelsberg**, Tel. 969 41 90, Tue-Sun 9 a.m.-12 noon, 12.30-5 p.m.

The cemetery **Stahnsdorfer Südwest-Friedhof**, on Bahnhofsstrasse, Stahnsdorf, is an overgrown area containing the graves of painter Heinrich Zille, architect Walter Gropius and other celebrities as well as pompous mausoleums of 19th century industrial magnates. Tel. 03329/623, daily 7 a.m.-8 p.m.

St. Nikolaikirche, Am Alten Markt, Potsdam, Tel. 29 12 19; Tue-Sat 10 a.m.-5 p.m., Sun 11.15 a.m.-5 p.m., Mon 2-5 p.m.

Palaces and Parks in Sanssouci

Information and Visitors' Center, Am Grünen Gitter 2, Tel. 969 41 90. **Sanssouci Park and Palace** are open daily (including holidays) 9 a.m.-12.30 p.m., 1-5 p.m. The palace is closed every first and third Monday of the month! The palace can only be visited on a guided tour (every 20 minutes); advance ticket sale begins at 9 a.m.; as tour groups tend to crowd round the ticket counters later on in the day, buy your ticket as early as possible. The various palace buildings within the park grounds have different opening times and admission prices.

Cafés and Restaurants

Gastronomy in Potsdam has been undergoing rapid changes. For special ambience and charm, try the cafés in the various palaces and parks. In downtown Potsdam, a visit to the **Café im Filmmuseum** is recommended, not least for its stylish atmosphere. The following restaurants in Potsdam are recommended for good meals: **Badische Weinstuben**, Gutenbergstr. 90, Tel. 280 04 29; **Stadtheide**, Zeppelinstr. 101, Tel. 97 20 33, very cosy; **Theaterklause**, Zimmerstr. 10, Tel. 29 23 64 and **Froschkasten**, Kiezstr. 4, Tel. 29 13 15 both have definite *Kneipen*-character.

Culture / Entertainment

Potsdam's proximity to Berlin has resulted in a certain amount of friendly cultural competition. The **Hans-Otto-Theater**, Am Alten Markt, Tel 280 06 93 is worth a visit, as well as the **Schloss-theater im Neuen Palais**, Sanssouci, where the ensemble of the Hans-Otto-Theater gives frequent performances, Tel. 29 30 38. Don't miss an evening in the cabaret **Am Obelisk** (in the Café Klatsch, 1st floor, Schopenhauerstr. 27, Tel. 29 10 69). Tue-Thur 11 a.m.-1 p.m., 1.30-8.30 pm; Fri 11 a.m.-10.30 p.m., Sat 4-10.30 p.m., Sun 4-8.30 p.m.

AROUND POTSDAM

Weisse Flotte (White Fleet), Lange Brücke, Tel. 4241/247. Ships leave for round trips and cruises to Caputh, Werder, Templin and to the Havelland.

Ketzin

Tourist information: City Council, Tel. 033233/203. **Heimatmuseum**, Ernst-Thälmann-Str. 32, Tel. 033233/203, Tue 3-5.30 p.m., Sat 10 a.m.-12 noon.

Werder

The City Council of **Werder** offers tips and information for tourists: Eisenbahnstr. 13/14, Tel. 03327/2331. The **Obstbaumuseum** (Museum of Fruit Growing), Karl-Marx-Platz 2, is open to visitors by appointment only, Tel. 03327/2331.

LANDSCAPES OF THE MARCH

Oranienburg

The memorial **Mahnmal Sachsenhausen**, documenting the history of the concentration camps and the atrocities committed under the Nazi regime, is open Tue-Sun 8 a.m.-6 p.m., Strasse der Nationen, Tel. 03301/80 37 15.

Bernau

The tourist information is located in the **City Hall**, Am Marktplatz 2, 16321 Bernau, Tel. 03338/87 34. Friendly staff give information on accommodation and restaurants.
Heimatmuseum Bernau, Im Steintor, Tel. 56 14, Tue-Sun 9 a.m.-12 noon, 2-5 p.m.

Eberswalde

Tourist information: **City Hall**, Heegermühler Str. 35, 16225 Eberswalde, Tel. 03334/231 68. Worth a visit are the **Stadt-und Kreismuseum** (Town and County Museum), with an exhibition of town history and the local metal industry, Kirchstr. 8, open Tue-Fri 8 a.m.-12 noon, 2-5 p.m., Sun 2-5 p.m., the **local zoo** and the **ship elevator**.

Strausberg / Buckow

Information about **Strausberg** and accommodation advice: Tourist information, Georg-Kurtze-Str., Tel. 03341/31 10 66, 15344 Strausberg.
In **Buckow**, the **Brecht-Weigel-Haus** is situated on Bertolt-Brecht-Strasse 29. Information about the **Naturpark Märkische Schweiz** (Nature Park Markish Switzerland): Wriezener Str. 5, 15377 Buckow, Tel. 033433/384.

Königs-Wusterhausen

The Tourist-Office supplies information about hotels and sights in the Spreewald, Am Nottekanal Ost, 15711 Königs-Wusterhausen, Tel. 03375/66 305. A good bus and train service connects Königs-Wuster-hausen with the immediate vicinity and the Spreewald.

Bad Saarow

Information from the local spa administration: Kur-verwaltung, Seestr. 5a, Bad Saarow-Pieskow, Tel. 033631/21 42. The ships of the **Weisse Flotte** (White Fleet) berth at the Schwanenwiese, Tel. 24 19.

Spreewald

Avoid visiting the **Spreewald** on Sundays or public holidays – during these times, restaurants and ships are packed with tourists! A charming, alternative way of exploring the Spreewald countryside off the beaten tracks is by bicycle or by hiking.

Lübbenau

Information about Lübbenau and the Spreewald region: **Fremdenverkehrsamt**, Poststr. 25, 03222 Lübbenau, Tel. 03542/22 63 and **Lübbenau-Infor-mation**, Ehm-Welk-Str. 15, Tel. 03542/22 25.
The **Spreewaldmuseum** in the palace park and the **Freilichtmuseum Lehde** (Open Air Museum), Tel. 03542/24 72, open Mai to October, are worth a visit. For a good meal try the restaurant **Zum grünen Strand der Spree** on Maxim-Gorki-Strasse, or the **Fröhlicher Hecht** in Lehde.
Various agencies offer **rental boats** between April and October: Bootshaus Kaupen, Am Kaupen 1, Tel. 2750 (at the footpath to Leipe). Bootsverleih Petrick, Tel. 3620, at the campsite Lübbenau), Paddelboot-verleih Hannemann, Am Wasser 1, Tel. 3647.

Restaurants in the March

Alte Klosterschänke, Am Amt 9, Chorin, Tel. 033366/433, hearty fare in a medieval cloister garden. **Holländische Mühle**, Berliner Chaussee 164, Werder, Tel. 03327/411 40, tasty Berlin food. **Mär-kisches Gildehaus**, Schwielowseestr. 58, Caputh, Tel. 033209/702 65, Berlin fare. **Schlosshotel Teu-pitz**, Kirchstr. 8, Teupitz, Tel. 033766/266, traditional German food in in the castle hall.

SHOPPING IN BERLIN

Berlin is expensive, Berlin is cheap: Shoppers in this city have a choice between expensive boutiques and flipped-out second-hand cellars, between huge department stores and shrill scene shops. In fact, all of Berlin appears to be one big and scrambled market where one can fulfil any and every consumer wish.

The Kurfürstendamm and its Side Streets

The Kurfürstendamm is still the great, glittering shopping boulevard, not only for tourists but also for many Berliners – even if they don't always want to admit it. The side streets have changed a lot in recent years, they've grown more chic and usually more attractive than the Ku'-damm itself.

Preceding page: The Pergamon Altar. Left: Way-out articles are to be had at Schrill's department store.

The most elegant side street is the **Fasanenstrasse**, particularly the section between the Ku'damm and Lietzenburger Strasse. Everything with name and rank in the fashion world has established itself here: **Cartier**, **Fred Perry**, **Roeckel Gloves**, **Paco Antique Jewelry**, **Louis Vuitton**; a tiny tailor's shop for fine shirts has also opened up here, and, recently, **Christie's Auction House** from London established a subsiduary.

Make a point of going window-shopping on the **Bleibtreustrasse**, especially near the Lietzenburger Strasse. On the corner of the Ku'damm, three first-class men's clothing stores, **Norbert's**, **SOR** and **Selbach**, keep top designer fashions in store as well as more usual – and somewhat less expensive – brands and models. Right next door, the small, exquisite lingerie store **Nouvelle** beckons seductively, and the shop **Fasetti** creates magnificent, superbly useless things of black leather, chrome and glass. Jeans fans with selective taste go to **City Jeans** on the other side of the street.

In the other direction, toward Kant-strasse, the stores offer everything the heart desires – not as elegant, but more odd-ball and at pleasing prices. The streets between the Ku'damm and Kant-strasse demonstrate that, in Berlin, the elegant and expensive can exist cheek-by-jowl with the way-out and cheap.

Fans of exotic threads have a ball in **Lila** and can buy the matching hat right next door in the **Kaufhaus Schrill**. For shoes, it's only a few steps to **Finn's** whose designs seem to be based on the motto: "Anything goes, as long as it is ec-centric." Meanwhile, gentlemen can fit themselves out from top to toe at **Hotch-Potch**.

Consumer Boulevard Tauentzien and KaDeWe

The Tauentzien is a street that is exclu-sively devoted to shopping and stretches between Breitscheidplatz and Witten-bergplatz. The eye-catcher here is the **Europa-Center** with its over 100 stores, a good place to explore on a rainy day (see p. 60).

Berlin's greatest and most famous temple of consumerism is the Kaufhaus des Westens (**KaDeWe**) on Wittenberg-platz (see p. 62). A visit to the KaDeWe is definitely worth it. It's true that many Berliners moan about the "Ossis" (as the ex-GDR Germans are disparagingly referred to) who walk through this elite department store as if it were a museum, getting in the way of the eternally stressed natives; but Berliners are still proud of the elegant establishment's fame. Opened in 1907, the store now has 24,000 square meters of sales floor space and supposedly 250,000 different articles of merchandise, making it the largest de-partment store on the continent. Its **gour-met floor**, opened in 1956, has once and for all proven its exclusiveness, attracting primarily the members of the "upper ten thousand." With its 5100 square meters and 25,000 different articles, including 400 kinds of bread and 1800 kinds of cheese, this department of KaDeWe is Europe's largest and the world's second-largest gourmet paradise.

Antiques and Art

Treasures from all periods are massed in Berlin's antique shops, illustrating the city's changing history. High quality an-tiques are concentrated on the **Keith-strasse**, just behind Wittenbergplatz. Here, and also in the **Eisenacherstrasse**, **Kalckreuthstrasse** and **Motzstrasse**, the stores are lined up one after the other. On **Suarezstrasse**, prices and usually quality are lower than on the Keithstrasse. With luck and a bit of talent, you can acquire a piece of furniture, Art-Deco and Art-Nouveau artwork at a reasonable price.

Browsers are welcome in Berlin's ex-cellent antique book and art shops con-centrated around the **Winterfeldplatz** and on **Motzstrasse**. In **Eckard Düwal's** on Schlüterstrasse, one of Berlin's reputed dealers, many a bookworm has lost track of time while reading old writings. **Kie-pert**, Berlin's largest book store, sells an-tique books and almost everything avail-able on the German book market. Unfor-tunately, Kiepert is very businesslike; the service here, while very competent and knowledgeable, is not particularly friendly. The Bücherbogen under the railway viaduct on Savignyplatz has much more atmosphere and specializes in exciting large-format art and photo books.

Since 1992 the brand-new multimedia department store **Herder** (on Tauentzien) has offered a mixture novel to Germany, friendly service and a gigantic selection of goods. Both vend a confusing wealth of CDs, LPs, books, hifi equipment, tele-vision sets, personal computers and vi-deos. The fnac, a French store, is located in the Meineckestrasse, and is worth checking out if only for its noble interior

decoration. Those who are keener of antique art can pick up the bust of Nefertiti for their living room from the **Plaster Casting Works of the Foundation of Prussian Cultural Heritage**. And if you want to dine like the Hohenzollern princes in your own livingroom, a shop on Unter den Linden sells **Meissen Porcelain**.

Second-Hand, Junk Stores and Markets

Berlin's off-scene offers old things of a completely different sort: Innumerable shops and mini-boutiques sell designer fashions by (as yet) unknown Berliner fashion designers or second-hand works by famous designers. The largest second-hand shops, like **Die Garage**, have quite a selection, most of it is unfortunately of miserable quality.

Above: The flea market on the Strasse des 17. Juni, one of many places in Berlin where one might find a genuine gem.

Berliners not only like to buy used merchandise, they also like to rummage, bargain and haggle. Thus, Berlin's **flea markets** and **junk stores** and many of the weekly **open-air markets** have all developed their own individual character. On the **Winterfeldplatz**, where one of Berlin's most attractive open-air markets takes place, vendors offer a wide spectrum of wares twice a week. From vegetables to ceramics, you'll find everything. On the **Reichspietschufer**, dealers pile up used things on folding tables. The flea market at the S-Bahn station Tiergarten on the **Strasse des 17. Juni** is even more popular.

The rules here are the same as all over the world: If you arrive early enough – 7 a.m. is best – you can find a real bargain. On the same side of the street, a little further in the direction of **Ernst-Reuter-Platz**, art conoisseurs mill around the **art market** held simultaneously. Here, artists and would-be artists offer very beautiful, tasteful things or absolute garbage: It is the customer's choice.

SHOPPING

In addition to the Ku'damm, the main shopping boulevards are **Wilmersdorfer Strasse** (pedestrian zone in Charlottenburg), **Schlossstrasse, Rheinstrasse** and **Hauptstrasse** in Schöneberg/-Steglitz and **Alexanderplatz** (Berlin-Mitte). Berlin's largest consumer temple is the Kaufhaus des Westens, better known as **KaDeWe** (Schöneberg, Tauentzienstrasse 21, Tel. 212 10).

Most small (but expensive) boutiques are located in the side streets around the Ku'damm, Savignyplatz und Ludwigkirchplatz. More colorful on the other hand are the shops on Kreuzberger-, Bergmann und Gneisenaustrasse.

Ladies' Fashions

Bramigk-Design, S-Bahn arches at Savignyplatz, Charlottenburg, Tel. 313 51 25. **Louis Vuitton**, Charlottenburg, Fasanenstr. 27, Tel. 882 52 72. **Nouvelle**, Charlottenburg, Bleibtreustr. 24, Tel. 881 47 37. **Pupi's Laden**, Charlottenburg, Schlüterstr. 54, Tel. 881 65 25. **Soft-Boutique**, Charlottenburg, Bleibtreustr. 6, Tel. 312 14 03. **Univogue**, Charlottenburg, Kurfürstendamm 25 a (on the 2nd floor), Tel. 882 71 99.

Men's Fashions

City Jeans, Charlottenburg, Bleibtreustr. 34, Tel. 882 56 42. **Fred Perry**, Charlottenburg, Fasanenstr. 27, Tel. 882 30 95. **Hotch-Potch**, Charlottenburg, Bleibtreustr. 17, Tel. 881 44 50. **Maggazino**, Wilmersdorf, Güntzelstr. 21, Tel. 87 99 46. **Manfred Klinke**, Charlottenburg, Kurfürstendamm 188, Tel. 883 47 30. **Masshemden**, Charlottenburg, Fasanenstr. 28, Tel. 881 65 15, shirts made to measure. **Mientus**, Charlottenburg, Wilmersdorfer Str. 73 and Kurfürstendamm 52, Tel. 323 90 77. **Selbach**, Charlottenburg, Kurfürstendamm 195, Tel. 883 25 26. **Veni Vici Vidi**, Charlottenburg, Leibnizstr. 40, Tel. 323 23 22.

Fashion by Berlin Designers

Collection Brigitte Haarke, Kreuzberg, Hedemannstr. 13, Tel. 251 90 98. **Durchbruch**, Charlottenburg, Schlüterstr. 54, Tel. 881 55 68. **Garage**, Schöneberg, Ahornstr. 2: second hand only. **Molotow**, Kreuzberg, Gneisenaustr. 112, Tel. 693 08 18. **Monella**, Charlottenburg, Ludwigkirchstr. 4, Tel. 883 18 45. Includes fashion by Claudia Skoda, Berlin's top designer.

Accessories / Gifts / Shoes

Ararat, Charlottenburg, Schlüterstr. 22, Tel. 312 44 45. **Budapester Schuhe**, Charlottenburg, Kurfürstendamm 199, Tel. 881 17 07. Elegant mens' shoes.

Cartier Berlin, Charlottenburg, Fasanenstr. 28, Tel. 882 16 00. **Fasetti**, Charlottenburg, Bleibtreustr. 24, Tel. 881 70 01. **Kaufhaus der Besten** (KaDeBe), Schöneberg, Hohenstaufenstrasse 68, Tel. 216 17 77. **Kaufhaus Schrill / Galerie Schrill**, Charlottenburg, Bleibtreustr. 46/49, Tel. 312 85 84. **Lila**, Bleibtreustr. 47. **Paco-Antiker Schmuck,** (antique jewelry) Charlottenburg, Fasanenstr. 73, Tel. 881 35 50. **Roeckel-Handschuhe**, (specializing in gloves), Charlottenburg, Kurfürstendamm 216, Tel. 881 53 79. **Schuhtick**, Schöneberg, Tauentzienstr. 5, Tel. 211 79 69 and Charlottenburg, Savignyplatz 11, Tel. 312 49 55. Unusual and classic shoes for men and women. **Tizian**, Charlottenburg, Kurfürstendamm 187, Tel. 883 36 55. Elegant Italian shoes.

Antiques / Books / Records

Art Deco, Charlottenburg, Leibnizstrasse 64, Tel. 323 17 11. **Bücherbogen am Savignyplatz** (books), Charlottenburg, Tel. 312 19 32. **Christie's-Auktionshaus**, Charlottenburg, Fasanenstrasse 72, Tel. 882 77 78. **Düwal**, Charlottenburg, Schlüterstr. 17, Tel. 313 30 30. **fnac**, Charlottenburg, Meinekestr. 23, Tel. 88 47 20. **Gipsformerei der SMPK** (plaster casts) Charlottenburg, Sophie-Charlotten-Str. 17/18, Tel. 321 70 11 (open until 4 p.m., Wednesdays until 6 p.m.). **Gelbe Musik**, Charlottenburg, Schaperstr. 11, Jazz, Rock, Pop. **Herde**, Charlottenburg, Am Tauentzien 13, entrance Rankestr. 4/5, Tel. 217 66 61. **Kiepert**, Charlottenburg, Hardenbergstr. 4/5, Tel. 31 10 09-0. **Meissener Porzellan**, Mitte, Unter den Linden 39b, Tel. 229 26 91.

Markets

Krempelmarkt am Reichspietschufer (open-air flea market), Kreuzberg, takes place Saturdays and Sundays 8 a.m.-3.30 p.m.

Kunstmarkt, Strasse des 17. Juni, (open-air art market), Tiergarten, Sat and Sun 11 a.m. -5 p.m.

Trödelmarkt, Strasse des 17. Juni (open-air flea market), Tiergarten, Saturdays and Sundays 10 a.m. until 3.30 p.m.

Wochenmarkt Winterfeldtplatz (weekly market), Schöneberg, Wed, Sat 8 a.m.-1 p.m.

Opening Hours

Large department stores and most shops are open from 9 or 10 a.m.-6.30 p.m.; every Thursday late opening until 8.30 p.m. for some shops and large department stores; first Saturday of the month until 4 p.m. (summer) or 6 p.m. (winter). As many small boutiques don't open before 11 a.m. or noon, telephone beforehand or check out opening times in one of the city's weekly magazines.

THE WHOLE WORLD IN A HALL: THE MUSEUMS

Many tourists in Berlin know *U-Bahn Linie 1* from the musical of the same name being performed by Berlin's Grips Theater, or from the film. The traveler partakes in an assortment of adventures on a journey from the genteel Westend to deepest Kreuzberg. 24 hours a day, a lot of peculiar people pass through the doors of the subway cars. This social mixture is typical for Berlin.

Meanwhile, another U-Bahn line over-shadows line 1: this is the old Line 2 which since 1994 has been running through all of Berlin as it did before the War, from the Krumme Lanke to Pan-kow. Now indeed ex-chancellor Willy Brandt's statement: "What belongs together will grow together" has become reality, and the three most important sites in the Berlin museum landscape, the historic **Museum Island**, the **Kulturforum** in Tiergarten and the museums in **Dahlem** will be united.

In the meantime, all state-run museums in the city have been placed under the aegis of the (one-time West-Berlin) Stiftung Preussischer Kulturbesitz. This foundation was created in 1957 and financed by the federal government. Since 1974 Germany's (western) states have carried the economic burden. Its principal task was to care for Prussian heritage – documents, paintings and art treasures from the Prussian provinces. And since unification when it was given responsibility over 30 museums, it has been able to perform its duties as never before.

The **Staatsbibliothek Preussischer Kulturbesitz** is housed in a building by

Left: The Pergamonmuseum on Museum Island boasts numerous treasures from antiquity, here a flight of rooms which is devoted to Egypt.

Hans Scharoun in the south-east part of the Kulturforum. The library has been designed to hold 8 million volumes, and stocks are already at 4 million.

Treasures of the World on One Island

Museum Island is presently in a worse than desolate state; specialists estimate that it will cost about 1.5 billion DM to renovate the buildings. But Museum Island's attractiveness remains unaffected by the general dilapidation, thanks primarily to the world-famous **Pergamonmuseum**, which took its name from the "Altar of Pergamon," erected as a victory monument sometime between 180 and 159 B. C.

Between 1878 and 1886, on a commission from the former Royal Prussian Museums Agency, archaeologists excavated the entire temple complex and brought it to Berlin. Shortly before the turn of the century, a museum had been built on the island between the Spree and the Kupfergraben. But this first building was too small for the altar, and so the present Pergamonmuseum was constructed between 1912 and 1930.

After the monumental Greek altar, the true crown of the collection from classical antiquity, the most popular attraction is the **"Market Gate of Milet"** in the hall of Roman architecture. The gate was built during the reign of Emperor Hadrian as the entrance to the city of Milet's southern market. In the well-lit and beautifully arranged museum hall, all the hustle and bustle of this ancient city in Asia Minor seems to echo in your ears.

Still, inspite of its prominence, the Pergamonmuseum, which also houses **Near Eastern**, **Islamic** and **Far Eastern collections** as well as the highly interesting **Museum für Volkskunde** (ethnographic museum), was the last museum to be opened on Museum Island.

The original core of the museum ensemble was the **Altes Museum**, built in

1830 across from the City Palace (Stadtschloss) as Berlin's first museum. It was joined by the **Neues Museum** – now a vegetating ruin requiring thorough restoration –, by the **National Gallery**, and by the **Bodemuseum**. The Bodemuseum, originally called the Kaiser-Friedrich-Museum and renamed in 1956 for its architect Wilhelm von Bode, was supposed to serve as home to the **Egyptian Museum**, the **Papyrus- and Sculpture Collections**, the **Museum for Prehistory and Early History** and the **Art Gallery**.

It is still unclear how the diverse collections are to be reassembled in accordance with modern museum practice. The museums were organized in the 19th century using a now obsolete system. This in itself will make their complete reorganization necessary. Museum specialists agree, for example, that the Bodemuseum

Above: The bust of Nefertiti, a coveted object of curiosity. Right: At the Art Gallery in Dahlem.

is completely unsuitable for exhibiting paintings.

The Kulturforum and the Dahlem Museums

A new art gallery is presently being built on the grounds of the Kulturforum on Kemperplatz, where it will join the **Neue Nationalgalerie** (New National Gallery) on Potsdamer Strasse, the **Kunstgewerbemuseum** (Museum of Handicrafts) and the **Musical Instrument Museum**, which is in an appropriate location beside the Philharmonie.

The New National Gallery with its modern architecture, built in the sixties according to plans by Mies van der Rohe and now regarded as classic, presents changing exhibitions of modern art and painting and has a permanent collection of art from the 19th and 20th centuries. The National Gallery, built between 1965 and 1968, is the only building which Mies van der Rohe designed in Germany after emigrating to the USA in 1937.

In the utilitarian Kunstgewerbe Museum (Museum of Arts and Crafts) built in 1985 four floors hold exhibits from all areas of European arts and crafts, from the Middle Ages to the present day. Since the collections were exhibited up until 1944 in the Berlin city castle, which was then destroyed, the best pieces have been on show at the **Kunstgewerbemuseum** on the **Schlossinsel** (Palace Island) in Köpenick.

Berlin's museum archipelago has a third base in **Dahlem**, where, at the beginning of the century, the State Museums of Berlin built an external branch of the Anthropological Museum. After World War Two and the construction of the Wall, Dahlem was systematically expanded to become West Berlin's museum center. Building after building was built, until the largest Berlin museum complex arose in Dahlem.

With the **Museums of Indian Art**, **Islamic Art** and **Far Eastern Art**, Dahlem displays a spectrum of fascinating exhibitions from our remarkably exotic world.

The new acquisitions are no exception. In 1989, the Islamic Museum purchased a "Relief Tile with Inscription in Quadratic Kufi" from West Turkestan (Samarkand), labelled A. D. 1386. The Museum of Indian Art is proud of a miniature from the heroic epic *Shahnama of Firdausi*, painted in the art school of a North Indian sultanate around A. D. 1450, while the Museum of East Asian Art boasts exhibits covering such topics as "Divine Providence and Earthly Happiness: Chinese New Years' Pictures from the Wallenstein Collection."

But the real "must" is a visit to the **Völkerkundemuseum** (Anthropological Museum), whose exhibits have impressed generations of visitors. With about 350,000 objects, it is the world's largest museum of its kind. Most of the exhibits are presented in skillfully arranged rooms. The unmoving faces of the sculptures glow in the midst of artificial darkness. Cones of light bring many a long-forgotten godhead back to life in almost frightening fashion.

The **Museum für deutsche Volks-kunde** (Museum of German Folk Life) will satisfy any curiosity about objects used in everyday life in Germany through the years. Whether you peruse the special exhibitions, accompanied of course by scholarly documentation, or the permanent exhibits, this museum elucidates how a culture arises, changes and eventually passes in the course of time – to the dismay of some, to the joy of others.

Dahlem is not only a storehouse of ancient cultures. The **Art Gallery**, the **Department of Sculpture** and the **Engraving Cabinet** also present artwork from the Middle Ages to the 18th century, in a cross-section of all styles and epochs from Lucas Cranach the Elder and Albrecht Dürer through the great Italian masters, such as Titian, Raffael and Botticelli, to Brueghel, Vermeer, Rubens and El Greco.

A short vacation hardly provides sufficient time to digest the entire spectrum of Berlin's state-run museums, whose cornucupia offers something for everyone – just ast he whole of Europe can't be seen in eight days. Each individual museum has its own special character and makes its own demands on the visitor to take in the great diversity of the history of art and culture, to the various epochs and schools of sculpture and painting, and to a world of peoples and communities.

Charlottenburg Palace, with its small and large orangeries also partakes in the cultural life of Berlin and Europe. It currently houses the famed **Gallery of the Romantic Era** and the **Museum for Prehistory and Early History**.

West Berlin's **Egyptian Museum**, located directly across from the palace on the Schlosstrasse, also belongs to this category of museum. For better or for worse, its greatest attraction for the public, the legendary bust of Nefertiti, will be

Right: The rich collection of porcelain in a room in the Charlottenburg palace.

returned to its original Berlin dwelling on Museum Island. Although the public cherishes the bust and buys its postcards by the hundred of thousands, museum director Dietrich Wildung, among others, emphasizes that no expert regards it as the most important treasure of the Egyptian collection.

Modern Painting in Berlin's Museums

Other Berlin museums cast light on completely different artistic dimensions. The **Bauhaus-Archiv**, which doesn't seem like a museum at all, fascinates even those not particularly enthusiastic about architecture. The exhibits demonstrate the complexity of the training at the Bauhaus School and what theater, film, design and such a practical piece of furniture as a rocking chair actually have to do with one other. The institution also possesses an outstanding archive on the Bauhaus School and its masters just in case scholars would like to deepen their knowledge of the movement.

Then there is the wealth of material in the **Martin-Gropius-Bau**, home of the **Berlinische Galerie**, the **Jewish Museum** and the **Werkbund-Archiv**. The Berlinische Galerie grew from the Berlin passion for collecting the city's artworks and ranges from the year 1870 to the present. The Werkbund-Archiv provides unusual insight into everyday life in the 20th century. And the Jewish Museum does not restrict itself to the period of German history infamous for the genocide committed on the Jewish people, but, beyond that, also recalls the great wealth of Jewish culture, once so alive in Berlin, that was exterminated in a mere 12 years.

The **Brücke-Museum**, on the other hand, specializes strictly in Expressionist art. It was named for the artists' group founded in Dresden in 1905, which later moved to Berlin. This group included not only Ernst Ludwig Kirchner, Max Pech-

stein and, for a time, Emil Nolde, but also Karl Schmidt-Rottluff, whose energetic initiative lay the foundations for the Brücke-Museum.

Another museum, the **Verborgenes Museum** (Hidden Museum), has also specialized in a very special branch of art that has all too rarely met the eye of the public, the immeasurable quantity and quality of art produced by women: Art that has been forgotten, suppressed, underestimated and has by and large gone unrecognized.

The **Georg-Kolbe-Museum**, in the sculptor's former studio, is not exclusively dedicated to the work of this artist, but does contain them. Kolbe, who lived from 1877 to 1947, was particularly influenced by the French sculptor Auguste Rodin. Georg Kolbe's sculptures are considered by art historians among the most important in the first half of the 20th century, and not solely because of his idealistic philosophy. Because of the vicissitudes of taste, they were nearly forgotten for a very long time.

The **Bröhan-Museum**, by contrast, is in no danger of being forgotten. This museum's paintings and sculptures as well as its glass and ceramic objects and even furniture, which are all fashioned in *Jugendstil*, the German Art Nouveau style, have kept it extremely popular over the years.

Discovering the World: Nature and Technology

Several other museums display fascinating exhibits of quite another character. Unconcerned with the artistic aspects of culture, they depict the world in which we live.

Topping the list is the **Museum für Naturkunde** (natural history), which has displayed its collections containing 60 million objects for 250 years. Its largest specimen is also the largest of its kind in the world: the 12-meter-high, 23-meter-long skeleton of a *Brachiosaurus brancai*. The museum also displays the unique fragment of pitchblende in which, in the

year 1789, the mineralogist Martin Heinrich Klapproth discovered uranium. A whole department is dedicated to meteorites, and in the ornithological department, all species of birds native to the region can be viewed without fear that they might fly away.

And don't be afraid to visit the **Hundemuseum** (dog museum); there is nothing here that bites, just everything you ever could have wanted to know about thoroughbred dogs, alongside cynological specimens and even medals and stamps.

The **Botanical Museum**, opened again in spring 1991, after a year of hiatus, is also all-encompassing. What nature has made small, like flowers, root hairs and leaf stems, is shown here in magnification – sometimes thousandfold. This technically enhanced presentation in no way spoils the beauty of a daisy or the mystery of a butterfly; on the contrary, it

Above: A Brachiosaurus skeleton in the Museum of Natural Science.

demonstrates just how brilliantly constructed Mother Nature really is.

Two Berlin **Post Office Museums** exhibit delicate little stamps, but dedicate more of their floor space to elucidating the post office system and precisely why it's so fast – that is, of course, when there are no foul-ups.

Many of the exhibits shown in the **Museum of Transportation and Technology** in the western part of the city are much more spectacular: for example, steam engines "live," full-sized and in all their splendor. The rooms of this museum also display outstanding historic automobiles and the technological devices which human beings have devised to compensate for their lack of wings. The industrial age is presented here in detail, in miniature and in full regalia.

The **Handwerksmuseum** (Crafts Museum) is somewhat similar but caters more to historical interest, portraying its subject's transformations from the Middle Ages through the 19th century.

The **Mahlsdorf-Gründerzeit-Museum** specializes in the 19th century period of German industrial expansion and its way of life. It began as a private initiative in former East Germany. Here, over the past 40 years, Lothar Berfelde resisted the GDR's predilection for recasting history to suit a single ideology. His living room embodies the style of the period exhibited as if no time had elapsed at all.

The spectrum of these museums, as varied as as the items on display, documents the extent of the Berliners' passion for gathering objects from all over the world. It is educational for some and entertaining for others.

You could spend your whole life looking at the objects on display in the Berlin museums, and still find something new to discover. Within their museum rooms, the citizens of Berlin find everything necessary to understand what holds the world together, materially and spiritually, close at hand.

STATE MUSEUMS AND PALACES

Ägyptisches Museum (Egyptian Museum), Charlottenburg, opposite Charlottenburg palace, Schlossstr. 70, Tel. 32 09 11, Mon-Thur 9 a.m.-5 p.m., Sat and Sun 10 a.m.-5 p.m. **Altes Museum** (Mitte), Bodestr. 1-3, Museum Island, entrance at the Lustgarten, Tel. 20 35 50, temporarily closed. **Alte Nationalgalerie**, Mitte, Museum Island, Bodestr. Tel. 20 35 53 07, open Wed-Sun 9 a.m.-5 p.m. **Bodemuseum** (Mitte), Museum Island, entrance at Monbijou Bridge, Tel. 20 35 50, Wed-Sun 9 a.m.-5 p.m. **Kunstgewerbemuseum Köpenick** (Handicrafts), in Köpenick palace, Palace Island, Tel. 657 26 51, Wed-Sun 9 a.m.-5 p.m. Guided tours Sun 1 p.m. **Kunstgewerbemuseum** (Handicrafts), Tiergarten, Matthäikirchplatz 10, Tel. 26 66 29 11, Tue-Fri 9 a.m.-5 p.m., Sat and Sun 10 a.m.-5 p.m. **Märkisches Museum** (Museum of the March of Brandenburg, Mitte), Am Köllnischen Park 5, Tel. 270 05 14, Wed-Sun 10 a.m.-6 p.m. **Museum für Naturkunde** (Natural History), Mitte, Invalidenstr. 43, Tel. 28 97 25 40, Tue-Sun 9.30 a.m. -5 p.m. **Musikinstrumentenmuseum** (Musical Instruments), Tiergarten, Tiergartenstr.1, Tel. 25 48 10, Tue-Sat 9 a.m.-5 p.m., Sun 10 a.m.-5 p.m. **Neue Nationalgalerie**, Tiergarten, Potsdamer Str. 50, Tel. 266 26 62, Tue-Fri 9 a.m.–5 p.m., Sat, Sun 10 a.m.-5 p.m.

Pergamonmuseum (Mitte), Museum Island, entrance at Kupfergraben: **Collection of Antiquities, East Asian Collection**: Tel. 20 35 50, Wed-Sun 9 a.m.-5 p.m., Mon, Tue architectural halls only (including Pergamon altar). **Vorderasiatisches Museum** (Museum of the Near East), Wed-Sun 9 a.m.-5p.m., Mon, Tue architectural halls only.

Schloss Charlottenburg, Schloßstr., Tel. 32 09 11, open Tue-Sun 9 a.m.-5 p.m.: **Belvedere** (exhibition of Berlin Porcelain), Mon–Thur 9 a.m.-5 p.m., Sat–Sun 10 a.m.-5 p.m.; **Galerie der Romantik** in the Knobelsdorff wing (early 19th century paintings), Tue-Fri 9 a.m.-5 p.m., Sat-Sun 10 a.m.-5 p.m.; **Schinkel-Pavillon**, Tue-Sun 9 a.m.-5 p.m. and **Museum für Ur-und Frühgeschichte** (Museum of Prehistory and Early History) in the western wing, Langhans Building, Mon-Thur 9 a.m.-5 p.m., Sat-Sun 10 a.m.-5 p.m.

State Museums in Dahlem: **Völkerkundemuseum** (Museum of Anthropology), **Indian and Islamic Art**, Tel. 830 11, Tue-Sun 9 a.m.-5 p.m.; **East Asian Art**, Lansstr. 8, 1/33, Tel. 830 11, Tue-Fri 9 a.m.-5 p.m., Sat-Sun 10 a.m.-5 p.m., **Kupferstichkabinett** (copper engravings), Tue-Fri 9 a.m.-5 p.m., Sat-Sun 10 a.m.-5 p.m. **Sculpture Gallery**, **Painting Gallery**, Arnimallee 23/27, Tue-Fri 9 a.m.-5 p.m., Sat, Sun 10 a.m.-5 p.m.

MUSEUMS AND EXHIBITIONS

Akademie der Künste (Academy of Arts), Tiergarten, Hanseatenweg 10, Tel. 390 00 70, Tue-Sun 10 a.m.-8 p.m. **Bauhaus-Archiv**, Tiergarten, Klingelhöferstr. 13, Tel. 254 00 20, Wed–Mon 11 a.m.-5 p.m. **Berlinische Galerie**, Kreuzberg, Stresemannstr. 110, Tel. 25 48 63 40, Tue-Sun 10 a.m.-8 p.m. **Berlin Museum**, Kreuzberg, Lindenstr.14, Tel. 238 09 00, Tue-Sun 10 a.m.-10 p.m. **Botanisches Museum**, Steglitz, Königin-Luise-Str. 6-8, Tel. 83 00 61 27, Tue-Sun 10 a.m.-5 p.m. **Brecht-Zentrum** (Mitte), Chausseestr. 125, Tel. 282 99 16, Tue-Fri 10 a.m.-12 noon, Thur 5 p.m.-7 p.m., Sat 9.30 a.m.-12 noon and 12.30-2 p.m. **Bröhan-Museum**, Charlottenburg, Schloßstr. 1a, Tel. 321 40 29, Tue-Sun 10 a.m.-6 p.m., Thur until 8 p.m. **Brücke-Museum**, Zehlendorf, Bussardsteig 9, Tel. 831 20 29, Wed–Mon 11 a.m.-5 p.m. **Deutsches Historisches Museum** (Zeughaus), Mitte, Unter den Linden 2, Tel. 21 50 20, Thur-Tue 10 a.m.-6 p.m. **Deutsches Rundfunkmuseum** (Broadcasting), Charlottenburg, Hammarskjöldplatz 1, Tel. 302 81 86, Wed-Mon 10 a.m.-5 p.m. **Ephraim-Palais** (Mitte), Poststr.16, Tel. 238 090 021, Tue-Sat 10 a.m.-6 p.m. **Forschungs- und Gedenkstätte Normannenstrasse ("Stasi-Museum")**, Lichtenberg, Ruschestr. 59, Tel. 553 68 54, Tue-Fri 11 a.m.-6 p.m., Sat, Sun 2-6 p.m. Exhibition at the former Stasi-headquarters. **Gedenkstätte "Haus der Wannsee-Konferenz"**, Zehlendorf, Am Grossen Wannsee 56-58, Tel. 805 22 94, Mon-Fri 10 a.m.-6 p.m., Sat, Sun 2-6 p.m., holocaust documentation. **Georg-Kolbe-Museum**, Charlottenburg, Sensburger Allee 25, Tel. 304 21 44, Tue-Sun 10 a.m.-5 p.m. **Gründerzeitmuseum Mahlsdorf**, Hellersdorf, Hultschiner Damm 333, Tel. 5 27 83 29, Mon-Tue, Thur-Sat by appointment, tours Sun 11 a.m., 12 noon. **Hamburger Bahnhof**, Tiergarten, Invalidenstr. 50-51, Tel. 394 96 11, modern art. **Haus der Kulturen der Welt** (World Cultures), Tiergarten, John-Foster-Dulles-Allee 10, Tel. 39 78 70, Tue-Fri 2-8 p.m., Sat-Sun 10 a.m.-8 p.m. **Jüdisches Museum** (Jewish Museum), Stresemannstr. 110, Tel. 25 48 65 16, Tue-Sun 10 a.m.-10 p.m. **Museum für Verkehr und Technik** (Traffic and Technology), Kreuzberg, Trebbiner Str. 9, Tel. 25 48 40, Tue-Fri, 9 a.m.-5.30 p.m., Sat, Sun 10 a.m.-6 p.m. **Postmuseum**, Mitte, Leipziger Str. 16, Tel. 22 85 47 10, Tue-Sat 10 a.m.-6 p.m. **Postmuseum Berlin**, Schöneberg, An der Urania 15, Tel. 21 71 17 17, Mon, Tue, Thur 9 a.m.-4.30 p.m., Sun 10 a.m.-5 p.m. **Verborgenes Museum**, Charlottenburg, Schlüterstr. 70, Tel. 313 36 56, Thur, Fri 3-7 p.m., Sat, Sun 12 noon–4 p.m. **Werkbund-Archiv** (Trade Union Archives), Stresemannstr. 110, Tel. 25 48 69 00, Tue-Sun 10 a.m.-10 p.m.

OASES OF NATURE

First-time visitors to Berlin generally explore the part of the city between the Ku'damm and the Reichstag and between Unter den Linden and the "Alex." In the middle of the city, Berlin seems grey. But this first impression is deceptive, for the city has quite a number of green areas, not including the parks and gardens inside the city, that are often an uninviting greyish green.

East or west, the Berliners' love of nature is undeviating. A genuine Berliner is someone who enjoys a "drive into the greenery" on the weekend or who withdraws into the petit bourgeois idyll of his *Laubenpieper* – the slang name for Berlin's typical small garden plots layed out in suburban colonies – even if it borders directly on the *Autobahn*. Unfortunately, this means that Berlin's better-known

Left: Sculptures in Charlottenburg Schlosspark. Right: Relaxing over beer, coffee or cake in the "Eierschale", Dahlem.

green areas are hopelessly overcrowded in summer and on weekends. Such conditions hardly promote a feeling for nature. But in addition to these smaller, artificial, park-like forests, Berlin also contains untouched and inspiring green idylls.

Palaces, Parks and Zoos

Berlin was fortunate in its misfortune: During its breathtaking rise to becoming the largest German industrial and residential city, its leading politicians acted with wise foresight, for once, and had public parks and gardens laid out. About a century ago, even the weary worker profited from this; today, the benefits have been transferred to stressed urbanites and surprised tourists.

Landscape gardening began even earlier in Berlin, when the Hohenzollern princes created enchanting parks behind their palaces. Berlin holds the claim to having Germany's first Baroque garden, which is behind **Schloss Charlottenburg**. In 1695 Friedrich I, Prussia's first

king, gave his wife Sophie-Charlotte a little palace as her summer royal residence. Later, this basic construction was repeatedly expanded on the model of Versailles. The park was re-designed as an English garden in the 19th century.

Aerial bombing in World War Two severely damaged the buildings and park facilities, so the park now gives only a faint idea of the original appearance. But a stroll through the park is still a refreshing conclusion to a tour of the museums in the palace (see p. 160). The path around the **Carp Pond**, past the **Mausoleum** and to the **Belvedere**, or a walk along the Spree shore can be quite charming. Many excursion ships cruising on Berlin's waterways toward Potsdam dock at the palace bridge.

In the twenties, the city had several parks laid out, among them the **Volkspark Jungfernheide**, located north of the palace below Tegel Airport. One bank of the park's lake is an open-air swimming area, the other boasts a small, artificial sand beach. In contrast to the Jungfernheide, the pleasing tranquility of the **Plötzensee** in the **Volkspark Rehberge** is seldom disturbed by airplanes landing at Tegel Airport.

Berlin's most famous park is, of course, the **Tiergarten** (see p. 70), which was designed by one of Europe's greatest landscape architects, J.P. Lenné. At the western tip of the Tiergarten is the **Zoological Garten**, Germany's oldest zoo. Today, with over 1700 species, it is also the zoo housing the most varied fauna in the entire world. Over the years, Berliners have developed an especially close relationship with these animals; some Berlin newspapers publish extensive reports on scenes of jealousy in the penguin house, on peace between the lions, or on the chimpanzees' newest offspring. And when a particularly old animal dies, whether it's an owl or a walrus, some papers don't hesitate to publish an extensive obituary.

The **Aquarium** next door is home not only to sharks, sea snakes and giant spiders, but also for the alligator hall,

169

where, from a wooden pier, visitors can watch the giant lizards dozing.

East Berlin has its own zoo, the **Tierpark Friedrichsfelde**, located in the park bearing the same name, which was also designed by Lenné. The Tierpark's longtime director, Prof. H. Dathe, cleverly adopted Lenné's design idea, providing a harmonious home for about 900 species of animals. The park, about 160 hectares in size, also enjoys a good international reputation. Berlin mourned when Dathe died at the beginning of 1991 – it is said that the 80-year-old man was heartbroken by the way his life-work was being "wrapped up" – the expression used to describe the systematic dissolution of East German institutions and businesses. In the meantime, the future of the Tierpark has been secured, although many employees will have to be laid off.

The **Botanical Garden** in the south of Berlin is a green idyll of a completely dif-

Above: Wintry landscape where the Spree ships berth on the Wannsee.

ferent sort. For almost three hundred years, species of plants from all over the world have been displayed and researched here. The botanical garden was originally over on the Potsdamer Strasse, where **Kleistpark** is now located. Shortly before the turn of the century, work began on the new garden in Dahlem. This botanical garden is one of the most important in the world, featuring about 18,000 species, many of which grow in their natural surroundings, sometimes arranged in huge glass arboretums. Anyone who can cope with the heavy moist air of the tropics should take a stroll through the Victoria house to see the royal water-lily from the Amazon basin.

Pure Nature in Berlin's North

Pristine nature as existed in Berlin's environs a hundred years ago is rare today: But if it can be found anywhere, then it is in the northern outskirts of the city, in **Tegel**, where the metropolis gradually fades into the March of Branden-

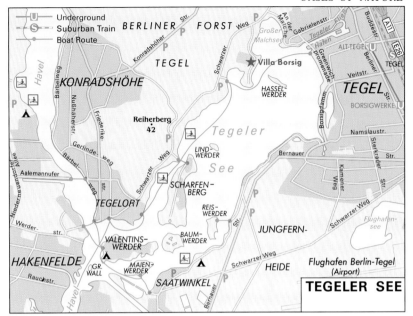

TEGELER SEE

burg. One of the most beautiful hiking routes leads around the **Tegeler See** (lake). An approximately three-hour hike along its shores is best begun at the **U-Bahn station Tegel** (line 6). From there, the route passes through the old village of Tegel, whose form still recalls the old village green, to **Greenwichpromenade**, which leads north along **Tegel Harbor**. After passing the little cove called **Grosse Malche**, the journey continues on the opposite shore on the **Schwarzer Weg**, an asphalt path. From here, trees block the view of the lake, so turn left onto the little shore path leading to a small peninsula. **Villa Borsig** hides there among shadowy trees behind a park wall. It was built in 1905 for the family of a captain of industry. Nowadays it is used by a research institute and, unfortunately, is closed to the public.

The trail along the shore continues south, past the open-air swimming area, the **Freibad Tegeler See** and the dock of the car ferry to **Scharfenberg**, the largest island in the Tegeler See. Scharfenberg is

reserved for the pupils of the boarding school that is located there.

The Schwarzer Weg continues to **Tegel-Ort** (Tegel Village), where every hour a ferry takes strollers across to the villages of **Valentinswerder**, **Maienwerder** and **Saatwinkel** on the other shore. Arriving in Saatwinkel, take a break in one of the restaurants or follow the shoreside trail to **Reiswerder.** This route leads past a swimming area in idyllic surroundings. The trip back to Tegel can be done on foot or with the Bus 113 on the **Bernauer Strasse**.

The U-Bahn station Tegel is also the starting point for a hike through the **Tegeler Fliess** conservation area, which extends to the northeast of Berlin. This little river has its source near Bernau and empties into the Tegeler See. It winds from Tegel to **Lübars** over a distance of nearly ten kilometers, and a three-hour hike along its shores, through meadows and small patches of forest, is among the most beautiful ways to experience the nature Berlin has to offer. In some places,

171

particularly on the other side of **Kienwerder**, the landscape is so spellbinding that you can easily forget you are hiking on the northern edge of a major city.

The Green South: Grunewald and Wannsee

In contrast to the landscape in Tegel, which is still relatively untouched and relatively free of masses of scurrying tourists, **Grunewald** and the shores of the **Wannsee** are so well known that you can never enjoy nature alone. It is seldom calm in Grunewald because shooting ranges, police exploding grounds, US Army barracks, maneuver grounds and even a radar station on the **Teufelsberg** (devil's mountain) in the middle of the forest create the impression that the forest is a testing ground made available to anyone for any purpose whatever.

Nonetheless, the Grunewald forest has its charms; its stock of game animals is nearly as large as it was 400 years ago, when Elector Joachim II first rode out to hunt in the *Grüner Wald.* Every year, boars emerge from the depths of the forest, only to show up in Zehlendorf's gardens where they tear up the flower beds – always a big event for the local press in the "silly season". It is even said that, in their search for food, boars have torn plastic bags from the hands of strollers. But these are isolated and heresay events; normally the only boars you will encounter are those kept in large enclosures. They prefer to doze in the mud.

Another popular destination in the Grunewald is Joachim II's **Jagdschloss Grunewald** (Grunewald hunting lodge) on Grunewald See (lake); it houses a museum with a collection of paintings.

To experience Grunewald by car, start from the **Havelchaussee**, which follows the shore of the Havel. This street was the site of one of Berlin's most amusing political farces. The "red-green" Senate, so called to describe the erstwhile ruling

coalition of Social Democrats and Green Alternative parties, had banned all car traffic from the Chaussee, but the local district office in Zehlendorf refused to put up the appropriate traffic signs. Finally the Senate Department – now with a conservative Christian Democratic majority – carried out the task in spite of the protests of the Zehlendorfers. In March, 1991, the new Senate had the signs rapidly removed again in a secret operation: This time the Senate was afraid of new protests from the opposite side.

The Havelchaussee leads past the **Grunewald Tower**, whose viewing platform offers a panorama of Berlin. Continuing south on the chaussee, you'll arrive at **Lieper Bucht**, whose lovely sandy

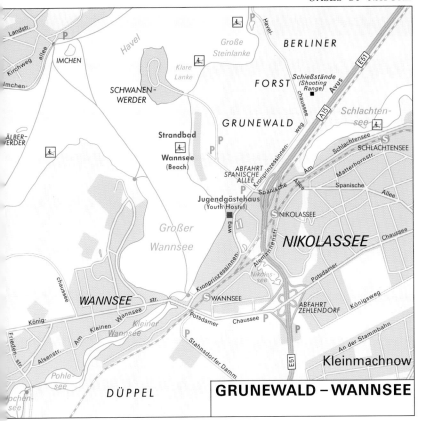

GRUNEWALD – WANNSEE

beach is great for swimming. The Havel-chaussee then meets up with the **Kron-prinzessinweg**, which quickly take you to the **Strandbad Wannsee** (Wannsee beach), Europe's largest inland swimming area. Up to 40,000 Berliners crowd together here on weekends. The nearby **Schlachtensee** and **Krumme Lanke** offer a real alternative to the masses on the Wannsee's artificial sand beach. Both lakes can be comfortably circled on foot; and while the best-known meadows are filled with sunbathers on warm summer weekends, there are also uncounted hidden swimming spots.

Leaving the southern cove of the Wannsee behind, the road goes past the excursion boat docking facilities and through Wannsee village. A bus shuttles along the **Pfaueninsel-Chaussee** to the ferry to **Pfaueninsel** (Peacock Island). In 1794, Friedrich Wilhelm II once again gave irrefutable evidence of the Hohenzollern dynasty's passion for palaces amid greenery, ordering the construction of a little palace in the form of an artificial ruin on the diminutive island. Two decades later, Lenné gave the island its finishing touches by creating a fashionable English garden. With its proud peacocks, the island is considered one of the most beautiful spots in all of Berlin.

The **Volkspark Klein-Glienicke,** accessible by the **Nikolskoer Weg**, sprawls south of the Pfaueninsel. Its real value has emerged with the fall of the Wall.

173

The park was originally part of the Sanssouci Palace grounds! It is hardly any wonder that the **Klein-Glienicke Palace** is reminiscent of the atmosphere in Sanssouci.

Nature in the East: Volksparks and Müggelsee

There are 14 large municipal parks in the eastern part of the city alone. The **Bürgerpark** in **Pankow** was laid out in 1854 as a private park. A three-part triumphal arch forms the entrance to this spacious park on Wilhelm-Kuhr-Strasse. Expansive sunbathing meadows, attractive flower beds and picturesque groups of trees extend on both shores of the **Panke river**, which gave the district its name.

In the middle of **Friedrichshain**, between the Friedensstrasse and Am Friedrichshain, is the **Volkspark** of the same name. Once again it was Lenné who drew

Above: The panda bear is still one of the zoo's most beloved dwellers.

174

up the plans, and in August, 1848, it was opened to the Berliners, but not before the casualties of the Revolution of March 1848 found their final resting place in the **Friedhof der Märzgefallenen**. Gustav Meyer, Berlin's first director of garden construction, had the park expanded between 1874 and 1875. Later the **Märchenbrunnen** (fairy tale fountain) provided it with a new entrance. The fountain, designed in Neo-Baroque style, sports sandstone figures from the fairy tales collected by the brothers Grimm.

After 1945, a million cubic meters of rubble from the city's ruins were piled up on the demolished Wehrmacht flak bunkers, thus producing two sizable hills. Maps designate them as **Grosser** and **Kleiner Bunkerberg** (big and small bunker mountain), but the Berliners nicknamed them **Mont Klamott**. A several hundred-meter-long sledding path winds its way down from the 48-meter-high plateau of the smaller mountain.

Treptow, bordered on the northeast by the Spree river, has three large green zones: the **Köllnische Heide**, near the S-Bahn station Oberspree, and the **Königsheide**, in the Johannistal quarter. Both are natural forest areas with trails suitable for long hikes. In 1896 Gustav Meyer began work on the **Treptower Park** beside the Spree. At the same time, the great Berlin Trade Fair was held here; its only comemmorative relic is the giant telescope in the **Archenhold-Sternwarte**. The "Neues Gartenhaus an der Spree," built in 1821-1822 across from the observatory, is now called "Haus Zenner" after its celebrated manager. Near the abbey bridge, rowboats or paddleboats are for rent for a row around the **Insel der Jugend** (Island of Youth). Treptower Park is also known for the **Soviet Memorial**, erected for 5000 Soviet soldiers laid to rest here, who died in the battle for the city.

The passenger ships of the **Weisse Flotte** (White Fleet) cruise from Treptow

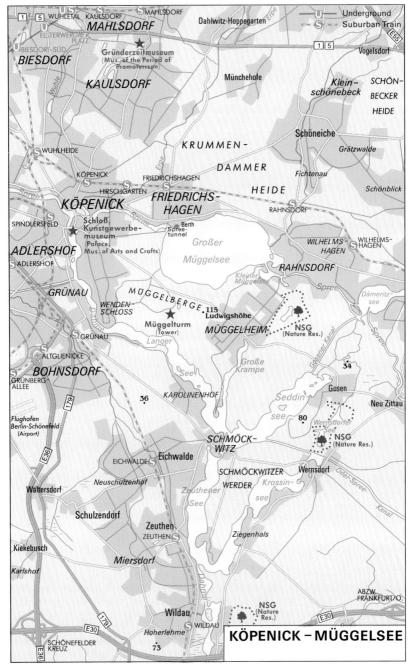

Harbor out onto the Spree and the Havel rivers, and into the countryside to **Köpenick**, one of Berlin's "green lungs," as it were. The **Langer See**, **Seddinsee**, **Dämmeritzsee** and finally **Kleiner** and **Grosser Müggelsee** are stops on its big lake journey. Of course you can take the same route on your own boat. Motorboats are prohibited on weekends in some areas.

Köpenick itself has only partially managed to retain its suburban character. When getting off at S-Bahn station **Köpenick**, you will find yourself surrounded by busy streets lined by very ugly buildings. But the atmosphere is rural around the **Köpenick Town Hall**, located in the middle of Köpenick's old town on an island in the Spree.

Across from the town hall, incidentally, **Weisse Flotte** ships also depart for cruises on the Spree. South of the old town is a peninsula, the **Schlossinsel**

Above: Friedrich Wilhelm II had this artificial ruin built on the Pfaueninsel.

(Castle Island) **Köpenick** with the **Köpenick Palace**, where East Berlin's Crafts Museum is now located. The **Müggelheimer Damm** and **Müggelschlösschenweg** both lead to the Grosser (Large) and Kleiner (Small) Müggelsee.

The conservation area of the **Müggelberge** lies in the middle of Köpenick's lake area. Crowning the Müggelberge is the 30-meter-high **Müggel Tower**, from which you can see for 50 kilometers on a clear day.

In the north, beyond the Grosser Müggelsee, you can make out Friedrichshain. That is where the typically provincial "Bolschestrasse" is located, with its buzzing market that attracts visitors from far and wide. The 120-meter-long Spree tunnel connects Friedrichshagen with the Köpenick forest region. Ships transport passengers to the Müggelsee's southern shore and the country inns **Rübezahl** and **Müggelseeperle**.

If you prefer exploring on foot, however, there is plenty of pristine nature in the environs of the Müggelsee.

PALACES, PARKS AND LAKES

Palaces / Parks / Zoos / Sightseeing

Botanischer Garten, Steglitz, Königin-Luise-Str. 6-8; second entrance at Unter den Eichen, Tel. 83 00 60; daily 9 a.m.-4 p.m., educational greenhouses daily 10 a.m.-3.15 p.m.

Britzer Garten (BUGA-site), Neukölln, Sangerhauser Weg 1, Tel. 700 90 60; entrances are at Buckower Damm, Mohriner Allee, Tauernallee, Sangerhauser Weg and Massiner Weg, daily 9 a.m.-4 p.m.; café and windmill Britzer Mühle. On this site, the *Bundesgartenschau* (National Garden Show) was held in 1985; in 1995 the BUGA will open in Berlin again with a new concept, incorporating the old park in Britz. Unfortunately, the BUGA-Park has been allowed to degenerate into a vast and uninspired park site.

Grunewaldturm, Havelchaussee, Auf dem Karlsberg, daily 10 a.m. until dusk. This tower is 55 m high, 200 steps lead to the observation platform.

Jagdschloss Grunewald, Zehlendorf, at the lake Grunewaldsee, Tel. 813 35 97, Tue-Fri 10 a.m.-2 p.m., Sat-Sun 11 a.m.-4 p.m., palace and museum, exhibition of hunting weapons.

Müggelturm, Köpenick; tower with an observation platform at a height of 30 m, 126 steps leading up, Tel. 656 98 12.

Schloss Charlottenburg, Luisenplatz, Tel. 32 09 11; **Palace Museums**: for descriptions and opening times see guidepost p. 167. The place is open to the public Tue-Sun 9 a.m.-5 p.m.

Schloss Friedrichsfelde, Lichtenberg, Am Tierpark 125, Tel. 513 81 42, museum, tours Tue-Fri 10 a.m.-12 noon and 12.45-4 p.m., Sat, Sun 1-4 p.m. (concerts see p. 2).

Schloss Klein-Glienicke, Zehlendorf, Tel. 805 30 41; closed to the public.

Schloss Köpenick, on castle island, Tel. 657 26 51, Crafts Museum open Wednesdays-Sundays 10 a.m.-6 p.m.

Schloss Schönhausen, Pankow, Schlosspark, Ossietzkystrasse. The park is open to the public. The palace is still being restored.

Schloss auf der Pfaueninsel, Zehlendorf, Tel. 805 30 42, visits to the Pfaueninsel (Peacock Island) daily 10 a.m.-4 p.m. (in winter), 8 a.m.-8 p.m. (in summer).

Spreepark Berlin, Treptow, Kiehnwerderallee, Tel. 68 83 50, daily from 11 a.m. New amusement park, ideal for families.

Tierpark Berlin (Zoo), Lichtenberg, Am Tierpark 125, Tel. 51 53 10, daily 9 a.m. until dusk.

Zoologischer Garten, Tiergarten, entrances at Hardenbergplatz (Löwentor) opposite Bahnhof Zoo

and at Budapester Str. (Elefantentor), Tel. 25 40 10, open daily 9 a.m.-5 p.m.

Aquarium, Tiergarten, Budapester Str. 32 (Elefantentor), Tel. 25 40 10, open daily 9 a.m.-6 p.m.

Country Inns / Restaurants / Cafés

Alter Dorfkrug Lübars, Reinickendorf, Alt-Lübars 8, Tel. 402 71 74, Wed-Sun 10 a.m.-9 p.m. Country inn with pleasant, cosy restaurant.

Forsthaus Paulsborn, Zehlendorf, at the Jagdschloss Grunewald, Tel. 813 80 10, Tue-Sun 11 a.m. until dusk.

Haus Zenner, Treptow, Alt-Treptow 14-17, Tel. 272 73 70, daily except Mon and Thur from 11 a.m.

Loretta am Wannsee, Zehlendorf, Kronprinzessinnenweg 260, Tel. 803 51 56, Mon-Sat 10 a.m.-1 a.m., Sun 9 a.m.-1 a.m. One of Berlin's most enjoyable beer gardens.

Müggelseeperle, Köpenick, at the lake Grosser Müggelsee, Tel. 658 820, daily 10.30 a.m.-10 p.m., the large terrace is open in summer, with a lovely view across the lake.

Müggelturm, Köpenick, In den Müggelbergen, for restaurant reservations: Tel. 656 9812, open Monday–Friday 10 a.m.-7 p.m., Saturday, Sunday 10 a.m.-8 p.m.

Rübezahl, Köpenick, at the lake Grosser Müggelsee, Tel. 65 88 20, Mon-Fri 10.30 a.m.-6.30 p.m., Sat, Sun 10.30 a.m.-7.30 p.m., large summer terrace with lake view.

Schlossrestaurant Glienecke, Zehlendorf, Königstr., Tel. 805 40 00, daily 10 a.m.-6 p.m. Small but elegant restaurant.

Wirtshaus Schildhorn, Zehlendorf, Havelchaussee/Strasse am Schildhorn 4a, Tel. 305 31 11, daily 10 a.m.-midnight. The best of all country restaurants with exquisite cuisine.

Zum Dorfkrug, Reinickendorf, Alt-Tegel 4, Tel. 433 85 35, Sun-Fri 9 a.m.-8 p.m.

Shipping Companies

City-Schiffahrt / Schiffs-Schillow, Charlottenburg, Bonhoefferufer, Tel. 344 41 64. Ships leave from the Schlossbrücke (palace bridge), Bonhoefferufer 14.

Reederei Bruno Winkler, Tiergarten, Levetzowstrasse 12a, Tel. 391 70 70.

Spreefahrt- und Kanal-Rundfahrten (for trips on the Spree river and canals), Charlottenburg, Geisbergstrasse 28, Tel. 394 49 54. Ships berth at the terrace by the old Congress Hall, Tiergarten.

Stern-und Kreisschiffahrt, Treptow, Puschkinallee 16/17, Tel. 617 39 00. The largest shipping company offering ship excursions from Treptow port.

SPORTS IN BERLIN: TRADITION AND RECORDS

Berlin's oldest sports club is a "shooting club," the Spandau Shooting Guild, founded in 1334. The "real" world of sports came to life only centuries later, and the place was once again Berlin. The world owes its first public gymnasium to Friedrich Ludwig Jahn, a sports teacher and "Father of Gymnastics," as he has since been known. It was dedicated in the spring of 1811, in the **Hasenheide**, a Neukölln recreation park.

Olympic Maelstrom

Could Berlin become sportsville besides being a world capital? Those committees in the Senat responsible for this sort of thing were intent upon proving this by having the summer Olympics held in Berlin in the year 2000. 56 million Deutschmarks

Above: The annual Berlin Marathon making its way around the victory column.

were forked out to oil Berlin's application – the Greens/ Bündnis 90 fraction in the Senat even came up with a total of 250 million – before everyone sobered up: IOC president Samaranch anounced on September 23, 1993, in Monaco that the Summer Games of the year 2000 would be held in Sydney, not Berlin. Those responding for promoting Berlin's candidacy had been out of touch with reality, had failed to notice that the mood in their own city was by no means euphoric about the idea. The IOC president on a visit to Berlin had made the oracular utterance that the Germans would always get what they want. Except that the Berliners, and many other Germans for that matter, did not really want the games. The Olympic stadium, which had already been in place since the "Nazi Olympics" in 1936, would have had to be thoroughly renovated. This project has now been put on the back burner. Building a new sports palace where the old Stadion der Weltjugend (Stadium of the World's Youth) used to be has also been cancelled. What has survived is the project to erect a new cycling stadium at the place of the old Werner-Seelenbinder-Halle.

Soccer Festivals with Türkiyemspor

Basically, the Berliners took the Olympic Committee's decision against their city with a sense of satisfaction rather than annoyance. Many thought the city has enough problems as it is, and that dealing with the Olympic Games would be an additional burden no one needed.

Local sports fans only fly off the handle when it comes to King Soccer. Berlin's traditional clubs, Hertha BSC and Tennis Borussia, are two rather mediocre clubs in the second league, whose performances only attract a thin crowd of fans. So, Berlin's soccer fans have turned to the games in the amateur leagues. Anyone looking for soccer with the vigor of the south should drop in on a game with Türkiyemspor. Players from at least four different nations beat the ball about with tremendous sucess. And the fans who attend in the Katzbach stadium are known for their their unbuttoned singing.

Ultimate Performances and VIPs

Don't cry for the Berliners. Great soccer is in fact an annual event, viz the German Soccer League (DFB) Cup Final which is held in the oval of the Olympic stadium, when a crowd of 76,000 shows up and turns the place into a veritable sea of colors. The place has well earned the nickname "the Wembley of Germany", recalling the London stadium where the British Cup Final is held. The city can offer its visitors a smörgasbord of 90 first league clubs, among which one finds quite a number of German champions.

Furthermore, at the last summer Olympics in Barcelona, Berlin produced about 70 starters and carried no less than 26 medals back home. The city's most popular and famous sportspeople are the swimmer Franziska von Almsick and the gymnast Andreas Wecker. Its teams have also proven their mettle by their numerous successes: BSC Preussen und die Eisbären Berlin, respectively from the eastern and western halves of the city, are in the national league. Preussen chases the puck in the Jafféstrasse rink and usually winds up in the play-offs for the title. Basketball fans should attend a game of Alba Berlin in the Sömmeringhalle. Handball enthusiasts will find the TSV GutsMuts more than adequate, and if you are interested in hockey, try watching the women of the SC Brandenburg.

The Berliner cannot complain of a dearth of major sporting events either.

The **Berlin City Marathon** reached its peak in 1990. Over 27,000 people wanted to run the course, which, for the first time, led through the Brandenburg Gate; only 25,000 were allowed for reasons of space. With this huge number of participants, the Berlin marathon is the third-largest in the world. Incidentally, the second marathon race ever to be staged in Germany was scheduled to take place in Berlin in 1904. It had to be called off; only seven runners had registered. Today, Berlin can be proud of other events as well. In August the city hosts the Republic's most important track-and-field competition (**ISTAF**) which attracts top athletes from around the world. The high-jump competition in February or March draws large and cheering crowds to the Schöneberger Sporthalle. Berlin also hosts the **German Trotting Derby** (August) and the **International German Tennis Championships for Women** (Whitsun).

One traditional event, however, will probably soon be a thing of the past: the **Six-Day Race**. It was invented at the zoo, and the first one started on March 15, 1909. The last so far was held in January, 1990, and ended with a loss of 1.5 million DM. 86 Six-Days-Races appear to be enough for the city.

On the other hand, the **Hoppegarten** will come to life again. This galloping track from the days of the Kaiser is once again justifying its reputation as the most beautiful riding facility east of Paris. In addition, there are also the **Trotting Rac-track Mariendorf** and the **Trotting Racetrack Karlshorst**.

Berlin Water Pleasures

Horse-lovers weren't the only sports enthusiasts who wished the Wall would fall. The Markish watercourses lured even Elector Friedrich III, who later became King Friedrich I, into buying so-called "pleasure yachts."

The pleasure yachts of today look very different. Most are registered in the 122 sailing clubs that have come into existence throughout Berlin. 20,000 sports boats (masted boats, sailboats, rowboats and windsurfing boards) ply the waves of

the innumerable lakes in and around Berlin. And that excludes sailing fans not registered in clubs! Other water sports fans are also well-off. At the beginning of the 19th century, Berliners who wanted to swim had to jump into the Spree or the Schafgraben (sheep ditch), known since as the Landwehrkanal. Today, in the western part of Berlin alone, over 30 open-air swimming sites in natural waters and over 20 open-air swimming pools offer Berliners a place in the sun, and there are over 40 public indoor swimming pools throughout Berlin.

In the western part of the city, the **blub** in Neukölln has been the big hit for long. But Europe's largest swimming pool is in the former East German capital, on the Leninallee in Friedrichshain: The **Sport and Recreation Center (SEZ)**, an early showcase project which the SED built "for the good of the people" in 1980. The SEZ also offers courses in dancing for senior citizen, aerobics for beginners, martial arts, body-building and ice skating in the building's own "polarium."

Above: Model-plane enthusiasts test their planes on theTeufelsberg.

SPORTS

Stadiums / Gyms / Ice Skating Rinks

Eisstadion Jafféstrasse, Wilmersdorf, Tel. 30 38 44 44. Playing field for BSC Preussen.

Eisstadion Wilmersdorf, Wilmersdorf, Fritz-Wildung- Str. 9, Tel. 823 40 60.

Erika-Hess-Eisstadion, Wedding, Müllerstrasse 185, Tel. 465 90 66.

Friedrich-Ludwig-Jahn-Sportpark, Prenzlauer Berg, Cantianstr. 24, Tel. 440 02 61.

Horst-Korber-Zentrum, Charlottenburg, Glockenturmstr. 3-5, Tel. 30 00 60.

Olympia-Stadion, Charlottenburg, Olympischer Platz, Tel. 304 74 72, ISTAF tournaments.

Radrennbahn Schöneberg (Bicycle Racetrack), Schöneberg, Sachsendamm, Tel. 781 17 22.

Sportforum Berlin, Hohenschönhausen, Weissenseer Weg 51-55, information Tel. 978 10. Most Eastern Berlin sports events take place here, especially the matches of the hockey team Dynamo.

Recreation Centers / Golf / Minigolf

Bahnengolfanlage Adelheidallee, Reinickendorf, Adelheidallee 1-3.

Freizeitforum Marzahn (Recreation Center), Marzahn, Marzahner Promenade 55, Tel. 54 70 40. Bowling, gyms, swimming, sauna.

Freizeit- und Erholungszentrum Wuhlheide (Recreation Center), Köpenick, An der Wuhlheide, Tel. 63 88 70. Ice skating rink, swimming lake, sunbathing meadow, cultural events.

Golf-und Landclub Stölpchenweg, Zehlendorf, Stölpchenweg, Tel. 805 50 75.

Sport-und Erholungszentrum (Recreation Center), Prenzlauer Berg, Landsberger Allee 77, information: Tel. 42 28 35 05; visitors' service: Tel. 42 28 33 20. Berlin's largest leisure center with seven pools, sauna, solarium, fitness center, bowling, billiards, ice skating, roller-skating, skateboard rink and restaurants.

Tennis-Squash-City, Wilmersdorf, Brandenburgische Str. 53, Tel. 87 90 97. Tennis and squash courts.

Public Baths / Outdoor Swimming Pools and Saunas

blub Badeparadies, Neukölln, Buschkrugallee 64, Tel. 606 60 60, Mon-Thur 10 a.m.-11 p.m., Fri 10 a.m.-midnight, Sun 9 a.m.-midnight.

Freibad Halensee, (outdoor swimming pool) Zehlendorf, Koenigsallee 5a, Tel. 891 17 03.

Freibad Oberhavel (outdoor swimming pool) Spandau, Havelschanze 29, Tel. 335 26 20.

Freibad Tegeler See (outdoor swimming pool) Reinickendorf, Schwarzer Weg, Tel. 434 10 78.

Haus Paulsborn, Wilmersdorf, Eisenzahnstr. 14, Tel. 892 70 20, offers traditional saunas as well as a "bio-sauna."

Stadtbad Charlottenburg, (municipal baths), Charlottenburg, Alte Halle, Krumme Str. 10, Tel. 34 30 32 14. These municipal baths, built in 1899, have been lavishly renovated and are today among the most lovely baths in Berlin: the walls are decorated with Art Nouveau couples gazing down at the swimmers.

Stadtbad Kreuzberg, (municipal baths), Kreuzberg, Baerwaldstr. 64, Tel. 25 88 31 24.

Stadtbad Neukölln, (municipal baths), Ganghoferstrasse 5, Tel. 68 09 26 53. First municipal baths in Berlin offering separate pools for men and women.

Stadtbad Tiergarten, (municipal baths), Tiergarten, Seydlitzstrasse 7, Tel. 39 05 40 11.

Strandbad Wannsee, (municipal lakeside beach and pool complex) Zehlendorf, Strandbadweg, Tel. 803 56 12.

Thermen am Europa-Center, Schöneberg, in the Europa-Center, Tel. 261 60 31, Berlin's largest sauna facilities.

Horse Riding

Hoppegarten, Dahlwitz-Hoppegarten, Goethestr.12, Tel. 559 61 02 (S-Bahn line 3, station Hoppegarten).

Trabennbahn Karlshorst (Trotting Racecourse,), Lichtenberg, Treskowallee 129, Tel. 509 08 91, Tue 5 p.m., Sat 2 p.m.

Trabennbahn Mariendorf, Steglitz, Mariendorfer Damm 222, Tel. 740 11, Wed 6 p.m., Sun 2 p.m., German Harness Derby.

The riding competition **Internationales Reitturnier** takes place every November in the **Deutschlandhalle**: Charlottenburg, Messedamm, Tel. 30 38 44 44.

Sport-Information / Advance Booking

Ausstellungs-Messe-Kongress-GmbH, Charlottenburg, Messedamm 22, Tel. 30 38 44 44; tickets for BSC Preussen matches.

Berliner Marathon-Büro, Charlottenburg, Meinekestr. 13, Tel. 882 64 05. Information and enrolment for marathon races in Berlin.

Landessportbund Berlin, Charlottenburg, Jesse-Owens-Allee 1-2, Tel. 300 02. Twice yearly the LSB publishes a sports calendar with information on important sports events.

Sportservice Berlin, Hohenschönhausen, Konrad-Wolf-Str. 45, Tel. 97 81 20 00, Mon, Wed 8 a.m.-5 p.m., Thur 8 a.m. - 3 p.m. and Fri 8 a.m. - 2 p.m. See guidepost on page 209 for a list of **Advance Booking Offices** in Berlin.

CULINARY DELIGHTS

The cuisine of Berlin has by no means reached metropolitan standard. To this day, Berliners prefer a good solid meal to fancy cooking. Accordingly, Berlin's cuisine has not yet progressed beyond *Eisbein* (marinated pork knuckle) with sauerkraut or mashed peas, *Buletten* (meat patties), and *Kasseler Rippchen* (smoked pork ribs) a 19th century invention by the Berlin butcher Cassel. The famous *Currywurst* (curried sausage) – pride of the snack bars and bottle shops – was also created here, amidst the expanse of rubble after the Second World War.

Plain Berlin fare can be had in most restaurants and innumerable snack stands, but hearty dishes (and ill-humoured waitresses) can best be enjoyed at **Hardtke**, in the Meinekestrasse. It opened during the 50s – as can be seen if you take a closer look

Preceding pages: Classical concert in the "Waldbühne". Above: Street-side café scenes on a summer day in Berlin.

at the slightly dusty décor – with its own butchery that still offers good meat and sausages à la Berlin.

Restaurants such as the **Alte Pumpe** in the Tiergarten district or **Leibniz-Klause** in Charlottenburg, where Berlin cuisine is combined with ideas that were propagated by the nouvelle cuisine, have more style and are more dependable in quality. The Alte Pumpe is located in a former water pumping station works and a dinner served in this 19th century building is sheer unadulterated Berlin. Many hotel restaurants are more elegant but still very German in their culinary creations; we may recommend, for example, the **Quadriga** in the Brandenburger Hof and the **Silhouette** in the Maritim Grand Hotel.

Berlin's Gourmet Temples

Hard to believe, but they do exist: gourmet temples and first-class cooks, even if you can practically count them on one hand. Siegfried Rockendorf and his restaurant **Rockendorf** in Waidmannslust is indisputably the number one. Even though the maestro only has one Michelin star left on his entrance, the average guests should not have noticed any drop in quality. In 1994, Siegfried Rockendorf even opened a small branch on the first floor of Café Leysieffer on the Ku'damm, the **Rockendorf Bistro**, which is reasonably priced and offers take-out food. **Frühsammer's Gasthaus**, a place that has taken second place to Rockendorf's for years, is in Nikolassee and the new German cuisine will amply repay the drive out there.

In the course of the last ten years, with the invasion of nouvelle cuisine, even the obstinate Berliners have discovered a taste for fine foods, usually combined with a soupcon of Italian and French cuisine. In many of these restaurants actually eating the food is often just one of the guests' activities. Typical of Berlin is the combination of an acceptable quality of fare at high prices, pub, bar and rendezvous of the fashionable and the trendy. After all, at dinner you should see and be seen.

This category especially includes the brightly-lit and bare-walled restaurants around the Ku'damm and Savignyplatz. The **Paris-Bar** has traditionally been a meeting-place for intellectuals and international stars passing through; and there you will find a respectable French menu and a good selection of wines. The waiters even speak French.

In the **Bovril** with its vaguely international menu, nobody, in contrast, could care less about nationalities. For years the Bovril has been a trusty haunt of journalists and artists, and even for people who take a pride in having a their own reserved place. The waiters are polite in an exemplary way, yet somewhat reserved. Just as popular and well-loved is another place for the more sophisticated palate, the **Florian**, which has become a home from home for all fans of South German cooking, a group which

inexplicably appears to be identical with film-makers and their entourages. *Riesling* (a fruity white wine) is what people tend to drink there and it is served until the wee hours of the morning. There are two excellent Italian restaurants downtown, **Tucci** and the new **XII Apostoli**, in both of which the waiters' attitude tends to be either self-sacrificingly friendly or haughty. Tucci's has been successful with the same menu for years, Apostoli really does offer twelve different kinds of pizza named after the twelve disciples – the most generously covered being the "Judas" pizza.

Doris Burneleit used to run an Italian establishment for GDR citizens in Köpenick. After the Wall fell, she moved to Charlottenburg and now receives her guests at the **Fioretto**, near Savignyplatz. This is a real address for gourmets.

Not far from the Fioretto is **Astir's**, which had protracted teething problems but has since become one of the nicest places in the city. The ambience is less chic and more informal than the Paris Bar, with very sound plain French fare on the menu.

The way to become acquainted with a country is by tasting its food, so that is what Berliners are doing more and more frequently. Exotic cuisine is in demand, and this is precisely what you will find at **Foyer** in Uhlandstrasse, which serves Turkish specialties outside in the open air. Then there's the very traditional **Fofi's Estiarotio**, where the world meets over Greek wine and food. The cooler city types will try out the imaginative dishes at the **Carpe Diem**, a Spanish restaurant where you can also enjoy tapas and a cocktail at the bar.

With the growth of the international community in the city it appears that there is now also a need for a more sophisticated American cuisine. Or at least, more and more restaurants are trying to fill the culinary vacuum on the other side of apple pie and hamburgers. Try the

Dschungel near the KaDeWe department store, or the **Lucky Strike** near the Pergamon Museum.

Amongst nocturnal revellers, the Dschungel was once known as the best discotheque in Berlin, but this establishment did not survive the 80s. Now it serves first-class American cuisine, even at lunchtime. The Lucky Strike is noticeable not only for its fancy hamburgers but also for its New Orleans Cajun cuisine, served amidst elegant architecture beneath three S-Bahn arches. The food is good, the West Berlin clientele sophisticated – unfortunately, the service is reminiscent of the GDR era.

Haute Cuisine in Kreuzberg

Kreuzberg residents prefer good solid food, which is why fine restaurants have been forced to leave the district in their entirety. In the past, Kreuzberg commu-

nards launched several attacks against posh establishments that allegedly were spoiling the Kiez. The most notable victim was **Maxwell**, which has recently reopened in Wilmersdorf and offers excellent German cuisine, without, surprisingly, any tendency to fattiness. All the same, enough good restaurants have remained in Berlin's rebels district, including the **Exil** on Paul-Lincke-Ufer which was founded by the legendary cabaret artiste Ossie Wiener. Then there is the **Altes Zollhaus**, the **Hasenburg** and the **Abricot**, which all serve better than average German or French fare at affordable prices.

Don't be lured into going to the popular meeting place of the trendy, the **Osteria No.1** in Kreuzberg. This restaurant's success remains a secret. Except for the pizza, nothing on the menu tastes good, not even the bread or the white wine, which is served lukewarm. Instead, check out the **Vineria Franzotti** next door, where perfectly trained sommeliers dispense a nobler drop.

Above: Fine dining in the elegant Baroque banquet halls in the Ermeler House.

186

RESTAURANTS

Top Quality Restaurants
with international Cuisine

For these restaurants, reservations are advisable and in some cases required.

Alt-Luxemburg, Charlottenburg, Windscheidstr. 31, Tel. 323 87 30, Tue-Sat 7 p.m.-1 a.m.

Bamberger Reiter, Schöneberg, Regensburger Str. 7, Tel. 218 42 82, Tue-Sat 6 p.m.-1 a.m.

Frühsammer's Gasthaus, Zehlendorf, Matterhornstr. 101, Tel. 803 27 20, meals served daily 7 p.m.-9.30 p.m.

Rockendorf's Restaurant, Reinickendorf, Düsterhauptstr. 1, Tel. 402 30 99, Tue-Sat 12 noon-2 p.m. and 7 p.m.-midnight.

Silhouette, Maritim Grand Hotel, Mitte, Friedrichstr. 158-164, Tel. 232 70, Mon-Sat 6 p.m.-1 a.m.

Traditional German Food
and Nouvelle Cuisine

Abricot, Neukölln, Hasenheide 48, Tel. 693 11 50, daily 11 a.m.-1 a.m.

Alte Pumpe, Tiergarten, Lützowstr. 42, Tel. 261 16 17, open daily 10 a.m.-midnight (meals served until 10 p.m.).

Altes Zollhaus, Kreuzberg, Carl-Herz-Ufer 30, Tel. 692 33 00, Tue-Sat from 6 p.m.

Bovril, Charlottenburg, Kurfürstendamm 184, Tel. 881 84 61, Mon-Sat 11 a.m.-1 a.m.

Exil, Kreuzberg, Paul-Lincke-Ufer 44a, Tel. 612 70 37, Tue-Sun 7 p.m.-1 a.m.

Florian, Charlottenburg, Grolmanstr. 52, Tel. 313 91 84, daily 6 p.m.-4 a.m. (meals served until 1 a.m.).

Hardtke, Charlottenburg, Meinekestr. 27, Tel. 881 98 27, daily 10 a.m.-0.30 a.m.

Hasenburg, Kreuzberg, Fichtestr. 1, Tel. 691 91 39, daily 6 p.m.-1 a.m.

Leibniz-Klause, Charlottenburg, Leibnizstr. 46, Tel. 323 70 68, daily 12 noon-1 a.m.

Maxwell, Wilmersdorf, Helmstedter Str. 9, Tel. 854 47 37, Tue-Sun 6 p.m.-1 a.m.

Offenbach-Stuben, Prenzlauer Berg, Stubbenkammerstr. 8, Tel. 448 41 06, daily 7 p.m.-1 a.m.

Quadriga in the Hotel Brandenburger Hof, Wilmersdorf, Eislebener Str. 14, Tel. 214 40 50, meals are served Mon-Fri 7 p.m.-1 p.m.

Reinhard's, Mitte, (in the Nikolai quarter), Poststr. 28, Tel. 242 52 95, daily 9 a.m.-midnight.

American Restaurants

Dschungel, Schöneberg, Nürnberger Str. 53, Tel. 218 66 98, Mon-Sat from 11 a.m., evening 7p.m.-11 p.m.

Jimmy's Diner, Wilmersdorf, Pariser Str. 41, Tel. 882 31 41, daily 4 p.m.-3 a.m., Fri, Sat until 5 a.m.

Lucky Strike, Mitte, Georgenstr., S-Bahn arches Nr. 177-180, Tel. 201 774 22, daily 10 a.m.-2 a.m.

French Restaurants

Astir's, Charlottenburg, Grolmanstr. 56, Tel. 313 63 20, daily 12 noon-3 a.m. Delicious food in lovely Bistro-restaurant.

Au bon Couscous, Charlottenburg, Bleibtreustr. 51, Tel. 313 32 78, daily 5 p.m.-midnight. French-Arabic cuisine.

Cour Carré, Charlottenburg, Savignyplatz 5, Tel. 312 52 38, daily 12 noon-2 a.m.

Paris-Bar, Charlottenburg, Kantstr. 152, Tel. 313 80 52, daily from 12 noon.

Vineria Franzotti, Kreuzberg, Kreuzbergstr. 71, Tel. 785 38 50, daily from 6 p.m.

Greek Restaurants

Fofis Estiatorio, Charlottenburg, Fasanenstr. 70, Tel. 881 87 85, daily 7 p.m.-1 a.m.

To Steki, Kantstr. 27, Tel. 313 40 59, Mon-Thur, Sun 5 p.m.-1 a.m., Fri and Sat from 5 p.m. Friendly Greek with live music.

Italian Restaurants

Fioretto, Charlottenburg, Carmerstr. 2, Tel. 312 31 15, Mon-Sat 6 p.m.-2 a.m.

Hosteria del Monte Croce, Kreuzberg, Mittenwalder Str. 6, Tel. 694 39 68, Mon-Sat from 7.30 p.m.

Osteria No. 1, Kreuzberg, Kreuzbergstr. 71, Tel. 786 91 62, daily 6 p.m.-2 a.m.

Tucci, Charlottenburg, Grolmanstr. 52, Tel. 313 93 35, daily 11 a.m.-1 a.m.

XII Apostoli, Charlottenburg, Bleibtreustr. 49, Tel. 312 14 33, daily 7 a.m.-5 a.m.

Spanish and Mexican Restaurants

Carpe Diem, Charlottenburg, Savingypassage, arch Nr. 576, Tel. 313 27 28, Tue-Fri 5 p.m.-1 a.m., Sat 11 a.m.-1 a.m., Sun 13 p.m.-1 a.m.

Los Tres Kilos, Kreuzberg, Marheinekeplatz 3, Tel. 693 60 44, daily 6 p.m.-2 a.m. Noisy, trendy Mexican.

Turkish Restaurants

Foyer, Charlottenburg, Uhlandstr. 28, Tel. 881 42 68, Mon-Sat 15 p.m.-3 a.m.

Hitit, Charlottenburg, Knobelsdorffstr. 35, Tel. 322 45 57, daily 11.30 a.m.-2 a.m.

KNEIPEN –
Brash Hang-outs and Zille's Dives

The place where the two halves of Berlin knitted back together fastest seems to be the Kneipen. For many Berliners, both from the East and from the West, the local Kneipe is simply an extension of their own living room. And if the beer is good, the pot roast is well done and the Korn is cheap, they'll even walk a couple blocks further. Old-fashioned Berlin *Gemütlichkeit* can be found even today in any bar on any corner. In all Berlin that includes the 5200 bars, Kneipen, dives, pubs, cafés and in-crowd joints.

The Charlottenburg Scene:
Cool as a Cucumber

The hub of Berlin's nightlife is around Savignyplatz, in the heart of West Ber-

Above: Berlin still has a number of typical, old-fashioned corner Kneipen.

lin's downtown. At least that is what those people think who like to frequent the bars and restaurants that exude an icy kind of elegance. One place the visitor will never find the Charlottenburg scene is on the Ku'damm. The boulevard may be an inviting place for a stroll in the evening, but do not expect more than a main drag for the group tourists.

Charlottenburgers like to meet around the Savignyplatz, which is also called, with double entendre, the "Savigny Triangle," for three streets (Grolmannstrasse, Knesebeckstrasse and Carmerstrasse) meet here and every kind of Kneipe can be found in this area.

Right next to the Savignyplatz, where Grolmanstrasse starts, there is the **Zwiebelfisch**, which still attracts veterans of the events of 1968 and other thirsty barflies. Most of the local places are restaurants, but some of them, like **Tucci**, are not to be despised as bars. Right next door is the diminutive **Le Bar**, which used to be an insider's tip, when its owner, Pascale Jean-Louis, still tended the bar. These days, on week-ends, it is usually frequented by a noisy nouveau riche clientele – but on weekdays it is an alternative to the standoffish bars in the Tiergarten district.

Café Savigny is a few steps further on and has a more casual atmosphere. It is one of the gay community's favorite and more elegant bars, but women too will enjoy themselves here.

Dralle's is on the corner of Pestalozzi and Schlüterstrasse and frequented by professional bar-hoppers. Night for night, you will see the same people, mostly from the media, yuppies and their classy girl friends. The leather benches are red, as are the walls, from which giant posters of American jazz legends stare down at the crowd, while their music booms from loudspeakers. The waitresses are as pretty as they are unpredictable, with the exception of Isabella, the bartender, who stands out with her cool poise and quickness.

On Knesebeckstrasse you will find two bars in close proximity that are diametrically opposed in style: **Rosalinde** and **CUT**. Rosalinde is a cozy place where plain (but mediocre) food is served and writers and intellectuals meet. In the CUT, a small bar right next door, middle-aged Charlottenburger beauties sip individually mixed cocktails.

At the end of the street, right on Savignyplatz, is the **Shell** – formerly a gas station – where narcissistic insiders gather. In summer the terrace is open and you can flirt to your heart's content – between a collection of modern art and avantgarde photography.

If you're still up to it, check in at the **Filmbühne** on Steinplatz, mostly frequented by students engaged in animated and intelligent conversations before taking in the latest arty movie at the adjacent cinema.

Don't miss the **Diener**, towards Ku'-damm at the beginning of Grolmanstrasse: since the post-war years, Berlin's

theater celebrities meet here to be harassed by moody waiters. But they are accustomed to the treatment, and the wine is good.

Zillemarkt on Bleibtreustrasse has a different kind of ambience. It used to be a stopping place for coaches. From this time only the cobblestone floor has survived, so watch out if you are wearing high-heeled shoes. Then there's **Ali Baba's Minipizza**, where, until the wee hours of the morning and in an easy-going atmosphere, you will be served the best minipizza in the city.

Before leaving Savignyplatz, don't miss checking out one of the Kneipen under the S-Arches between Bleibtreustrasse and Knesebeckstrasse. The **Bogen** is particularly pleasant when it is not frequented by boisterous West German school classes that have gotten lost – an irritation to both the regular customers (mostly elderly) and the waiters.

Schöneberger Kiez: A Somewhat Different Scene

Schönebergers tend to turn up their noses at Charlottenburg. They think that the elegant Westerners are much too snobby to know how to enjoy a real Berlin Kneipe. And thus the Schöneberger scene is less elegant than elsewhere in Berlin West, but not quite as eccentric as in Kreuzberg.

The focal point of Schöneberg's nightlife is around the Winterfeldplatz and the Nollendorfplatz. **Café Swing** is where rock musicians, students and married men from Schöneberg out on their own rub shoulders. Then there's **Café M** on Goltzstrasse, the entertainment street of the neighbourhood and favoured particularly by the young and the unconventional. Cafè M tends to be crowded and during the summer customers simply move outside.

Café Sidney, a spacious establishment on Winterfeldplatz also moves its steel tables out into the street during the summer. Diagonally across the square is the traditional **Slumberland**, which once housed the Dschungel. The scene starts to gather here on market Saturday as early as mid-afternoon in an attempt to forget the cold: you cross over to the bar on genuine white sand.

The **Rössli-Bar** is situated a little out of the way, yet is ideal for skiing fanatics: one of the walls is covered by a panorama of the alps made of paper-mâché. And at the **Pinguin-Club** you will meet all of the names from Berlin's music scene who, against the background of rock'n'roll and blues from the jukebox, would have the 50s come back to life again if they could.

Kreuzberg Tradition

According to one alley hit which has been sung to death "Kreuzberg nights are long". What is true about this statement is that Kreuzbergers are perhaps a little more inclined to celebrating than other Berliners. What is even more true is that there is a number of traditions that coexist alongside one another in Kreuzberg. There are the old corner Kneipen, which the in-crowd avoids like the plague; there are the pretentious bars for the district's social climbers; and then there are the Kneipen for the punks and the university students.

Leydicke is a Kreuzberg institution, even though it is actually situated in Schöneberg. This centegenarian drinking establishment is still a meeting-place today for Berliners, as also for tourists and school classes. It is less noisy on weekdays, and also more authentic. The strawberry and rasperry wines are home-made productions served in simple drinking glasses and thus taste even better.

Which is something one would turn up one's nose at the **Bar Centrale** or the

Right: The 1900, a trendy meeting place in Prenzlauer Berg with Art Nouveau flair.

Café Wirtschaftswunder, both frequented by successful yuppies, while outside someone or other is usually ripping the star off their Mercedes.

If you want to experience unadulterated Kreuzberg, go check out the **Bierhimmel** at Oranienstrasse and Heinrichplatz. It is the alternative scene's most popular meeting place. Just what is heavenly here, as the name "Himmel" would seem to suggest, no one actually knows, especially as the wall candles are more reminiscent of a funeral.

There are a lot of other Kneipen in the area, in particular **Max und Moritz**, **Café am Heinrichplatz** or **Rote Harfe**. Their clientele generally consists of old communards from the late sixties who sit at the rustic tables philosophizing about the end of communism.

The Oranienburgers

Very quickly after the fall of the Wall, the once deserted Oranienburger Strasse turned into one of the fastest-paced and most exciting night streets in Berlin. Curious night owls and the alternative scene from West Berlin, which were beginning to tire of Kreuzberg, as well as artists and prostitutes, started discovering the area. Since the days of the East's new beginning much has changed in the area: the street-walkers have disappeared and bus loads of tourists are shepherded along the Oranienburger.

Yet this Kiez at the heart of Spandau (sometimes also referred to as the "*Scheunenviertel*", or barn district) remains exciting. Much will probably change in the future, too, as it has one of the best locations in downtown Berlin. The **Silberstein** is still a place where DDR intellectuals and artists meet. Further on are the **Café Orange** and the **Café Oren**, where you can get kosher food until the small hours. In summer the café is virtually hidden by the crowd out on the street, but this crowd happens to

be trying to get into the **Obst und Ge-müse**, a bar-cum-Kneipe. Why hundreds of pleasure-seekers are standing around in the hope of getting in, no one really knows. Maybe it is due to the many beautiful young East Berlin women drinking cheap white wine or DDR beer here.

Right across the street is the **Tacheles**, a combination of café, bar and discotheque in the ruins of an old department-store.

In the side streets, especially August-strasse and Tucholskystrasse, there are other bars, including the **Verkehrsberu-higte Ostzone**, which means the "reduced-traffic eastern zone", its décor an amusing collection of old bus seats. Then there's **Hackbarth's**, frequented by Humboldt University students. Not far from here you will find numerous discotheques (s. P. 187).

Clärchens Ballhaus, a real Berlin institution, is a little way up Auguststrasse: this place has been around since the 30s. Elderly gentlemen still slide their ladies with fancy hairdos over the polished dance floor. Petit bourgeois happiness in the midst of chaos.

Prenzlauer Berg: Scene for Scene's Sake

So far Prenzlauer Berg has mostly been spared by tourism and curious West Berliners. The scene here seems to rotate around its own axis anyway. The night-life is increasingly concentrated in the streets around Kollwitzplatz. If you go to **Café Kyril** on Lychener Strasse, you will get an (unintentional) idea of what life was like before the Wende and the fall of the Wall: here a great number of bookish types, still living in the past, meet to reminisce about the old days of inner resistance in the underground. Frequently there are readings at the weekends, which are quite bearable if you take them with a glass of beer.

On the other hand, the guests at the **Café Anita Wronski** and the **Kommandandatur**, both on Knaackstrasse, are more relaxed and quite free of ideo-

logy. Even though the names of these cafés are political, the guests are young and apolitical – despite one or two preferring to wear a flat cap and red star.

On the other hand, the clientele in the **Café Westphal** – which almost deserves mention for its venerable age alone – tends to be a little more heterogenous. During the Wende, this establishment, which used to be a store called "Ost- und Westpreußische Spirituosen- und Likörhandlung C. Westphal" was occupied by the scene. This scene has since disappeared, and isn't to be found at the **Krähe** either, which – especially during the warmer months – tends to be frequented by successful East Berlin businessmen and snobby west Germans.

The Schönhauser Allee, the center of the district, seems deserted and abandoned at night. But nowhere else can you observe so closely the contradictions in the East Berlin scene. The décor and the

Above: The beer is still brewed on the premises in this Berlin Kneipe.

clientele of the two Kneipen **Lolott** and **Zum Räwier** could hardly be more unlike in character. While East Berlin yuppies toast one another in an artfully arranged scenery of rubble at Lolott's, not one of these people would escape being physically chucked out of the punky Räwier.

Zum Oderkahn and **Schlot** have a more common touch. Oderkahn greets the guest with a genuine Berlin Kneipe atmosphere, with solid Berlin-style food on the menu. The Schlot, located on one floor of an old factory, is the meeting-place for Prenzelberger alternative-type artists who all the same will not do without a proper beer and bockwurst.

If you think the crowd is too noisy here or elsewhere in Prenzlauer Berg, try the Husemannstraße: there you will find the **Restauration 1900**. Even when it is crammed full, it's guaranteed to stay quiet and decorous. Faces from the old DDR days pop in, visitors from the West lean against the bar and slowly the two sides come closer: Cheers, then!

CAFÉS AND KNEIPEN

Ali Baba, Charlottenburg, Bleibtreustr. 45, Tel. 881 13 50, daily 11.30 a.m.-3 a.m.

Bar Centrale, Kreuzberg, Yorckstr. 82, Tel. 786 29 89, daily 4 p.m.-3 a.m., Sat, Sun from 12 noon.

Bierhimmel, Kreuzberg, Oranienstr. 183, Tel. 621 74 34, Mon-Thur 10 a.m.-3 a.m., Fri, Sat 10 a.m.-4 a.m.

Bogen, Charlottenburg, Savignypassage, arch Nr. 597, Tel. 313 77 04, daily 4 p.m.-2 a.m.

Café Anita Wronski, Prenzlauer Berg, Knaackstr. 26-28, Tel. 609 75 89, daily 9 a.m.-2 a.m.

Cafe Kyril, Prenzlauer Berg, Lychener Str. 73, Tel. 449 80 73, daily 11 a.m.-3 a.m.

Café M, Schöneberg, Goltzstr. 7, Tel. 216 70 92, daily from 8 a.m.

Café Savigny, Charlottenburg, Grolmannstr. 53, Tel. 312 81 95, daily 2 p.m.-1 a.m.

Café Sidney, Schöneberg, Winterfeldtstr. 40, Tel. 216 52 53, Mon-Fri 9 a.m.-4 a.m., Sat, Sun until 6 a.m.

Café Swing, Schöneberg, Nollendorfplatz 3-4, Tel. 216 61 37, daily from 10.30 a.m.

Café Westphal, Prenzlauer Berg, Käthe-Kollwitz-Str. 64, Tel. 448 32 89, daily 9 a.m.-3 a.m.

Clärchens Ballhaus, Prenzlauer Berg, Auguststr. 24/5, Tel. 282 92 95, Tue-Thur 7 p.m.-midnight, Fri and Sat 7.30 p.m.-1 a.m.

CUT, Charlottenburg, Knesebeckstr. 16, Tel. 313 35 11, daily 10 p.m.-6 a.m.

Deichgraf, Wedding, Nordufer 10, Tel. 453 76 13, daily 9 a.m.-4 a.m., a bit out of the way, frequented mainly by students.

Diener, Charlottenburg, Grolmannstr. 47, Tel. 881 53 29, daily from 6 p.m.

Dralle's, Charlottenburg, Schlüterstr. 69, Tel. 313 50 38, daily 12 noon-3 a.m., Fri, Sat unil 4 a.m.

Filmbühne am Steinplatz, Charlottenburg, Hardenbergstr. 12, Tel. 312 90 12, daily 10 a.m.-4 a.m.

Geierwally's Stieftochter im Ausland, Prenzlauer Berg, Prenzlauer Promenade 3, Tel. 965 50 702, daily 2 p.m.-3 a.m.

Grossbeerenkeller, Kreuzberg, Grossbeerenstr. 90, Tel. 251 30 64, Mon-Thur 2 p.m.-3 a.m., Fri-Sun 2 p.m.-4 a.m., Kreuzberg Kneipe with original flair, here local politicians like to chat over a beer.

Hackbarth's, Mitte, Auguststr. 49a, Tel. 282 77 06, daily 9 a.m.-3 a.m.

Kastanie, Charlottenburg, Schlossstr. 22, Tel. 321 50 34, daily 12 noon-2 a.m., Kiez and media people meet under chestnut trees. Near the palace.

Kleine Weltlaterne, Wilmersdorf, Nestorstr. 22, Tel. 892 65 85, Mon-Sat 8 p.m.-4 a.m., popular with artists, worth a visit.

Kommandantur, Prenzlauer Berg, Knaackstr. 20, no phone, daily 2 p.m.-4 a.m.

Krähe, Prenzlauer Berg, Kollwitzstr. 84, no phone, Mon from 5 p.m., Tue-Sun 9 a.m.-2 a.m.

Lentz, Charlottenburg, Stuttgarter Platz 20, Tel. 324 16 19, daily 10 a.m.-2 a.m., Kneipe with relaxed atmosphere, families are welcome.

Leydicke, Schöneberg, Mansteinstr. 4, Tel. 216 29 73, daily from 5 p.m., Sat from 12 noon.

Lolott, Prenzlauer Berg, Schönhauser Allee 56, Tel. 448 44 15, Tue-Fri 10 p.m.-6 a.m., Sat and Sun 8 p.m.-6 a.m.

Max und Moritz, Kreuzberg, Oranienstr. 162, Tel. 614 10 45, daily 6 p.m.-1.30 a.m.

Obst und Gemüse, Mitte, Oranienburger Str. 48/49, no phone, daily from 6 p.m.

Oren, Mitte, Oranienburger Str. 28, Tel. 282 82 28, Sun-Fri 10 a.m.-1 a.m., Sat 10 a.m.-2 a.m.

Pinguin-Club, Schöneberg, Wartburgstr. 54, Tel. 781 30 05, daily 10 p.m.-4 a.m.

Restauration 1900, Prenzlauer Berg, Husemannstr. 1, Tel. 449 40 52, Mon-Sat 4 p.m.-midnight.

Rössli-Bar, Schöneberg, Eisenacher Str. 80, Tel. 784 63 45, daily 4 p.m.-8 a.m.

Rosalinde, Charlottenburg, Knesebeckstr. 16, Tel. 313 59 96, 9.30 a.m.-3 a.m.

Rost, Charlottenburg, Knesebeckstr. 29, Tel. 881 95 01, daily 9 a.m.-2 a.m., trendy bar for actors.

Rote Harfe, Kreuzberg, Oranienstr. 13, Tel. 618 44 46, Tue-Sun 10 a.m.-3 a.m.

Schlot, Prenzlauer Berg, Kastanienallee 29, Tel. 208 20 67, daily from 10 p.m.

Shell, Charlottenburg, Knesebeckstr. 22, Tel. 312 83 10, Mon-Fri 9a.m.-1 a.m., Sat, Sun 10 a.m.-2 a.m.

Slumberland, Schöneberg, Goltzstr. 24, Tel. 216 53 49, daily 9.30 a.m.-4 a.m.

Tacheles, Mitte, Oranienburger Str. 53-56, Tel. 282 61 85, daily.

Tucci, Charlottenburg, Grolmannstr. 52, Tel. 313 93 35, daily 11 a.m.-3 p.m.

Van Loon, Kreuzberg, Urbanhafen/Carl-Herz-Ufer, Tel. 692 62 93, Tue-Sun 10 a.m.-1 a.m.

Verkehrsberuhigte Ostzone, Mitte, Auguststr. 93, no phone, open daily 24 hours.

Wirtschaftswunder, Kreuzberg, Yorckstr. 81, Tel. 786 99 99, daily 3 p.m.-5 a.m.

Zillemarkt, Charlottenburg, Bleibtreustr. 48a, Tel. 881 70 40, daily 9 a.m.-1 p.m.

Zum Oderkahn, Prenzlauer Berg, Oderbergstr. 11, Tel. 449 44 62, Mo-Sa 16-1 Uhr.

Zum Räwier, Prenzlauer Berg, Schönhauser Allee 20, no phone, daily from 8 p.m.

Zwiebelfisch, Charlottenburg, Savignyplatz 7-8, Tel. 313 73 63, daily 12 noon-6 a.m.

Most of these *Kneipen* offer tasty food or snacks. Many restaurants too have a definite *Kneipen*-atmosphere, see page 187.

BERLIN NIGHTLIFE –
THE SCENE GOES BERSERK

When national and international TV cameras broadcast Berlin's Love Parade, the world came to realize that Berlin is not only the city with the largest annual dancing event in Europe but also the German capital of night owls, ravers, dance fanatics and pleasure-seekers. Hundreds of thousands of young people from all over Germany and Europe came to participate in the Love Parade and danced frenetically along the Kurfürstendamm. Young girls in jeans shorts and bikini tops, and gays in leather letting their naked muscular bodies sway to techno-music – in broad daylight!

These pictures only showed the top of a bubbling volcano of partying whose hottest chunks are hidden in the Berlin

night scene. There, "in the heat of the night", new clubs, parties with new mottoes or parties with the same motto but a constantly changing location or a constantly changing clientele, are ceaselessly dreamed up.

During the weeks after the Parade, the night-clubbers hogging the scene gossip were the same ones who were at the Love-Boat parties celebrated on old barges that were crossing the rivers and canals of Berlin: a ticket to ride cost DM 35. Anyone who missed it only had to wait a few weeks to take part in another all-night trip: a techno-train that hurtled through the Berlin and Brandenburg night with a couple of hundred dancers aboard.

If you have just recently moved to Berlin, or are a tourist, you'll have a difficult time discovering the depths of Berlin's party-volcano without the assistance of a Berlin night owl. Or take a look at the city magazines *Tip*, *Zitty* or *Prinz* that are available at newspaper stands, or the two free events and "scene" magazines *[030]*

Above: The city's best cocktails are served at Harry's New York Bar. Right: Showgirls at the La Vie en Rose.

and *Weekly*, which can be picked up in cinemas, bars and clubs.

Berlin Bars – Cool and Wild

Among the 7,500 various gastronomic operations in Berlin a number of bars and discotheques have developed which are nearly always worth a visit.

Modern cocktail aficionadoes begin their evening at the **Bar am Lützowplatz** at about 10 p.m. Many a guest has the first-class cocktails to thank for ending his evening once again here juiced. A bar like this was long overdue in Berlin as the architecture, drinks list and staff are mixed into a classic fun cocktail in this long tube of a bar. Behind the 50 foot bar the bartenders shake their shakers. In front of the bar the chic clientele relaxes on bar stools of dazzling chrome. The preferred topic of conversation: the difference between Jim Beam and a 12-year old whiskey from the Scottish highlands, or which aluminium rims go best with the new convertibles.

If you are not in the right age bracket for its yuppyish atmosphere, just stroll over to Hotel Esplanade, which is right around the corner. There you will find the Berlin branch of the legendary **Harry's New York Bar**. The bartenders, male and female, wear white uniforms and the walls are adorned with pictures of all 43 American presidents. And every night of the week, in real Dixie style, American jazz pianists or tubby Afro-American soul singers sit down at the piano and entertain the over-forties.

The **Bristol Bar** in the Hotel Kempinski on Fasanenstraße is less crowded and slightly more elegant.

Another bar that attracts students and all other artists (in the school of life) from about 10 p.m. onwards is the small **Zoulou Bar**, which is somewhat reminiscent of the African bars Hemingway describes in his novels.

Then there's the **Caracas** in a basement on Kurfürstenstraße with its hundreds of plastic roses on the ceiling and its perpetually crowded bar.

The **Fischlabor** ("Fish Laboratory") is also located in Schöneberg. Its décor – if that is how one can refer to it – is in grey. Grey furry rugs hang from the walls, and the curtains are in grey, too. The fridge is well stocked with "Space" beer.

Even before midnight Schöneberg's **Kumpelnest 3000** is a lively place, but things get really steamy at about four a.m., when the bartender plays wild 70's music on his cassette deck and guests start to dance spontaneously at the bar while holding on to their glass of Beck's beer. If you are in the mood for something more swank, try the discotheque in the **Lucky Strike Restaurant**.

Small Cabarets and Hot Shows

There are plenty of cabarets such as **Chez Nous** and **La Vie En Rose** where

*Above: The famous "Dschungel" stairway.
Right: Customers at the in-place 90° – a special kind of meeting place.*

you can simply lean back comfortably and let yourself be entertained in style. When the "Ladies" at Chez Nous aren't on tour in the west German provinces, they like to joke around with the audience and tell all kinds of anecdotes from the transvestite daily grind. La Vie En Rose offers various performances several times a night – a mixture of travesty and magic show, dancing and tasteful striptease. Under the bright red lights you'll see lots of naked skin, bare breasts and gyrating derrières only fleetingly covered by feather boas.

Discotheques in the West Part of the City

Nights spent on Berlin's dance floors are even more strenuous, especially since the scene in the eastern districts has blossomed and become a paradise for DJs and owners of new clubs. Since then, thousands of dance fanatics from all over the city set out every weekend on their pilgrimage to the wild East.

One of the most prominent places that has suffered from this change is the legendary discotheque **Dschungel**, once the favourite disco of West Berlin's in-crowd. Today it can only manage to survive as a restaurant. However, this club's ageless interior décor is still worth a visit. Especially when the "After Dinner Dance" program begins after midnight, memories of the old days stir between the fountains, the aquarium and the spiral staircase.

New First, formerly the First, on Joachimstaler Strasse, is still the number one for Berlin's wealthy celebrities. For over ten years the discotheque's owner Jochen Strecker has looked after his most affluent guests in person, including celebrities like Gitte, Frank Zander, Udo Lindenberg, Brigitte Nielsen and Harald Juhnke and Juhnke junior.

It doesn't cost anything to get in, the doorman simply checks out the quality of your clothing. The drinks are what brings in the money: Just take a look at the more than 40 coolers for sparkling wine and

champagne on the shelves, and you will know what people prefer to consume every weekend after 1 a.m. The cheapest price for a bottle of champagne is 140 Marks.

If that isn't your price range and if you are at least ten years younger, try **Blue Note**, where men must wear a dinner jacket and the ladies sip champagne. But it is somewhat more affordable, even if getting in does cost the 10 Marks usual in Berlin.

Even though the Indian guru Bhagwan Shree Rajneesh has passed away some time ago, the disco **Far Out** on Lehniner Platz is indestructible and is still operated by his Berlin disciples. It looks bright and airy like all the other Bhagwan discoes: from Thursdays to Saturdays believers and non-believers alike put their glasses don on gleaming marble counters, the floor vibrates under hundreds of dancing feet and powerful day-strength lighting promotes direct eye contact, while the DJ starts playing the hits of yesterday's and today's charts.

Kreuzberg Discotheques

During the summer months, Far Out regulars prefer tovisit Kreuzberg's **Golgatha**, which is a mixture of beer garden, discotheque and daytrip pub. It lies right on Kreuzberg's "slope" and is definitely worth seeing, if only because it is so close.

If you continue on to Kreuzberg's downtown area, you will hit the **Turbine** on Glogauer Strasse. Thursdays the mood here reaches such a frenetic pitch that normal party goers are totally exhausted for the rest of the weekend. Like in most Kreuzberg scene places, at first glance the color black dominates a gloomy atmosphere. But the female DJ is a genius and the mixture of disco beat from the 70s, beat and rave, and an exuberant dance crowd that knows it won't

Above: Dance floor in Sox – especially popular with Kreuzberg night birds. Right: Facial artwork in Kreuzberg.

be going to work on Friday make for a boisterous atmosphere.

Although Berlin's under-18 student crowd has to get up early in the mornings, there is nothing that will keep them from meeting at the **Rockit** on Tuesdays and Thursdays for some headbanging after 10 p.m. You will see Berlin's sweetest little teeny girls, and the boys are Curt-Cobain lookalikes. They all dig grunge rock and are anti-establishment, but of course next morning they will all be sitting in their classrooms again. School classes should not miss this dance floor!

Downtown Berlin: Techno Beat and House

On weekends, house music and techno fans tend to go to one of their techno temples **Tresor**, **E-Werk** or **Bunker**. Tresor used to be number one among Berlin's techno-dance floors for a couple of years. Top international DJs worked here, and more often than not one would hear the British accent of young house fans; once the American rap icon, Guru, from the band Gang Starr, even stopped by. He grabbed the microphone and launched into a rap-song about the problems American cities have.

Then came the **E-Werk** and along with it a genuinely metropolitan night-life. Now that the young ravers have gotten used to paying ten to fifteen marks to get in, the doorman asks for twenty marks. Nevertheless, it's mobbed every weekend. Between three and eleven a.m., the atmosphere in this discotheque, formerly a transformer station, screams as if a thousand power cables had burst.

On the other hand, sometimes too much popularity can keep the clientele away. Gay trendsetters in particular like to celebrate at tomorrow's party places, for instance, at **Café Moskau**. This is where you can hear the best house music in the city. Berlin's heteros have meanwhile become aware of this, and like to check in on Fridays.

The **Bunker** is on Allbrechtstrasse, where the disc jockeys exploit the windowless walls to play the hardest kind of techno: they play Gabba. One story lower, in the **Ex-Kreuz-Club**, formerly the Rot-Kreuz-Klub, Berlin's sado-masochists indulge in wild SM orgies once a month – including chains, doctor's chairs, lots of leather and a tiny dance floor. Be careful: this is not a place for just watching.

Friendly Clubs for People who Like to Talk

As a consequence of this party inflation, many night clubbers who are older than twenty long for a fair amount of intimacy and a chat at the bar. They don't want to just dance their feet hot, they want to move their tongues too. Berlin's party volcano immediately spat out the right kinds of clubs for those wanting communication together with their beer

at the bar, and gave these clubs a new label: Creative Clubbing.

Bob Young's **90*** is one of them. He turned an old garage and its mechanic's atmosphere and uneven cement floor into an insider's place with a parquet dance floor. On weekends, people that have a membership card have a better chance to get past the doorman than those who don't. The DJ plays soul and house, and at the crowded bar regular guests discuss the interior decoration of the bar, which has changed yet again.

Boogaloo gives its guests enough space for some small talk, too – either in cosy old living-room armchairs or up on a small gallery which looks over the dance floor. There, dancers gyrate their bodies to the good old soul and acid jazz records.

Things got a little quieter here when **Delicious Doughnuts** opened on Rosenthaler Strasse. This place is the epitome of creative clubbing. Weeknights Doughnuts sometimes stages "Jazz Poetry Performances" for insiders and enthusiasts,

or even a small concert with the world's fastest rap poet JC 001 from London.

You had better get there before midnight on weekends, otherwise you don't have a chance to make it past the inevitable long queue in front, as this place is now one of the most popular spots to dance and talk.

When you're inside, your first impresssion is that you have entered a cozy Kneipe, where you have paid eight marks at the door to get in: yellow walls, a couple of wooden tables and a copper-topped bar. Some of the guests actually are eating the doughnuts that are sold here, and washing them down with Afri-Cola. Even the friendly bartender with his small moustache and wooden pearl necklace confides that they "taste awful." Behind the narrow swing doors, the creative club guest will finally discover the acid jazz he can listen and dance to.

If this music is far too modern or too extravagant for you, just remain in the neighbourhood and continue on to the **Noa**, one street further in the Joachimstrasse. There the DJ still plays "Sunday Bloody Sunday" by U2, followed by Police and Madness. Noa's owners took a lot of trouble to give their ancient underground vault a real noble-trash design. First the brick walls were plastered properly, then laid bare in some places, or broken right through in others. This gives the surroundings quite a pleasant, medieval quality, and especially young women like to come here, ever since the magazine *Elle* ran an article about Noa. Men will like that as much as the price for a Budweiser – about 4 Marks 50.

At the end of their tour of Berlin's party scene, dance tourists will have an additional 40 miles on their car clocks and at least the same amount of marks less in their wallets. If you don't have at least two club stamps on the palm of each hand, you will probably have missed the hottest party in town.

Above: Sweating it out in East Berlin – on the tiny Sophienclub dance floor.

NIGHT BARS

Bar am Lützowplatz, Tiergarten, Lützowplatz 7, Tel. 262 68 07, daily 4 p.m.-5 a.m.

Berlin Bar, Wilmersdorf, Uhlandstr. 145, Tel. 883 79 36, daily 10 p.m.-7 a.m.

Caracas, Schöneberg, Kurfürstenstr.9, Tel. 261 56 18, daily from 10 p.m.

Champussy, Charlottenburg, Uhlandstr. 171, Tel. 881 22 20, daily 7 p.m.-3 a.m., elegant champagne bar in the city.

Fischlabor, Schöneberg, Frankenstr. 13, Tel. 216 26 35, daily from 11 p.m.

Hafenbar, Mitte, Chausseestr. 20, Tel. 282 85 93, Mon, Tue 8 p.m.-3 a.m., Fri, Sat 8 p.m.-4 a.m., Kneipe with East Berlin charm.

Harry's New York Bar, in the Grand Hotel Esplanade, Tiergarten, Lützowufer 15, Tel. 26 10 11, daily from 12 noon.

Kumpelnest 3000, Tiergarten, Lützowstr. 23, Tel. 261 69 18, daily 5 p.m.-5 a.m.

Lucky Strike, Mitte, Georgenstrasse, S-Bahn arches Nr. 177-180, Tel. 201 77 422, Fri and Sat disco with live band 9 a.m.- midnight, then DJ until 4 a.m.

Morena, Kreuzberg, Wiener Str. 60, Tel. 611 47 16, daily from 9 a.m., Mexican bar.

Niagara, Kreuzberg, Gneisenaustr. 58, Tel. 692 61 72, daily from 8 p.m.

Tom's Bar, Schöneberg, Motzstr. 20, Tel. 213 45 70. Favorite meeting place of the young gay scene.

Zoulou Bar, Schöneberg, Hauptstr. 1, Tel. 784 68 94, daily 10 p.m.-6 a.m.

REVUE THEATERS

La Vie En Rose in the Europacenter, Charlottenburg, Tauentzien, Tel. 323 60 06. Tue-Thur, Sun show at 9 p.m.; Fri and Sat show at 10 p.m.

Cabaret Chez Nous, Charlottenburg, Marburger Str. 14, Tel. 213 18 10, shows daily at 8.30 p.m. and 11 p.m.

Kleine Nachtrevue, Schöneberg, Kurfürstenstr. 114, Tel. 218 89 50, shows daily except Sun at 10.30 p.m. and 0.30 a.m.

DISCOTHEQUES

Abraxas, Charlottenburg, Kantstr. 134, Tel. 312 94 93, Tue-Sun 10 p.m.-5 a.m. Pleasant small disco for fans of Latin and Afro music.

Blue Note, Schöneberg, Courbièrestr. 13, Tel. 247 248, daily 8 p.m.-5 a.m., white funk music.

Boogaloo, Mitte, Brückenstr. 1, Tel. 279 13 70, daily from 11 p.m.

Bronx, Kreuzberg, Wiener Str. 34, Tel. 611 84 45, daily 10 p.m.-4 a.m., for ardent Kreuzberg fans.

Bunker / Ex Kreuz Club, Mitte, Albrechtstr. 24/25, Tel. 87 40 97, Fri-Sun from 2 a.m.

Cosmopolitan Club, Kreuzberg, Oranienstr. 39, Tel. 618 15 22, daily 8 p.m.-2 a.m. Pleasant club, music from jazz to funk and salsa.

Delicious Doughnuts, Mitte, Rosenthaler Str. 9/ corner Auguststraße, Tel. 283 30 21, Tue-Sun 10 p.m.-5 a.m.

Die Halle, Weißensee, An der Industriebahn 12, Tel. 609 63 70, irregular parties, phone for dates and times.

E-Werk, Mitte, Wilhelmstr. 43, Tel. 251 32 14/251 57 90, Fri and Sat from midnight.

Far Out, Wilmersdorf, Kurfürstendamm 156 (at Lehniner Platz), Tel. 320 007 23, daily 10 p.m.- 3.30 a.m., Fri and Sat until 5.30 a.m.

Golgatha, Kreuzberg, Dudenstrasse 48-64, (at the Kreuzberg), Tel. 785 24 53, daily 10 p.m.-6 a.m.

Loft im Metropol, Schöneberg, Nollendorfplatz 5, Tel. 215 54 63, small disco, concerts, live music.

Knaack Club, Prenzlauer Berg, Greifswalder Str. 224, Tel. 436 23 51, Fri-Mon, Wed 10 p.m.-6 a.m.

Lipstick, Charlottenburg, Richard-Wagner-Platz 5, Tel. 342 81 26, daily 10 p.m.-5 a.m., relaxed gay disco.

Metropol, Schöneberg, Nollendorfplatz 5, Tel. 216 27 87, Fri and Sat from 10 p.m. One of the largest Berlin discos, for teenies.

90°, Schöneberg, Dennewitzstr. 37, Tel. 262 89 84, Wed-Sun from 11 p.m.

New First, Charlottenburg, Joachimstaler Str.26, Tel. 882 26 86, daily except Mon, 11 p.m.-6 a.m.

Noa, Mitte, Joachimstr.11, no phone, Fri and Sat from 11 p.m.

Orpheuo, Schöneberg, Marburger Str. 2, Tel. 211 64 45, daily from 11 p.m.

Rockit, Schöneberg, Lützowstr. 105, Schöneberg, Tue, Thur-Sat from 10 p.m.

Sophienclub, Mitte, Sophienstr. 6, Tel. 282 45 52, daily from 9 p.m.

Tränenpalast, Mitte, Reichstagsufer 17 (at the S-Bahn station Friedrichstrasse), Tel. 321 10 22, irregular parties are held in this former East German border checkpoint.

Tresor / **Globus Bar**, Mitte, Leipziger Str. 128a, no phone, Fri-Mon from 11 p.m.

Turbine, Kreuzberg, Glogauer Str. 2, Tel. 611 38 33, daily from 11 p.m.

Zoo Club, Schöneberg, Nürnberger Str. 50, Tel. 242 447, daily from 11 p.m., elegant disco for fans of funk and soul music.

Please note: The entrance fee for most discos is 10 DM (this does not include drinks or snacks). You can wear what you like, except in classy bars and discos. Most clubs are open to all age groups.

WORLD THEATER AND
THEATRICAL BERLIN

One thing that has made Berlin unique since reunification is the cohesion and conflict between *two* theater cultures, which have undergone different development since 1945.

Compared with the theaters in the west, the stages in the east were more certain of the approval of their audiences. In a fairly subtle manner they functioned as forums for political information and frequently even as a substitute for newspapers. Now, since political theater lost its *raison d'être* by virtue of the change of systems, the stages in the city's eastern section are in search of a new identity. It may be that before long there won't be much to distinguish them from the stages in Berlin's western section.

As the capital city, East Berlin attracted the best directors of the former GDR, whereas West Berlin was just one theater city among others. The nearly 30 stages in unified Berlin *could* serve as the foundation for turning the city back into what it once was before the Nazis closed the theaters in 1944 and roughly half of Berlins stages were destroyed during the war: Germany's theater capital (as it had been called since the turn of the century). In the twenties it was even *the* European theater metropolis. Today the houses and the performances they offer differ widely. Everything is represented from world-class theater to specialty stages to mercurial "off-theater." Nonetheless, the city hasn't yet managed to step back into its former role as a true theater metropolis. This was especially apparent during the **Berlin Theater Competition**, which takes place annually in May. A jury selects what it deems to be the best German-language production. For the most part only the productions of the

Right: The Schauspielhaus served as a theater until 1944, then as a concert hall.

Schaubühne have made it through this competition, and since 1989 those of East German director Thomas Langhoff have always been at the top. However, in 1991 Berlin was represented with six productions – half of all the nominations.

Major "Talk Theater"

The **Schaubühne am Lehniner Platz** is a private theater whose players enjoy extensive co-determination in the creation of the performances. As a cultural showpiece, it is heavily subsidized and was for a long time thought of as one of the best theaters in the world. It was founded in 1962 as a left-leaning, socially critical private theater, and named simply after its location, *Schaubühne am Halleschen Tor*.

In 1970 a troup of actors and actresses centered around Peter Stein moved into the building. Their programming was generally in accord with the goals of the protest movements of 1968. The reputation of the Schaubühne is primarily based on the directing work of Peter Stein, who remained artistic director until 1985, and of Luc Bondy and Klaus Michael Grüber – as well as the professionalism of the players themselves.

However, many critics believe that the Schaubühne broke with its political tradition and developed into a "boulevard theater" when it moved from Kreuzberg to the Ku'damm. Nonetheless, many spectators travel from around the world to enjoy its productions, and for the Berlin money-and-culture crowd, attending every production goes without saying.

In the five years since the fall of the Wall the **Deutsches Theater** in the former eastern section of the city has developed into the premier theater in Berlin. There is hardly another German-speaking theater which so enthuses critic and public alike. This is due not least to a unique combination of sheer excellence in acting with provocative stage manage-

ment. The name might bring to mind associations with a "national theater," but since the merger with the former West Berlin state theaters the Deutsches Theater has had to take over, albeit involuntarily, the role of Berlin State Theater. Although at its foundation in 1883 programming along these lines played a role, today, however, both classical and contemporary pieces from around the world are on the performance schedule. The theater has an unusually broad repertoire including some 30 lengthier productions.

Another rather unusual fact is that almost all of these productions have been worth the ticket fee. Moreover, the carefully decorated interior walls seem to exude 100 years of theatrical history. When Max Reinhardt, the Deutsches Theater's owner, emigrated in 1933, he chose Heinz Hilpert to carry on with the good work. Hilpert was aware of the fact that the Nazis needed the Deutsches Theater and its accompanying *Kammerspiele* playhouse as a liberal "alibi," and lead both theaters with innocuous pro-

ductions of classics through the war. Even so, occasionally Joseph Goebbels threatened: "Hilperts' stagings are concentration camps on vacation." However, Hilpert would then counter: "Then you'll have to put Goethe in Oranienburg and Hebbel in a concentration camp." Soon after the war's end, the Deutsches Theater dared to leap into the political fray with contemporary dramas. The tradition of subtle political innuendo was continued by Thomas Langhoff, who in 1991 became general director.

Of course, just as it has always been, star actors and actresses like to perform at the Deutsches Theater, but the spirit of the ensemble is also highly developed. An excellent new generation is growing alongside the venerable acting greats. The old separation between the Deutsches Theater and the Kammerspiele, which was almost exclusively used as an experimental stage, no longer exists. In both houses classics, contemporary drama and good "boulevard" pieces are performed today. In addition to Heiner

Müller, who from time to time produced his own work here, Alexander Lang was one of the most important directors ever, both in the Deutsche Theater as in the old GDR.

In the west of the city however the time of the major productions has gone – since the end of 1993. It was then that the Senat suddenly and suprisingly decided to close the state-run **Schauspielbühne** together with its flagship, the Schillertheater, due to the city's grave financial situation. After weeks of protests and protracted legal proceeedings the Berlin House of Representatives confirmed the senator's decision. Ironically an audit one year later showed that this overhasty closure had in fact cost the taxpayer ten million DM more than a gradual close-down would have. The theater will probably be opened as a stage for musicals.

The **Maxim-Gorki-Theater**, though small, is also among the most successful

Above: Hamlet in the Deutsches Theater.
Right: The great Max Reinhardt.

stages. The name-patron Gorki is also representative for the many other dramatists from the Soviet Union and other East European states whose pieces are lovingly produced in this theater. Alongside its meritorious director (and actor) Albert Hetterle, producers Rolf Winkelgrund and Thomas Langhoff, who made theatrical history with George Tabori's political farce *Mein Kampf*, have shaped the house's style. In addition to the political theater, good "boulevard" pieces with excellent casts have become important in the repertoire.

On the other hand, the **Berliner Ensemble** has been relying primarily on its past worldwide reputation since it drove away producer and director Ruth Berghaus in 1977. The Ensemble was founded by Bertolt Brecht in 1949, right after his return from exile. In 1954 the Ensemble received its own performance space, the **Theater am Schiffbauerdamm,** which Brecht developed into an avant-garde stage. After his death in 1956, the Berliner Ensemble remained specialized in Brecht dramas. It has also consistently tried out works written in his spirit by other dramatists. Despite the interesting concept and the dedicated work of its players, this stage – predestined for experimentation – has congealed into a kind of theater museum, although the renowned directors Fritz Marquardt and Christoph Schroth are now at work on resurrecting the Berliner Ensemble's battered prestige.

"Art for the people" was the motto for the 1890 founding of the **Volksbühne** (People's Stage). Germany's first theatergoers' association erected its own building in 1914 on Bülowplatz – the present-day Rosa-Luxemburg-Platz – from pennies donated by workers. Max Reinhardt was the first director; later Erwin Piscator became chief producer. After initial success the Volksbühne's pedagogical dramaturgy began wearing down the spirit and patience of its proletarian audience. At a time when Reinhardt was making great art at the Deutsches Theater, essayist Hans Sahl mocked: "The workers went to Reinhardt to edify themselves with beauty after dull labor; the bourgeoisie went to Piscator to applaud the portrayal of their impending downfall."

Piscator's revolutionary impetus finally lead to a break with the Social-Democratic attitudes of the Volksbühne's directorate. He founded his own theater on the Nollendorfplatz, where his *agitprop* productions of the time – toward the end of the Weimar Republic – made the theater hall into a battlefield. In 1954 after its reconstruction as the municipal theater – it had only the name in common with the older institution – the Volksbühne, under the direction of Brecht student Benno Besson, became the most innovative theater of the former GDR during the seventies. It failed, however, to maintain this status on its own. Today the directorate is seeking a new profile for the repertory and currently

PROFESSOR MAX REINHARDT.

more popular pieces are being considered. The Volksbühne already attracts the ideal public for that kind of repertoire, a representative cross-section of Berlin's wide-ranging social strata.

In 1953, when the Volksbühne was dissolved in the GDR because the Free German Union Alliance took over the management of theater attendance, several of the former members in West Berlin founded their own peoples' stage association.

It managed to open its own theater by 1963: the **Freie** (Free) **Volksbühne**. Piscator worked here for a while after his return from exile, directing plays like *Der Stellvertreter* by Rolf Hochhuth; *In der Sache J. Robert Oppenheimer* by Heinar Kipphardt and *Die Ermittlung* by Peter Weiss, among others. Under the direction of Kurt Hübner there were further signs of a critical peoples' theater, with political and social contents that interested a broad spectrum of the public. *Ghetto* by Joshua Sobol, for instance, sparked a vehement discussion.

Since 1986, the name Freie Volks-bühne has been nothing more than a fake label. The old members of the audience association rejected the highly individ-ualistic direction of Hans Neuenfels, and audience numbers sank dramatically. Fi-nally the musicals producer Friedrich Kurz took over the Volksbühne and turned it into the **Musical Theater Ber-lin**. Currently the production imported from London is showing here: Shake-speare and Rock'n'Roll.

The **Theatermanufaktur** is a remnant of the '68 upheaval, when it was good, renowned and significant. Meanwhile the epic-didactic style with socialist inten-tions has become somewhat dated, and since the fall of the Wall, one might say almost insultingly silly.

The elegant **Renaissance-Theater**, built in 1926, is oriented toward the tastes of a broad public, serving up dramas by Molière, Arthur Miller and Dürrenmatt in

Above: The world-famous musical Line 1 at the Grips-Theater.

easily digestible form. Berlin's popular star Harald Juhnke has lent several of the productions a pinch of the "boulevard" theater. Occasionally on Sundays, cele-brities from culture and politics deliver commentaries as part of the "Berliner Lectures" series; a workshop stage per-forms private theater as well; **das studio** presents contemporary drama.

The **Hebbel-Theater** primarily hosts productions which stand slightly oblique of the commonplace, established theater. Here they find a distinctive, intellectual and mostly youthful public, who – be-yond the major guest productions – are interested in the latest currents from around the world, from plays via pan-tomime and on to really off-the-wall per-formances.

Small Stages and "Boulevard" Theater

The **Hansa-Theater**, the **Vaganten-Bühne** and the **Tribüne**, founded in 1919 as an attempt at a proletarian theater, favor more-or-less pretentious entertainment and popular pieces, but also hark gladly back to the tradition of the cellar theater of the fifties, confronting their audiences with Beckett or Sartre.

The **kleines Theater** is a self-designated specialty stage. The unknown is rescued from oblivion there and presented with a good helping of irony, some sarcasm, and frequently music as well. They may even be setting a record with over 1400 performances of the production of *Das Küssen macht so gut wie kein Geräusch* (which translates as "Kissing hardly makes any sound at all").

Almost every theater in Berlin's eastern section includes intelligently produced "boulevard" pieces in their repertoires. West Berlin, on the other hand, has two theaters which specialize in this sort of production, the **Theater am Kurfürstendamm** and the **Komödie**, which are part of the Wölffer entertainment dynasty. Neither, however, have managed to pull off a production which could persuade the genre's dyed-in-the-wool opponents that boulevard theater isn't by definition stuffy. The audience backs up this impression: Crowds of tourists are carted in on busses so that they can catch a few winks after a day filled with stress of sightseeing. A more aggressive approach was tried out once with Alan Ayckbourn's *From now on* directed by Peter Zadek in 1989, featuring Otto Sander and Susanne Lothar; unfortunately to date it has remained only a fluke. On the other hand, the **Magazin,** an offshoot of these two "old aunties," is a ray of hope. The theater does manage to pull in people who otherwise would have gone to one of the Ku'damm cinemas.

Beyond the Big-Time: Off-Theater

During the past 15 years many independent groups have come into being and disappeared again, since only few have managed to hold their ground and drum up a regular financial support. Among the more durable "off" stages are the **Theater zum Westlichen Stadthirschen**, the **Transformtheater**, the **Zan Pollo Theater** and the **Freie Theateranstalt Berlin**. The latter is an exceptional phenomenon, having put on well over 1000 performances of *Ich bin's nicht, Adolf Hitler ist es gewesen* (*It wasn't me, it was Adolf Hitler*). Most of the other independent groups have no performance space of their own, and only few of them are up to the task of creating good, unconventional or even daringly experimental theater.

Cultural activities not closely connected to the state were always suspect to the GDR's regime, therefore independent troups have only now begun to spring up in the city's eastern section. One of the trail blazers is the **Zinnober** troupe, another the **Theater unterm Dach**. The Kreuzberg address, Hasenheide 54, houses three independent troupes simultaneously: the **Etage**, the **Stükke** troupe, and the **Fliegendes Theater**. They also present excellent pieces by out-of-towners. The **bat-Studiotheater** in Prenzlauer Berg is, of course, hardly an off-theater, nonetheless it embodies all of the charming characteristics of the independent groups. Student directors do most of the productions, and graduates of the Ernst Busch school give high-quality performances.

It is evident with each performance that unseasoned but enthusiastic young theater people are plying their trade here. One of the few productions of Brecht attempted in the GDR in which the directors were not paralyzed with awe for the master was done at the bat with the assistance of the professionals Peter Schroth and Peter Kleinert. The bat (*Berliner Arbeiter* (worker) *und Studententheater*) originated in 1961, when Wolf Biermann set up self-regulated *subotniks* with workers and students who wanted to do

performances as an independent group. However, their very first première was forbidden, and the Communist GDR regime expropriated the workers' theater.

Theater for Children and Adults

The **Grips** is an independent (free) but regularly supported group. Since the end of the sixties, it has been brewing up a powerful blend of children's and youth productions. Its musical *Linie 1* (Line 1) made it world famous. It is dedicated to political problems such as youth unemployment, alienation and estrangement in the big city, environmental protection, as well as historic topics such as Germany's infamous Nazi past.

Several members of the ensemble were displeased with the agitating style of the Grips theater, which is setting out to shape minds. They started their own group, the **Theater Rote Grütze** (refer-

ring to a fruit pudding). Indeed, they deal with society problems such as the abuse of children in the family, however they don't give their themes an abstract and general treatment, but rather begin by examining the psychic consequences for both children and adults. Sexual education is also a favorite of the theater; many pieces want to encourage audience participation.

In addition to these two well-known theaters, there is a good number of other independent troups of the Berlin's whipper-snappers offering entertainment and information to children and young-at-heart adults. This of course not only includes numerous puppet and marionette theaters, but also known names such as the **Klecks-Theater** of Neukölln.

Naturally the theaters are all competing for the public's favor. Competition enlivens not only business, but the arts as well. Accordingly Berlin *is* on the right road to becoming the theater metropolis of Europe and a cultural turntable between east and west.

Above: Ubiquitous street theater – an attentive audience is guaranteed.

THEATERS

Berliner Ensemble, Mitte, Bertolt-Brecht-Platz, Tel. 282 31 60.

Deutsches Theater and **Kammerspiele**, Mitte, Schumannstr. 13a/14, Tel. 287 12 21. Tickets: Tel. 287 12 22/26.

Freie Theateranstalt Berlin, Charlottenburg, Klausenerplatz 19, Tel. 321 58 89, 325 50 23.

Freie Volksbühne, Charlottenburg, Schaperstr. 107, Tel. 881 37 42. Ticket reservations Tuesday-Sunday 10 a.m.-2 p.m. and one hour prior to the beginning of the performance.

Hansa-Theater, Tiergarten, Alt-Moabit 48, Tel. 391 44 60.

Hebbel-Theater, Kreuzberg, Stresemannstr. 29, Tel. 251 01 44.

Junges Theater, Kreuzberg, Friesenstr. 14. Entrance Schwiebusser Straße, Tel. 692 87 35.

Kleines Theater, Steglitz, Südwestkorso 64, Tel. 821 30 30. Ticket sales Tuesdays-Fridays 6-8 p.m. and one hour prior to the beginning of the performance.

Komödie, Charlottenburg, Kurfürstendamm 206, Tel. 882 49 41.

Magazin, Charlottenburg, Kurfürstendamm 206, Tel. 882 10 72.

Maxim Gorki Theater und Studiobühne, Mitte, Am Festungsgraben 2, Tel. 208 27 83.

Renaissance-Theater, Charlottenburg, Hardenbergstr. 6, Tel. 312 42 02.

Schaubühne am Lehniner Platz, Wilmersdorf, Kurfürstendamm 153, Tel. 89 00 23.

Theater am Kurfürstendamm, Charlottenburg, Kurfürstendamm 209, Tel. 882 49 41.

Theatermanufaktur, Hallesches Ufer 32, Tel. 251 09 41. Ticket sales Tuesday-Sunday from 2-8 p.m.

Tribüne, Charlottenburg, Otto-Suhr-Allee 18-20, Tel. 341 26 00.

Vagantenbühne, Charlottenburg, Kantstr. 12a, Tel. 312 45 29. Ticket sales Mondays 10 a.m.-4 p.m., Tuesdays-Saturdays 10 a.m.-7 p.m., Sundays and public holidays 5-7 p.m.

Volksbühne am Rosa-Luxemburg-Platz, Mitte, Rosa-Luxemburg-Platz, Tel. 282 89 78.

OFF-THEATERS

bat-Studiotheater, Mitte, Rosa-Luxemburg-Platz, Tel. 442 79 96.

Die Etage, Kreuzberg, Hasenheide 54, Tel. 691 20 95.

The independent theater companies **Stükke** (Tel. 692 32 39) and **Fliegendes Theater** (Tel. 692 21 00) show performances here.

Freie Theateranstalt Berlin, Charlottenburg, Klausener Platz 19, Tel. 321 58 89.

Garn-Theater, Kreuzberg, Katzbachstr. 19, Tel. 786 43 46.

Grips-Theater, Tiergarten, Altonaer Str. 22 (at the U-Bahn station Hansaplatz), Tel. 391 40 04.

Klecks-Kindertheater (Childrens' theater), Neukölln, Schinkestr. 8-9, Tel. 693 77 31.

Modernes Theater Berlin, Schöneberg, Merseburgerstr. 3, Tel. 781 55 04.

Ratibor Theater, Kreuzberg, Cucrystr. 20, Tel. 618 61 99.

Theater am Halleschen Ufer, Kreuzberg, Hallesches Ufer 32, Tel. 251 09 41.

Theaterforum Kreuzberg, Kreuzberg, Eisenbahnstr. 21, Tel. 618 28 05.

tik-Theater im Kino, Friedrichshain, Proskauer Str. 19, Tel. 589 80 13.

Theater o. N., Prenzlauer Berg, Knaackstr. 45; home of the performance group **Zinnober**, Tel. 442 11 26.

Theater Rote Grütze, Kreuzberg, Mehringdamm 51, Tel. 692 66 18.

Theater Schmales Handtuch, Friedrichshain, Frankfurter Allee 91, Tel. 558 46 59.

Theater unterm Dach, Prenzlauer Berg, Dimitroffstr. 101, in the cultural center Kulturhaus Ernst-Thälmann-Park, Tel. 42 40 10 80.

Theater Zerbrochene Fenster, Kreuzberg, Fidicinstr. 3, Tel. 694 24 00.

Theater zum Westlichen Stadthirschen, Kreuzberg, Kreuzbergstr. 37, Tel. 785 70 33.

Zan Pollo Theater, Steglitz, Rheinstr. 45, Tel. 852 20 02.

Zaubertheater Igor Jedlin, Charlottenburg, Roscherstr.7, Tel. 323 37 77.

ADVANCE BOOKING

Berlin Ticket im KaDeWe, department store Kaufhaus des Westens. Schöneberg, Tauentzienstr. 21, Tel. 24 10 28.

Berlin Ticket bei Wertheim, Charlottenburg, Kurfürstendamm 231, Tel. 882 53 54.

Centrum, Charlottenburg, Meinekestr. 25, Tel. 882 76 11.

Concert Concept, Steglitz, Hauptstr. 83, Tel. 852 40 80.

Die Erste, Mitte, Unter den Linden 36, Tel. 223 12 93.

Theater-und Konzertkasse Berliner Morgenpost/City Center, Charlottenburg, Kurfürstendamm 16, Tel. 882 65 63.

Theaterkasse im Europacenter, Schöneberg, Tauentzienstr. 9, Tel. 261 70 51.

Top Ticket, customers' service organized by the theaters' advance booking offices, Tel. 882 70 11.

209

OPERAS, ORCHESTRAS, VARIETY SHOWS, CABARET

Opera Houses

The **Deutsche Oper** may not be considered the most revolutionary of German opera stages, but no one would accuse it of being hackneyed. Director Götz Friedrich has, after all, succeeded in getting young people interested in Wagner with his *Ring of the Nibelungen*. In the eyes of some of the more conservative opera-goers, Friedrich is considered merciless in his tendency to première the operas of contemporary composer Hans Werner Henze. The controversial stagings of Hans Neuenfels, John Dew and Günter Krämer seldom appear in the repertoire, however.

Hitherto, the Deutsche Oper has had greater artistic significance, but the **Deut-**

Above: A performance at the German State Opera on Unter den Linden. Right: The Philharmonic in the Kulturforum.

sche Staatsoper Berlin, the state opera, also referred to as the Lindenoper, has the more beautiful domicile. It is a veritable temple to the muses, created by Knobelsdorff in 1740 in the North German Classical style. Today it stands a good chance of once again resuming its duties as a representative opera house.

Unfortunately, nothing very moving has taken place within this pretty shell for the past few years. Only the cantankerous conductress Ruth Berghaus has drawn a wild cacophony of boos and bravos from the audiences. All hopes are on Daniel Barenboim, who has taken over the musical and artistic direction of the Staatsoper, if the opera is to stand its ground against the Deutsche Oper in the west.

The **Komische Oper**, the Comic Opera, where only German is sung, is one of the most interesting in all of Germany. It became famous because of the work of Walter Felsenstein. Its current standing it owes to the innovative principal director Harry Kupfer. Audiences who are less interested in the actual con-

tent of the operas and prefer applauding the vocal calisthenics of the interpreters aria for aria or who wait with bated breath for the soprano to reach that high C, do not, of course, patronize this particular opera house. Kupfer relies mainly on his youthful ensemble. Any imperfect vocal performance is easily counteracted by the accurate filling of roles according to age, as in Kupfer's cycle of six Mozart operas. The ballet corps under the direction of choreographer Tom Schilling has elevated the Comic Opera to the number one place among Berlin's three opera houses.

On the other hand, Berlin has remained cut off from developments in modern dance. The **Tanzfabrik**, or dance factory, is the only institution that has had any kind of international acclaim in the field of free dance.

Other independent troups include the **Neuköllner Oper** and the **Berliner Kammeroper** (chamber opera), both of whom perform lesser-known works in inspired stagings.

The Philharmonic and other Orchestras

The world famous **Berlin Philharmonics** have gathered much superlative acclaim. This orchestra was born over a hundred years ago, and is considered today one of the world's finest orchestras. It is housed in one of the most beautiful concert halls, the **Philharmonie,** built by Hans Scharoun, inaugurated in 1963. It is probably one of the century's most important constructions and has, to boot, superb acoustics. The tent-like building has been nicknamed "Karajan-Zirkus" after Herbert von Karajan who acted as its music director for decades, and shaped the orchestra's even interpretative style. The musicians also seem to have inherited – by some kind of collective memory – the musical qualities of the ensemble's earlier conductors Hans von Bülow, Arthur Nikisch and Wilhelm Furtwängler. Claudio Abbado, who took over after Karajan's death, places greater emphasis on contemporary works.

The **Berlin Symphony Orchestra** (BSO), whose musical expression was shaped by conductor Kurt Sanderling, is housed in the Schauspielhaus, designed by Schinkel, where Iffland, Jessner and Gründgens made theater history. The Schauspielhaus is used now and then by the **Staatskapelle Berlin**, the orchestra that usually performs in the state opera. Finally there are two orchestras affiliated with Berlin radio stations that frequently travel abroad for guest performances: The **Radio Symphony Orchestra** (RSO) under Vladimir Ashkenazy and the **Rundfunk Sinfonie Orchester Berlin**, from the eastern part of the city.

Music aficionados might even find more than they bargained for during **Berlin Festival** weeks. The event, which takes place in September, has been a part of the cultural scene for over 40 years now. The program usually devotes itself to a single theme, tending to a kind of earnest thoroughness. For example, works of Schönberg and Brahms might be contrastingly played side-by-side. For Berlin and its performing artists, the festival weeks serve as an important meeting point for eastern and western Europe.

The **Arts Academy** (Akademie der Künste) and the **Bethanien Artists House** (Künstlerhaus Bethanien) concentrate their efforts on contemporary music. The **Freunde guter Musik** (friends of good music), on the other hand, confront their audience with radically avant-garde works that, mostly, escape any form of categorization. The organizers of the **Berliner Kabarett-Anstalt** have come up with some intelligent compromises with regard to new music. Every Tuesday they put on a show called **Unerhörte Musik**, or unheard (of) music. Because it is so unheard of, i.e. shocking, the musical works are explained and discussed in a congenial atmosphere.

Right: Variety show in the Friedrichstadtpalast, in the eastern part of Berlin.

Jazz and Rock Scene

Exactly the place where you would expect to find space for some serious boundary crossing has fallen victim to the demands of the dreaded lowest common denominator. At the **Berlin Jazz-Fest**, which is consistently put on in November, the program is largely tailor-made for the stars who just happen to be on a European tour at the time. You rarely discover anything new there. At the **Total Music Meeting** (TMM), jazz musicians gave expression to their protest against the status quo in general – and the established Berlin Jazz Festival in particular – with the medium of free jazz. Today the one-time "anti-festival" is considered a complement to the established one. In the **Quasimodo** jazz-cellar, many international greats of the genre make guest appearances; a portion of the Berliner jazz musicians have found a place to a perform in public at the **Flöz**.

Musicals, Variety Shows and Cabaret

The **Theater des Westens**, situated in a 19th-century palace, has developed into one of the best musical repertory stages in Europe through the efforts of director and choreographer Helmut Baumann. Also, revues and even operettas have been made entertaining, even for those who otherwise would more likely turn up their noses at them. The presentations range from the *Kurt Weill Revue* to *Porgy and Bess* and the captivatingly silly transvestite fairy tale *La Cage aux Folles*. In the eastern section of the city the **Metropol-Theater** is busy covering the catch-up demand for *My Fair Lady* and *West Side Story*. Now it's adjusting to the audiences which have been showing up in the last year and in the future will devote itself entirely to operetta. In general, on those stages in East Berlin which have sold out to plain entertainment a certain philistine tendency is unmistakable. Or-

gies of petty bourgeois conventionality are still held on the stages of the **Friedrichstadtpalast**. The "greatest revue in Europe", as it promotes itself, has improved only marginally, despite new directors and professional support from the US. For people who might enjoy seeing, say, *Strapse und Gänsehaut* ("garters and goosepimples") the much more intimate **Kleine Revue** ("Little Revue") in the Friedrichstadtpalast offers an exciting variety show including some thoroughly erotic numbers around the witching hour.

In the twenties, Berlin was *the* European entertainment metropolis par excellence. There were over 150 variety theaters. Two very different establishments have resuscitated this tradition: the **Wintergarten** and the east Berlin **Variete Chamäleon**. International artists under the direction of the great magician Andre Heller and Roncalli-founder Bernhard Paul present impressive performances: one of the program titles was *Donnerwetter, Tadellos!* (something like "Faultless, by Jove"). The Chamäleon re-

jects the idea of arid reconstructions of the twenties, offering instead a modern and witty variety, presented at the **Hackesche Höfe** with great elan and increasing professionality by groups of young performers. A younger but very popular sister of these two is the **Bar jeder Vernunft im Spiegelzeit**. The Berlin cabaret artist Holger Klotzbach has turned this venue into a Berlin nightscene contender with appearances by scene stars Tim Fischer, Meret Becker and Max Raabe. In the meantime others are daring enough to put on unusually large stage productions: in the Weißes Rößl, performers from the state stages play alongside culture critics and off-stars.

The 40 hobbyist acrobats and clowns of the **UFA-Fabrik** have meanwhile achieved an admirable degree of professionalism. In 1982 the alternative UFA-Circus opened. According to their own advertising, their only predatory animal sits in the ticket booth.

In the twenties, Berlin was also a true metropolis of the political-literary ca-

baret as well. Among the most renowned of these was Max Reinhardt's *Schall und Rauch* (Sound and Fury). In the cellar of the **Theater des Westens**, Trude Hesterberg's cabaret became famed as the "Wild Stage;" Claire Waldoff and Ernst Busch sang Tucholsky chansons in the Kabarett der Komiker (Cabaret of the Comedian) – Kadeko for short.

Nowadays the tone is set in Berlin's cabarets by glib-tonged word rapists like Martin Buchholz, who as a master of the stale political joke has recently become a Berlin institution. Like many other one-man cabarets he appears mostly at the cabaret **Wühlmäuse**.

The best cabaret, inasmuch as it's still truly satirical in the sense of Heinrich Heine ("Wit without seriousness is only a sneeze of the intellect"), is **Die Distel** (The Thistle) in the city's eastern section. And, though it lost its favorite pincushion – the Communist regime – it certainly hasn't lost its spines. Die Distel is refreshingly biased, in stark contrast to the "balanced" cabaret of the **Stachelschweine** (Porcupines). An insider tip for people with a soft spot for crazy thinking is the **Berliner Kabarett-Anstalt** (BKA). Anstalt is a double-entendre: institute or sanatorium, take your choice. In the **Haus der Jungen Talente** (House of Young Talents), **Die Reizzwecken** have their home base. Just like the **Mehringhoftheater**, **the Podewil** is a place for all kinds of productions. Here is the legendary place where rebellious artists from east and west appeared when the house was still under the thumb of the Communists. Entirely new in the city's eastern section is the café-restaurant **Kartoon,** in which semi-pro cabaret artists wait the tables and then, in lieu of dessert, serve up nourishment for the intellect. Perhaps this is a first indication of a renaissance for that mixture of cabaret and amusement locale that was once so typical of the city. Indeed, the Berlin of today is far from having the diversity it then did.

Above: The highly recommendable Berlin cabaret Die Distel in the east of the city.

OPERA AND CONCERTS
VARIETY SHOWS AND CABARET

Opera Houses and Musical Stages

Berliner Musicalbühne, Wilmersdorf, Schaperstr. 24, Tel. 884 230 884. The musical *Shakespeare & Rock 'n Roll* is currently staged here.

Deutsche Oper Berlin, Charlottenburg, Bismarckstr. 35, Tel. 341 02 49.

Friedrichstadtpalast, Mitte, Friedrichstr. 107, Tel. 283 62 474. Ticket sales daily 10 a.m.-6 p.m., Information: Tel. 232 62 203.

Komische Oper, Mitte, Behrenstr. 55-57, Tel. 220 27 61.

Metropol-Theater, Mitte, Friedrichstr. 101/102, Tel. 20 36 41 17, tickets Mon-Thur 10 a.m.-6 p.m.

Staatsoper Unter den Linden, Mitte, Unter den Linden 7, Tel. 20 35 44 94.

Theater des Westens, Charlottenburg, Kantstr. 12, Tel. 31 90 31 93, Advance tickets available in the pavillion opposite the theater.

Concerts featuring Berlin Orchestras

Hochschule der Künste, Charlottenburg; concert hall at Hardenbergstrasse 33, chamber music hall at Fasanenstrasse 1, Tel. 31 85 23 74, advance ticket sales Tue-Fri 3-6.30 p.m., Sat 11 a.m.-2 p.m.

Max-Beckmann-Saal, Wedding, Luxemburger Str. 20, Tel. 457 25 40.

Otto-Braun-Saal (in the Staatsbibliothek – State Library), Tiergarten, Potsdamer Str. 35, Tel. 26 61.

Philharmonie und Kammermusiksaal, Tiergarten, Kulturforum, Matthäikirchstraße 1, Tel. 25 48 80. Ticket sale Monday-Friday 3.30-6 p.m., Saturday, Sunday and public holidays 11 a.m.-2 p.m.

RIAS Berlin, Schöneberg, Kufsteiner Str. 69, Tel. 850 30.

Konzerthaus Berlin, Mitte, Gendarmenmarkt. Visitors' service in the courtyard behind the theater. Tel. 20 90 21 05.

Schloss Friedrichsfelde, Lichtenberg, Am Tierpark 125, Tel. 513 81 42. Ticket sales Tuesday-Friday 11 a.m.-1 p.m. and 2-5 p.m., Saturday 10 a.m.-1 p.m. and 2-5 p.m. Ticket office at the palace entrance of the Zoo.

SFB (Radio Free Berlin); concerts in the large and small broadcasting studio; Charlottenburg, Haus des Rundfunks, Masurenallee 8-14, advance ticket sales in the SFB-Pavilion, Mon, Tue and Fri 9 a.m.-1 p.m. and 2-5 p.m., Wed 2-8 p.m., Tel. 30 31 11 23.

Jazz / Rock / Contemporary Music

Akademie der Künste, Tiergarten, Hanseatenweg 10, Tel. 30 00 70.

Alabama, Wedding, Genter Str. 65, Tel. 453 69 52, blues, jazz, rock music.

A-Trane, Charlottenburg, Bleibtreustr, 1, Tel. 313 25 50. Popular jazz bar with excellent acoustics, featuring famous jazz musicians.

Eierschale I – Landhaus Dahlem, Zehlendorf, Podbielskiallee 50, Tel. 832 70 97. Jazz.

Eierschale II an der Gedächtniskirche, Charlottenburg, Rankestr. 1, Tel. 882 53 05. Jazz.

Flöz, Wilmersdorf, Nassauische Str. 37, Tel. 861 10 00.

Künstlerhaus Bethanien, Kreuzberg, Mariannenplatz 2, Tel. 614 80 10.

Loft, Schöneberg, Nollendorfplatz 5, Tel. 66 83 44 65.

Metropol, Schöneberg, Nollendorfplatz 5, Tel. 216 41 22. Rock and pop concerts.

Tacheles e.V., Mitte, Oranienburger Str. 53-56, Tel. 282 61 85, unusual live concerts.

Quasimodo, Charlottenburg, Kantstr. 12a, Tel. 312 80 86. Jazz sessions.

Variety Shows / Dance / Cabaret

Bei jeder Venunft, Wilmersdorf, (tent on the parking deck of the Freie Volksbühne), Schaperstr. 24, Tel. 883 15 82.

Berliner Kabarett-Anstalt (BKA), Kreuzberg, Mehringdamm 32-34, Tel. 251 01 12.

Chamäleon Varieté, Mitte, Rosenthaler Str. 40/41, Tel. 282 71 18. Vaudeville stage in an old cinema hall.

Die Distel, Mitte, Friedrichstraße 101, Tel. 200 47 04.

Die Reizzwecken, Mitte, (Podewil), Klosterstr. 68-70, Tel. 240 32 25.

Kama-Theater, Kreuzberg, Friesenstr. 14, Tel. 692 87 35. Private music theater with good house productions.

Kartoon, Mitte, Französische Str. 24, Tel. 229 93 05.

Mehringhof-Theater, Kreuzberg, Gneisenaustr. 2a, Tel. 691 50 99.

Scheinbar, Schöneberg, Monumentenstr. 9, Tel. 784 55 39, cabaret.

Die Stachelschweine, Charlottenburg, Europa-Center, Tel. 261 47 95, satirical cabaret.

Tanzfabrik, Kreuzberg, Möckernstr. 61, Tel. 786 58 61.

Tempodrom, Tiergarten, In den Zelten, Tel. 394 40 45.

UFA-Fabrik, Tempelhof, Viktoriastr. 10-18, Tel. 752 80 85.

Unart, Oranienstr. 163, Tel. 614 20 70. Absurdly comical dance theater, changing program.

Wintergarten, Tiergarten, Potsdmer Str. 96, Tel. 262 70 70/261 60 60.

Die Wühlmäuse, Wilmersdorf, Nürnbergerstr. 33, corner Lietzenburger Str., Tel. 213 70 47.

It is advisable to book tickets for all above mentioned stages at least a few days in advance. **Advance booking agencies** see guidepost page 209.

FILM STUDIOS AND BIG SCREENS

Once a year, in the midst of the murky Berlin February, black sunglasses suddenly start turning up on the street scene. They are the unmistakable sign of the international film jet-set, who invade the city for ten days during the International Film Festival. The one or two film stars, directors and a gigantic retinue of PR people arouse in the city the deceptive feeling that it is again a major film industry metropolis. Certainly, the **Berlinale**, as the festival performance is casually referred to, has evolved into one of the major film festivals since its founding in 1951. However, as is true for the other major European festivals in Cannes and Venice, Berlin suffers from the general feebleness of the European film and the outright bankrupty of the German

Above: Taking a break between shots during on-location filming in Berlin.

cinema. The **Forum des Jungen** (newer) **Films**, established in 1971, did not change the situation much: The works of unknown directors were well-meaningly accepted, but the broader public was more interested in productions from the dream factories in Hollywood. Nonetheless, the festival *is* an important event, especially since you are more likely to discover unusual and gripping small productions in Berlin than in Cannes, Venice or Hollywood.

Within the framework of the festival some 800 films are shown in Berlin's cinemas. The number of screens available has fallen dramatically since 1945, from some 200 then to 87 in the west and 21 in the east today. At any rate, altogether they add up to almost 30,000 seats, thus making Berlin Germany's cinema capital. Nonetheless, these figures appear rather modest in comparison with the cinemas during the twenties. In 1932 one could choose from among 358 cinemas. The major movie houses, in which – now as then – the premières are run (sometimes even with the director and actors present) are located on the Kurfürstendamm (see p. 69).

Film City Berlin

There was a time when film history was made in Berlin's studios. The pictures learned how to walk in Pankow, when the brothers Emil and Max Skladanowsky began experimenting with the bioscope beginning in 1892. In 1900, Berlin's first film producer, Oskar Messter, took Berlin's movie houses by storm with his silent films.

Beginning in 1919, the German film industry developed a style of its own in Berlin based on Expressionism on the stage and in literature. Famous examples are Robert Wiene's *Das Cabinet des Dr. Caligari* and Fritz Murnau's equally bizarre *Nosferatu*. In the mid-twenties this style was extended to portray the extremity of a modern, technologized world, as in Fritz Lang's *Metropolis* (1926).

The model for these and other films was partly Berlin's babylonian vivacity, as reflected in Walter Ruttmann's *Berlin, die Sinfonie einer Großstadt* (1927) or social criticism as in *Mutter Krausen's Fahrt ins Glück* (1929). At the beginning of the thirties, German film was a big export success; 52 percent of all foreign films in the USA came from Germany – from Berlin at that! However, with the advent of the Nazi regime German film collapsed. The majority of directors had already emigrated to the United States. Films shot during the war were either harmless comedies, musicals or morale boosters. After the war, a new German cinema only started up hesitantly. With *Die Mörder sind unter uns* or *Die Sünderin* (both of them featuring Hildegard Knef), Wolfgang Staudte remained a maverick. And, after a brief renewal of the cinema in the sixties, films like *Berlin Alexanderplatz* or *Der Himmel über Ber-*

lin only appeared to be blazing a new trail – they turned out to be exceptions.

Today there are the **German Academy of Television and Film** in Berlin and the **College for Film and Television** in Potsdam as well as the **Deutsche Kinemathek** and the **Arsenal**, its affiliated cinema house. All of these institutions offer the opportunity to get good training. In addition, the Senate's plans to construct (for 60 million DM) the **Filmhaus Berlin** out of the ruins of the **Esplanade** on Potsdamer Platz could give the city a new impulse – even though the realization of this idea has been repeatedly shelved. However, the few German directors who have achieved international success unfortunately prefer to work abroad, and producers prefer to spend their money in Munich.

While waiting for a new beginning, the studios are slowly decaying, consumed by their own myth. Whether the acquisition of the **DEFA studios** in Potsdam-Babelsberg by a major French investor will secure the future of Berlin as a filmmaking city is still uncertain. All the same the star director Volker Schlöndorff has taken over the management of the new Babelsberg studios, which are intended to tie into the good old days of the UFA studios. However the artist sees himself in the unwilling role of the broker who is forced to canvas from door to door just to have the films made in Babelsberg and thus bring in the big money.

The once so proud studios, which cover an area of 43 hectares, and include the largest inventory of props in the world (over 600,000 pieces), survive today on on television and video productions. So far only one major movie has been made here: The Neverending Story III, not exactly an advertisement for Berlin. Perhaps Babelsberg will join the ranks of the minor Berlin film studios, such as the **CCC-Ateliers**, the **Havelland Studios** or the **Adlershof**. The great days of the Berlin film seem past forever.

THE ART SCENE: TRADE AND TRIBULATION

Berlin's gallery landscape, which has weathered a lot of change through the storms of history, is distinguished today primarily for its almost incomparable diversity. Its perpetual metamorphosis is its most impressive characteristic. One thing is guaranteed: The galleries of Berlin have something for every taste and pocketbook. Since the reunification of the two Germanies this has become even more true than ever before.

Really interesting artists from Leipzig, Dresden or the districts of the old capital of the GDR are making their way to those places which are still intact or the places where the developments have remained on home soil; where things are not being busily imitated, rather where individual ability and knowledge is demonstrated; where an entirely special life experience

*Preceding pages: Summer lunch break.
Above: The Berlin artist J. Grützke.*

and standard of living has survived, namely in East Berlin.

Berlin galerists are still, even after reunification, complaining about the insular location of the city, the money which the customers do not have, and the remoteness of its position on the edge of eastern Europe far from the major European and American art exhibitions. The conversation still revolves around the importance of Frankfurt, Zürich and Chicago. People are a little overkeen to complain that the city is dead.

Here, in the metropolis of the future, the members of the Association of German Galerists squabble over appearances, feuds are cultivated because one galerist allegedly holds a very negative opinion of another. At the same time the art scene has a liveliness which is due to the constant supply of new faces from the master classes and the exchange of artists. To find out how good they are, go to the changing exhibitions at the **daad-Galerie** (Tiergarten, Kurfürstenstraße 58, Tel. 261 36 40).

What is apparently a disadvantage – the sheer volume of work – should change into the advantage of having in stock precisely what the interested party in question is looking for. The only thing you need in the this city of art is what people apparently have the least of: time. And since time is money, art lovers can leisurely look at pictures in those galleries – and with a bit of patience might find some genuinely new and promising talents.

Galleries in East Berlin

As thoroughly worn out as the comparisons between the milieus of Prenzlauer Berg and Kreuzberg may be, it does not make it any less true that here, just as there, a special lifestyle exists, expressed by peoples' unbroken will to realize their own wishes. The Oderberger Strasse, formerly located hard up against the edges of the "anti-fascist defensive wall," cut off and degraded to a dead-end street, can more or less be thought of as a model example of such conceptions. In this "biotope", which has luckily up to now been neglected by official interests, four or five galleries have established themselves: The **Zentrale PGH Glühende Zukunft** (Nr. 17; the name means glowing future) or the **Galerie OderForm** (Nr. 27). In a tiny storefront – once used as a stock room – the **Galerie am Dreieck** (Nr. 2-6) was established as the first private gallery. It was opened, designed and is run by painter Wolfgang Krause, who still maintains his studio next door. His target audience hasn't changed significantly, however, it has greatly expanded as he consistently maintained contact with artists who tried to realize their own concepts and ideas even if they were in crass opposition to the state-supported arts. The well-attended openings in Krause's gallery naturally attract a lively and openminded crowd, and these gatherings always tend to spread out onto the broad sidewalk. It's hardly surprising that Wolfgang Krause primarily likes to show the works of artists whose scope is not strictly defined by the canvas, such as avantgarde artists using the media of performance, video or installations to express their ideas in totally unconventional ways.

Diagonally opposite the Galerie am Dreieck, Johannes Zielke, one of East Berlin's best-known gallery owners, used to cultivate his life's dream. Unfortunately the sharp rise in rents forced him to move to a new location in Berlin-Mitte where he now offers a brilliant meeting place for artists as he did before in Prenzlauer Berg (Gipsstr. 7, Tel. 282 98 02). At the end of 1991 two new galleries opened here specializing in artists from eastern Germany. The **Galerie T&A-Edition** (Wallstr. 60, Tel. 275 29 49) does not shrink before the challenges of modern art, and it is even trying its hand in the field of art consulting. A short way away, two women opened a gallerie, **leo.coppi**, (Wallstr. 90, Tel. 200 41 29) where they offer artworks at reasonable prices.

Besides these galleries, the former State Galleries in the city's eastern precincts are following the downhill course of liquidation. Hardly comparable with the communal galleries, they were places of unencumbered effortlessness. Here the Good, the Beautiful and the True were cultivated. Here the colors of the flowers were discussed and landscapes revelled in, which were supposed to be theoretically beautiful, but were perfectly unattainable from a practical standpoint. This is not meant to damn the work of those who made a sincere effort to bring the proletariat of a country a bit of culture. And, obviously there's no need to quarrel over whether creativity should be state-supported. Nevertheless, the gallery-landscape will not be decisively truncated by the elimination of several establishments for the exhibition of "positive humanity."

In contrast, one has to take pleasure at how much initiative it takes to present art over which opinion might differ, as, for example, in the gallery of **Dr. Christiane Müller** (Mitte, Clara-Zetkin Str. 90, Tel: 236 82 63), a gallery offering womens' art exclusively, but where anyone, male or female, can scrutinize the female brush-stroke. Ideas from east and west are fused together here, and cooperation with the commercial galleries from the Kurfürstendamm is also sought and found.

Galleries in West Berlin

The **Galerie Vier** (Prenzlauer Berg, Wilhelm-Pieck-Straße 25, Tel: 437 05 06) is working in cooperation with the **Galerie Wewerke-Wiess** (Charlottenburg, Pariser Str. 63, Tel: 882 66 39). They are able partners without the compulsive effort required to be compliant to

the needs of the other. It might be that in his gallery – in contrast to such "joint ventures" – East Berliner Johannes Zielke is a dreamer, even an amateur, though in this case only with the connotation of enthusiast. One thing is certain: He has brought with him the energy necessary to transform his dream into reality, and he possesses enough passion to allow comparisons with the West Berliner Rudolph Springer (**Galerie Springer**, Charlottenburg, Fasanenstr. 13, Tel: 313 90 88). He is one of the small number of gallery owners in Berlin who has steadfastly continued to work in the Fasanenstrasse during the last 45 years. Unimpressed by passing fashions, trusting only his own standards of quality, this gallery owner still mourns the passing of the days when things revolved more around art than money.

Times have changed indeed; nowadays there are plenty of galleries where one can stand longer than a half-hour in front of a new painting in order to gain a full grasp of it. This is the amount of time you

Above: K. Mühlenhaupt and his sculpture.
Right: Renovation á la Kreuzberg.

need to come to grips with the works not on sale which are either painted or perhaps only projected on the walls of the **Galerie Fahneman** (Charlottenburg, Fasanenstr. 61, Tel: 883 98 97).

On the whole, the range and breadth of Berlin's gallery landscape can be experienced in the Fasanenstrasse as well as in the neighboring streets. Located there are also the gallery of **Anselm Dreher** (Charlottenburg, Pfalzburger Str. 80, Tel: 883 52 49), the **Galerie Georg Nothelfer** (Charlottenburg, Uhlandstr. 184, Tel. 881 44 05) and the **Galerie Nikolaus Sonne** (Charlottenburg, Kantstr. 138, Tel: 312 23 55).

These are galleries which represent – with a certain commitment – artists who, on the one hand, are popular like Andy Warhol at **Sonne's**, or thoroughly experimental, like Jochen Gerz at **Dreher's**. You will really be well taken care of at these places, and you can rely on their professional knowledge. These are places that also cater to unconventional tastes. Obviously this applies just as much to those galleries that sell paintings perfectly suiting exquisite furniture, among them the **Raab Galerie** (Schöneberg, Potsdamer Str. 58; Tel: 261 60 98). They have to be modern, but they may be exciting as well. The people there know what they have acquired and can display it without hesitation.

This society of galleries wouldn't be complete without **Eva Poll** (Tiergarten, Lützowplatz 7, Tel. 261 70 91) who remained loyal to realists like Ulrich Baehr or represented Schang Hutter's delicate wood sculptures. She also looks after the daughter of Fred Thieler, H. C. Gabriel, just as she does with several painters who already made their departure from the GDR quite a while ago. You will find Russians there who have had a broad public in Berlin for a long time. And if you should want to purchase even more geographically defined art after surveying this vast selection, you will also find

it, if you ask for Latvian artists, for example, represented in the gallery **InterArt** (Schöneberg, Potsdamer Str. 93, Tel: 262 88 10).

The Eccentric and Grotesque

The architecture gallery **Aedes** (Charlottenburg, Tel, 312 25 98 in the S-Bahn arcade at the Savignyplatz is a gem in its own right. In one of the arches you will find an exposition that deals with more than just Berlin's future architectural development. Models provide information on the ideas of both students and professors. It is possible to gain a real understanding from these models. Drawings illlustrate their aesthetic concepts, and the adjacent café is by no means the worst place to mull over and discuss the possiblities of these interesting artistic designs.

The combination of café and gallery, incidentally, is popping up more and more often. The economic pressures involved in financing the exhibition spaces

223

as well as providing the artists with a monthly existence – just running the gallery, with the constant maintenance of the salespeople and buyers – forces owners like Manfred Giesler with his **Café Mora** (Kreuzberg, Großbeerenstr. 75a, Tel: 785 05 85) or Heidi Springfeld in the **Galerie Neue Räume** (Kreuzberg, Lindenstr. 39, Tel 251 48 12) to take up side-occupations by transforming their cafés into extensions of their galleries by hanging artworks on their walls for the edification of the guests.

The painter Dieter Fenz and the sculptor Michael Schuh have come up with a new and unusual way of combining a café and a cultural experience. Their **Café Phillis** (Tiergarten, Pohlstr. 70, Tel. 261 90 60, daily from 10 am – 2 am) attracts a variegated crowd of cocktail hounds, art fans and coffeehause intellectuals. It is a bunch that according to Dieter Fenz should be "lively, cosmo-

politan and a little off-color." Fenz and his partner spent years working away at the dilapidated junk store ultimately turning it into a chic cultural meeting place. The bar is downstairs, the gallerie upstairs. Once a week there is a special show, a jazz concert, a lecture, a performance or the opening of an exhibition.

Anybody wishing to move beyond all the popular conception of what a gallery is and confess to the consumption of cheap art should feed a few coins into the **Blumenautomat** (flower vending-machine) at Dresdner Straße 9, in Kreuzberg: For five marks this machine will provide that unusual gift you needed for that birthday party you forgot you were invited to.

If you prefer unusual combinations, you can also make your acquisition in the **Gelbe Musik** (Charlottenburg, Schaperstr. 11, Tel. 211 39 62) for a slightly higher price. Records and scores from visual artists are the unusual round-up of this gallery, which operates just as spectacularly as it does reclusively.

Above: Living with art on an everyday basis in the streets of Berlin.

On the other hand, two other galleries are rather aggressive in their handling of the remains of a great past. The photography guild, which once had its home in Berlin, has to be satisfied with two addresses at the moment. In the eastern section of the city the **Fotogalerie am Helsingforser Platz** (Friedrichshain, Tel. 588 62 13) still has its lens cap off, while in the western section of town only Ernst Volland with his **Galerie Voller Ernst** (Schöneberg, Innsbrucker Str. 37, Tel. 782 68 03) provides the public with primarily humorous photographs.

One of the most unusual places imaginable for an art exhibition could certainly have originated only in Berlin, where, as must be obvious by now, anything goes. The artery beginning in Steglitz which feeds the inner-city *Autobahn* runs parallel to the S-Bahn. The bus lines which used to operate here (since the Berliners couldn't use the S-Bahn during the construction phase of the artery) required the construction of a covered concrete staircase near the Steglitzer traffic circle. Since the re-connection of the train line and the discontinuation of the bus service, the staircase has stood empty.

So, the **Galerie Treppenhaus** (stairway) was installed here (Steglitz, Albrechtstr. 129, Tel. 792 84 29) which has caused artists to show up in Steglitz, a precinct which is not exactly famous for its activities in the field of art and culture.

Berlin and Literature

In the 20s almost 1000 publishing houses were located in Berlin and one quarter of all publications in German came from Berlin.

Today there are less than 200, and those mostly small publishing houses. Publishing novels today doesn't bring in big money; more important are the large scientific and education publishers, including Julius Springer, Walter deGruyter, Cornelsen and Langenscheidt who together publish one fifth of all German-language scientific works.

Many of the traditional, large publishing houses are returning. For example, after reunification Rowohlt opened up a branch publishing house in Berlin which specializes in Eastern European culture and literature. And one of the riskiest new ventures, by Klaus Wagenbach, has turned into a publishing house of renown. This, together with the rather garish *edition dia*, has maintained West Berlin's old reputation of being an interesting mixture of high culture and the off-scene.

At the same time in the east of the city all the major publishing houses of the former GDR have lost readers as well as authors. Many of these houses are still fighting to survive. Publishing in Berlin is a modest business and the great writers have stayed away but there is no lack of opportunities for literary discussion.

There is, for example, the **Literaturhaus Berlin** founded in 1986 (Charlottenburg, Fasanenstr. 23, Tel. 882 65 52) with its literary readings, moderated discussions and exhibitions.

Even the venerable **Literarische Colloquium Berlin** (Am Sandwerder 5, 816 99 60) which used to be the meeting place for *Gruppe 47* is still a place where heated literary debates take place between authors, who sometimes live in this elegant villa at the Wannsee too. Every year the city rents rooms to young writers who have received scholarships.

And there is the **Buchhändlerkeller** (Charlottenburg, Carmerstr. 1, Tel. 31 01 51), where almost all German authors have read from their first works, supervised by multi-talent K.P. Herbach. Traditionally readings take place here on Thursday evenings.

Literaturwerkstatt Berlin (Majakowski-Ring 46/47, Tel. 482 47 65) opened fairly recently. Stop by, maybe you will be there when Berlin's next great literary talent is discovered!

225

THE ALTERNATIVE SCENE

Almost everybody in Berlin complains about the "scene," but nobody, allegedly, is a part of it. The "scene" is always the *others*. Nevertheless, there is some concern making the rounds that it could dissolve into thin air, that the little niches in which it ekes out its subsidized existence might dry up, because the Senate is turning off the money-faucet.

For all that, the "scene" – which fills the Joe Sixpacks of Berlin with fear – has since become quite tame. In fact the "scene" is dead. Berlin, stronghold of the "scene," rang in the era of the alternative conformist already ten years ago.

How it all began

At the end of the '60's, when the **extra-parliamentary opposition (APO)** was at its zenith, the alternative scene

Above: Student leader Rudi Dutschke in 1968. Right: Punkers with their favorite pets.

was going for the jugular of convention. They made a ruckus in an effort to banish the stench of the Adenauer era from peoples' living rooms. At the head of the pack was the **Socialist German Student League** (SDS), then headed by Rudi Dutschke. They took to the streets in a broad offensive against the national emergency laws (*Notstandsgesetze*), for democracy at the universities, the liberation of the so-called Third World, and against the Vietnam War. In Berlin, the tension, which had already been long dammed-up, exploded during the 1968 International Vietnam Congress.

12,000 adherents of the SDS participated in its concluding demonstrations against the USA's war in Vietnam. The Springer Press mobilized against the the protesters and proclaimed Rudi Dutschke an enemy of the people. On April 11th, 1969, one Jürgen Bachmann fired shots at Dutschke – his injuries brought about his untimely death ten years later. There was a spontaneous reaction to the attempted assassination, committed by

Bild-reader Bachmann. The same evening, thousands of students blocked deliveries of the *Bild* newspaper.

With this act they triggered a wave of violence that washed over other major cities. West Berlin became the driving force of the students' movement. However, slowly the protest generation withdrew from the universities into grassroots and trade union groups. Grandiose plans for a world revolution faded in favor of more modest changes in daily life. Self-administered day-care centers and youth centers were established in this way, as well as the – at that time exotic, but today entirely normal – *Wohngemeinschaften* (communes).

House-to-house Battles

In July 1971 the first successful squat began at the Mariannenplatz in Kreuzberg, in the **Georg-von-Rauch-Haus**. The squatters wrote: "Hands off the Rauchhaus, otherwise City Hall will go up in smoke." (*Rauch*=smoke). How-

ever, the real wave of squatting began eight years later, when the housing shortage became intolerable in West Berlin, while at the same time 20,000 apartments stood empty. The majority of these were the objects of speculation by owners who simply allowed the buildings to decay and were awaiting demolition permits so that they could erect new apartment blocks, and then demand enormous rents. Within two years 170 buildings were occupied, and at the high point of the movement the number reached 281. The squatters, who were in favor of upkeep, waged a veritable war against the speculating landlords. Since the beginning of the eighties the street battles have had less and less to do with political protest. Every May 1st, the so-called chaotics celebrate for their own amusement a "street slaughter-festival", which alludes to an old country custom when pigs were slaughtered and their meat eaten.

In 1981 Hans-Jochen Vogel, the governing Social-Democratic mayor at that time, drafted a set of rules which still apply today. According to these, the Senate makes a difference between the squatters who are willing to negotiate and those who refuse to do so. The ones willing to negotiate are offered rental contracts. The Senate speculated that the *occupation* mentality might eventually metamorphose into an *owner* mentality. The Berlin rules were also taken up by the Christian Democrats, who won the election in May 1981, partly as a reaction against the squatters. In the meantime virtually all squatters have made tenancy agreements with the city districts and renovated the houses by their own efforts and Senate funding.

A new generation has grown up which accuses the old squatters – meanwhile owners themselves – of being speculators. Thus, the 150 occupants of the oldest self-adminstered buildings in Berlin had to look on as their unused attics were stormed by 20 young people in April, 1990. After a couple of days the building owners called in the police.

Newly Squatted Houses in East Berlin

Endless re-runs, or something entirely new? In the eastern section of the city there was a new edition of the squatters' movement in the spring of 1990. With 25,000 unoccupied apartments in a situation of unclarified ownership – a legacy of the former Communist state – the squatters forced their way in. The scattered remains of the West Berlin scene and their younger successors also made their way to the east. Along with them came all sorts young people from Bavaria and Baden-Württemberg, who were revealed – with relish – by the media as being "sons of the middle class with daddy's money in their pockets".

The squatters from the east rapidly became a minority. 126 buildings were oc-

cupied, the largest part of them in the Friedrichshain district, the remainder in Prenzlauer Berg and Lichtenberg.

The focal point of the protests was the Mainzer Strasse, a block of 13 occupied buildings in a "state of emergency" with sofas and tables on the sidewalks, information cafés and in-house militias. The squatters had high-flying plans: They wanted to combine living and working together in one building with self-managed alternative businesses in the back yards and womens' apartments in the front buildings. The city council offered the squatters who were willing to negotiate individual rental contracts. However, there was division in the "scene", and a portion refused to negotiate. On November 14, 1990, the situation escalated; squatters, autonomist elements and police wound up in a bloody street battle when the Senate decided to have the houses forcibly vacated. Since then the squatter scene is just another chapter in the history of East Berlin too.

Alternative culture: A Village Idyll

Pragmatism is perhaps the decisive catchword to best describe the changes in the squatters' scene. Great ideals are no longer the primary concern, rather small, concrete projects. Meanwhile, there are some 2500 of these in Berlin, mostly in cultural or social areas. The alternative movement has, over time, moved into every nook and cranny of the general culture. However, even in the public eye the "scene" locations were soon no longer decried as meeting places for rabble-rousers, but were welcomed as spots of color in the grey uniformity of the city, as an appealing attribute for an open-minded Berlin. After reunification, however, many of the projects faced doom since they depended on a steady trickle of subsidies. Not much remains of the original concept of creating an area free of rulership, in which everything was to be

Right: Squatters are no longer part of everyday political and social life in Berlin.

decided with equal voting rights – except for the uniform wages, which many of the projects have retained.

THe **UFA-Fabrik** (Tempelhof, Viktoriastr. 13, Tel. 7 52 80 85) is one of the few projects which is making the challenge of living and working together into a reality. On a plot of land some 18,000 square meters in size, where the UFA films were produced in the twenties, there are now an organic bakery, a circus school, a theater and cinemas, a café, workshops and the residential buildings of the 60-member UFA commune. However, with its recognized cultural offerings the UFA Fabrik has long been part of the establishment. Berlin, as a cultural capital, found the major European Theater Festival which the commune organized in 1988 worthy of a public boast; even the bread from the UFA bakery has become a household word in Berlin which is by all accounts no small feat.

With 227 individual projects the **Mehringhof** (Kreuzberg, Gneisenaustr. 2a, Tel: 691 50 99) is also a major self-administered project with a bookstore, bicycle shop, ecological bank, a *Kneipe* and a theater. Demonstrations are planned in the Mehringhof, discussions are held, and people threatened by legal proceedings consult with each other.

In the former eastern section of the city there is a self-administrated cultural center, the **Tacheles** (downtown, on Oranienburgerstr. 53-56), situated in the **Camera**, which was until 1981 the only program-cinema of the former GDR's capital. During the last five years the Tacheles has developed into the leading address of the alternative art scene. Parties and performances are held, and the rapt people who look on forget that all of this – just like the entire off-scene in the Oranienberger Strasse – is merely an interlude. The Swedish concern which would like to build on the Tacheles site has indicated it is willing to negotiate but sooner or later this ruin will have to be pulled down. Quite possibly the Tacheles will have to go elsewhere, but it will then most probably lose all of its old charm.

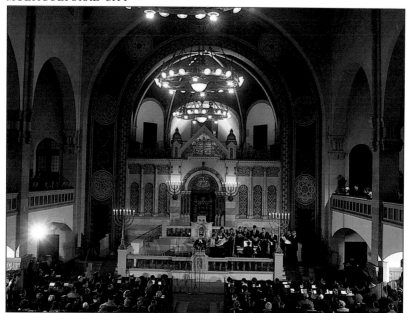

THE MULTICULTURAL CITY

There is no other German city where as many different nationalities live together as in Berlin. This is not just a fact of the recent past, either: The history of Berlin is also the history of waves of immigration that began in the 17th century. At that time it was especially the Huguenots, who, by 1700, numbered 5800 people and composed one-fourth of Berlin's population; in the 18th century about 2000 Bohemians also migrated to the city. Both of these peoples were persecuted for their religion in their native countries. The difficulties the Huguenots and Bohemians had in becoming accepted were rather slight in comparison to the Jews, who emigrated from Vienna to Berlin at the end of the 17th century: The Jews, branded as "murderers of Christ" by the churches, suffered from discrimination and weren't allowed to

Above: The Prenzlauer Berg synagogue.
Right: Turkish Muslim before prayers.

work in most professions. In the fields remaining to them, such as trade and finance, they learned how to find loopholes in the market beyond the reach of the guilds and corporations. In the course of time, however, the economic success, which many of Berlin's Jews achieved, also increased the distrust – and sparked the envy – of the remaining population. The Jews were not given equal rights until 1812, after which they could participate relatively unhindered in Berlin's economic and cultural development. Not only were many well-known Berlin firms founded by Jews, they also produced an above average number of the most progressive artists and scientists of the day.

Toward the end of the 19th century more Jews, mostly poor, came from Russia to Berlin, fleeing the brutal pogroms in their homeland. And, as the last immigrants before World War Two some 300,000 exiled Russians settled in Berlin, although they almost all left the city again after 1923. The Nazi's seizure of power in 1933, with their brutally enforced ideologies and their mass murder, particularly directed against the Jewish people, brought the diversity of religion and nationality in Berlin to an end.

Berlin without the Allies

With its occupation by the victorious powers, Berlin became perforce somewhat more multi-cultural. Of course, at the beginning any contact between the Allied soldiers and the Germans was strictly forbidden. Nonetheless, the needs of both sides brought them closer together. Not only were the long-deprived troops surrounded by the widows of war, but the American GI's were in possession of goods, such as whiskey and cigarettes, that were sorely missed in the devastated city and served as a valuable medium of exchange. The American allies brought about the triumphal advance of the Anglo-American lifestyle. While in Berlin the radio broadcasters continued to slog away with German pop-songs, the programming for the US soldiers by AFN (broadcasting from Zehlendorf to this day) was already lighting quite a fire in their listeners with rock'n'roll music. Any Berlin kid with a claim to being with it only listen to AFN and the British BFBS. Because of the Allies' presence, Berliners were the first to develop enthusiasm for American sports like football, baseball and basketball. When the allied forces left Berlin, despite the festive spirit many Berliners, especially the older, had a lump in their throats. Not only was a chapter in history closed but also many ties of friendship and culture sundered. The 4000 or so apartments which thus became free in West Berlin were moved into by students, and the German armed forces took over the empty allied barracks. In the old US Army cinema, the Outpost, a temporary museum of the allied forces has opened which commemorates this chapter of Berlin history. Its fitting name is

"More than a suitcase remains" (Clay-allee 135, Tel. 32 90 11 53).

Turks and Other Foreign Workers

While the soldiers continue to the present to live in their housing areas, the recruitment of guest workers has left behind an indelible mark on the texture of Berlin's population since the mid seventies. That the integration of Italians and Greeks (of which there are some 9000 of each nationality living in Berlin) is considered particularly successful, is due especially to their home countries, which are members of the European Union and familiar to the many Germans who vacation there. A large number of people who came as simple laborers have worked their way up the ladder, and are now respected businessmen. Berlin's second-strongest group of foreigners, the roughly 34,000 ex-Yugoslavs, have a harder time as non-EU citizens. Permits for residency and employment are more complicated to obtain.

The largest group of foreigners in Berlin, the some 128,000 Turkish people, still face a struggle for acceptance. In contrast to the other immigrants, they are Muslims and bound by the strict rules of the Koran. Especially the first generation arrivals, who have often come from remote villages of Anatolia, are conspicuous because of their way of life, which has been shaped by an unbroken patriarchal tradition. They have tried to preserve their cultural identity by residing close to each other in districts such as Kreuzberg, Wedding and Neukölln.

As a result, the Turkish minority composes 19 percent of the population in Kreuzberg. A typical infrastructure has also developed there: Besides Turkish restaurants there are Turkish banks, physicians, travel agencies and countless shops. The religious involvement of the Turks is much less conspicuous than their economic activities.

Above: Turkish children. Right: Monk at the Buddhist monastery in Frohnau.

In Berlin, Islam has risen to become the second-largest religious community after Christianity, even though the city's roughly 35 mosques are often hidden away in former factories and apartments above stores. Since the Turkish community has neither been able to reach agreement among themselves nor with the Senate on the matter of religious instruction in public schools, many children and youths attend Koranic schools in the afternoons after their regular classes. This means that the second and third generations of young Turks people, who, as far as their interests go, see themselves more as Berliners than as foreigners, are thrust yet again into a separate role. Young Turkish people experience more than enough exclusion in their day-to-day lives. Their opportunities on the job market are fewer; even an innocent visit to a discotheque may often run aground on the resistance of the doorman. It's no wonder that many young Turks withdraw in frustration and sometimes found more-or-less aggressive youth gangs.

Discriminated Minorities in the East

In contrast to the western part of the city, the presence of foreigners has hardly had any impact on daily life in East Berlin, or in the former GDR as a whole. The approximately 11,000 guest workers – primarily from Vietnam, although also from Angola and Mozambique – who were working in the eastern part of the city on bilateral contracts, lead isolated lives in cramped apartment complexes. The "peoples' friendships" decreed by the GDR regime existed only for official occasions. After the opening of the Wall it became clear how damaging this separation had been to the psyches of many citizens of the former GDR.

With the absence of restrictions, many citizens and right-wing extremist groups that have suddenly sprung up are allowing their resentments to run free. Also, on the official side, labor contracts still in force have been frequently cancelled with little or no notice. After only a few months of "freedom," an increasing number of foreigners left the east. To be sure, several of the youth clubs are making efforts to foster understanding between quite different cultures. However, as long as foreign residents have to fear being attacked by right-wing hoodlums, especially at night, they feel more comfortable in the west. The availability of international culture is also far greater.

Last Hope Berlin: The Refugees

Since the end of the seventies, the increasing number of people seeking asylum here have brought about the formation of new communities of foreigners. Until 1986, the refugees went to West Berlin via Schönefeld Airport, since they didn't need to present a visa for their further travel into West Berlin and the Federal Republic. Until the West managed to get the former GDR to apply stricter regulations, Berlin was the major

gateway to the West, especially for asylum-seekers from the Middle East and Africa.

Since Berlin didn't have much interest in this form of immigration, the applicants' living conditions were made harder during the often several-year-long waiting period for a decision on the petition for asylum.

It will probably be primarily the refugees who determine the composition of nationalities in Berlin in the future as well. A first indication of this already appeared at the beginning of the eighties, as an increasing number of Poles fled to Berlin because it was the closest western city. After the fall of the Wall they were followed by the "consumer tourists" who sought to improve their meager incomes by working illegally or retailing goods purchased in the West. That foreigners are welcome in Berlin – despite the increasing violence of the radical right – is shown by the frequently forgotten but very friendly way different cultures live alongside each other in the city.

SCIENCE AND RESEARCH

During the mid-90s, Berlin's scientific landscape is undergoing a radical change: the old institutions in the East have been dissolved and reintegrated, but the future of Berlin as a center of research is still unclear.

And yet Berlin, like no other city in Germany, can look back on a great scientific tradition: between 1870 and 1933 scientists such as Dr. Rudolf Virchow and the Nobel Prize Laureate Robert Koch worked here. Physicians such as Max Planck, Max von der Laue and Albert Einstein revolutionized the world; Otto Hahn and Lise Meitner did research on radioactivity in Berlin.

Although Berlin has never been one of the old university cities, its modern and enlightened atmosphere has attracted countless scientists since the beginning of the 19th century. However, after twelve years of National Socialism not much remained of this fruitful era, as many Jewish scientists were forced to emigrate or were brutally murdered.

The Mass Universities

Today the unified city of Berlin has a difficult time tieing back into such grand traditions. The two oldest universities in Berlin, the Friedrich Wilhelm University, which was founded in 1810 and today is called Humboldt University, and the Technische Universität (TU), which was founded in 1879, have had to undergo many changes during the course of their history.

Nowadays the TU and the Freie Universität (Free University) represent Berlin's university image. The FU was founded in 1948 by former students of the Humboldt University, who, for political reasons, were personae non gratae.

Right: The Siemens research laboratory, one of the high-tech centers in the city.

Spoonfed with funds from the American Henry Ford Foundation, this copybook university of the Free West turned into a center of the student movement at the end of the 60s.

Today more than 140,000 students – more than a third from West Germany – are enrolled at a total of 82 universities, polytechnics or other institutes of higher education. This makes Berlin the German university capital. But the mass universities, the FU (58,000 students) and the TU (38,000 students) are suffering from cuts and are having a hard time maintaining research and teaching, despite the city's enormous 2.5 billion DM science budget.

By 2003, the two universities must make savings of 135 billion DM and the number of students must be cut back by then to 100,000. As a consequence of Berlin's status as a divided city, some faculties were represented at two or even three universities. They are now being combined.

The Humboldt University (HU) is developing into a relatively small university (21,000 students), after its much-debated political and scientific restructuring program. A lot of people consider it to be a university for the elite.

For a long time Berlin's universities, above all those in the western part of the city, had the reputation of expelling radical students who supposedly were more interested in demonstrating than in studying. But that is not the whole truth: even though the situation at both the Technical and the Free University is catastrophic, the two universities publish more scientific publications than anywhere else in Germany.

Many faculties, such as machine construction and industrial engineering at the TU, or biochemistry and history at the FU, are internationally renowned. Quite a few fields of study, such as culture management or ecotrophy, can only be studied in Berlin.

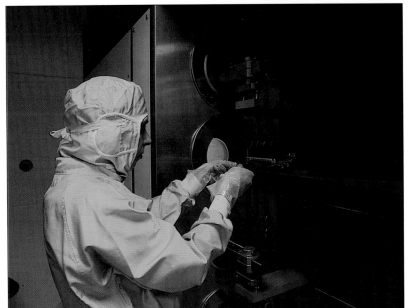

The City and its State-of-the-Art Technology

Meanwhile, almost unnoticed by the public, Berlin has worked its way up to becoming Germany's high-tech capital: in the whole city 50,000 scientists work at 250 different research institutions. The Max Planck Institute and its Hahn Meitner Institute, the Berlin Scientific Center and the German Institute for Economic Research are particularly renowned.

During the early 80s, cooperative projects betweeen state-funded research, universities and industry gave new stimuli to the city. The *Produktionstechnisches Zentrum* (production engineering center) is a classic example of this co-operation.

In the meantime, Berlin has become the German leader in genetic engineering and computer technology: accordingly it was scientists from the Rudolf-Virchow-Klinikum who, in 1994, launched the first treatment of cancer using gene therapy in Germany. And in cooperation with the German chemical firm Schering, the FU started its first open-air reseach with genetically manipulated plants. Berlin is also the leading location for laser and materials research.

The institutions of the former DDR regime, which were "wound down", will play a leading role in the future of Berlin as research capital. Both private and state institutions are benefiting from the huge potential of the former Research Academies of the DDR.

At least two places in Berlin are demonstrating what research may be like in the next century: at the Research and Technology Park Adlershof, 160 companies and institutes are jointly testing new technologies. And at the Innovations Park in Wuhlheide research and industry have come together in innumerable projects. The construction and testing of new solar collectors is only one example among many.

Thus Berlin in the mid-90s seems to be right on course to pick up where its last great era left off.

SCIENCE AND INDUSTRY

A few years after the Wall came down and Berlin was reunified, it is still a city with a somewhat unusual industrial and economic structure. However, the unique industrial history of the city, which has always been the power behind the city's development, is not quite what it once used to be.

Berlin once again has superlatives to offer: there are almost 3000 industrial companies, making it into the largest industrial city in Germany. Berlin-Brandenburg brings in a gross domestic product of 176.5 billion DM (1993), which represents 5.6% of Germany's total economic performance. Berlin is thus the sixth largest German industrial region.

The relocation of government and parliament to Berlin could result in the creation of 700,000 new jobs.

But these impressive numbers should not hide the fact that Berlin is still in a difficult period of transition: the industrial sector is, as yet, far from being reunified, and West Berlin's industry is presently experiencing a painful weaning process. This is because until the Wall came down, the Western part of the city was always considered a capitalist showroom which was on the whole kept alive on a diet of generous federal subsidies, tax benefits and direct investment contributions.

Berlin lacks the production chains that developed naturally elsewhere, and its economic structure today still has something of that artificial quality due to its old island-like situation in the sea of the DDR. Hence the Berlin cigarette industry supplies almost 80 percent of Germany's requirements.

But West Berlin also has a few trump cards up its sleeve. Corporations such as

Siemens or Schering have remained in Berlin with their company headquarters and are even extending their commitments.

The times when the economy operated under the Wall's shadow are over and traditional Berlin industrial branches such as electrical and mechanical engineering are hardhit by worldwide competition. Accordingly, large companies such as Siemens, Nixdorf, Mercedes or Mannesmann do have their headquarters in Berlin, but all the same Berlin's companies have had to fire approximately 1,200 employees a month during 1993 and 1994 alone.

East Berlin, formerly the capital of the DDR, used to be the pride of the East German industry. But that is all part of the past. The eastern half of the city has still not recovered from the after effects of 40 years of socialism. In the next few years the unemployment rate will be considerably higher here than in the rest of Germany, and thus will be a burden on the Berlin public purse.

Almost all large industrial companies in East Berlin, mainly those that specialize in micro- and electrical engineering, have been "finalized", sold and privatized by the Treuhand. Of course the East with its reasonable property and land prices has great development potential. Even today, East Berlin's economy is growing 7% faster than in the west of the city.

Berlin – the Booming Metropolis?

The East and the West are slowly becoming a unified economic metropolis, although it still must contend with problems of location and image.

Berlin's industry is still dominated by the old sectors such as electrical engineering (45,400 people employed), mechanical engineering (14,400 people employed) and the automotive industry (14,200 people employed). In total, these

Right: A brilliant idea – Osram light bulbs being produced in Wedding.

three sectors represent 42 percent of all of jobs in Berlin.

Unlike other major West German cities such as Hamburg, Frankfurt or Munich, the service sector in Berlin is still completely underdeveloped. Commerce, banks and insurance companies – after a brief boom during the first few years after the Wall came down – have virtually stopped moving to Berlin. Economy too is waiting for the government's relocation from Bonn to Berlin.

The few large projects in this area, such as the building of the service center of debis, the Mercedes Benz subsidiary, on Potsdamer Platz, or the construction of Sony's European headquarters, also on Potsdamer Platz, are simply trend-setters. Whether they will find companies willing to imitate them is still an open question.

Although foreign investors have been streaming into Berlin since reunification of the city, most of these projects, such as the American Business Center, are still in the planning stages. Berlin has the image of being too expensive, inflexible and rather unwelcoming for investors. The current logistical problems in Berlin are probably an additional reason for potential investors to shun the city. The debate about Berlin's application to host the Olympics and the constant postponement of Bonn's move to Berlin have not improved matters.

Some investors who have been drawn to Berlin end up settling outside the city in Brandeburg. Some politicians in the city already are afraid that in the next few years Berlin will be surrounded by a belt of prosperity as Brandenburg can offer considerably lower wages and production costs.

Furthermore, unlike other German cities such as Cologne or Hamburg, Berlin can now feel the geographical proximity of the low-wage countries of eastern Europe, especially Poland. Berlin's function as the connecting point between East and West will soon decline to the city being simply a transit station which brings little profit to Berlin and its people.

BERLIN'S TEMPO: TRANSPORTATION

"What on earth gives this city its charm? In the first place, its tempo. No city is as restless as Berlin. Everything is in motion." So wrote the English journalist Harold Nicolson, who spent the twenties in Berlin. The rhythm of life in this city was set by its industrialization in the late 19th century.

After the invention of the electric motor in 1879 it took about 20 years before all the horse-drawn train routes had been electrified and the horse-drawn omnibuses had been replaced by motorized buses. Simultaneously, between 1871 and 1877, the Stadtbahn (urban train) was constructed; unique in Europe at the time, it connected the various Berlin train stations in a loop laid around the inner city. By 1925 this 12-kilometer stretch had been electrified. Against resistance from the city's in-

Above: Berlin's extensive network, here the U-1, connecting Ruhleben and Kreuzberg.

habitants and officials, Werner von Siemens managed to prevail with his idea of an underground railway, and in 1902 the first U-Bahn (subway) line was opened between Zoo and Stralauer Gate.

The Division and New Perspectives

Only a short while after the end of World War Two, the S-Bahns (suburban train lines) and U-Bahns were in operation again, as were the streetcars and buses. However, the construction of the Wall in 1961 divided public transportation into two separate systems. Many lines ended as dead tracks at the Wall, and the stations in East Berlin remained closed to trains traveling through from the West. Only the S-Bahn in West Berlin was operated by the GDR's Reichsbahn, until it was sold to the BVG (the West Berlin office of transportation) in 1984. The Reichsbahn had already shut down its operation on the city-ring line four years earlier, after a tenacious strike by S-Bahn employees.

Since the reunification of Berlin the public transportation systems have been fusing back together. And since the **BVG** of West Berlin swallowed up its eastern partner BVB, the extension work on the U-Bahn and S-Bahn networks is going on a little more briskly even though the Berliners will as always have to endure the bare-faced impertinence of their bus drivers and ticket collectors. In 1990/91 all the "ghost" stations were put back into service, the entire bus network was reorganized, and "dead" tracks reconnected.

Today, Berlin has a 127-km subway network and 245 km of S-Bahn routes. The reestablishment of service on the entire city ring is more problematic. The BVG has been renovating these routes since 1984, but it will hardly be able to complete the billion mark improvements by the year 2000. Actually, the future of the Berlin S-Bahn is endangered, since neither the city of Berlin nor the Bundesbahn (the federal railroad) wants to maintain this expensive means of transport alone. Berlin's request for special assistance for the S-Bahn remains unfulfilled. As a result, the Berliners are developing a sort of love-hate relationship with it: They complain halfheartedly when the trains are late, but, especially in summer, they enjoy riding in the wobbling cars, several of which have been rumbling over the tracks since before the war.

Berlin: Europe's Intersection

Since September 22, 1838, when the first Prussian railroad went into operation between Zehlendorf and Potsdam, tracks have been laid to Berlin from every point on the compass. As a result, in the late 19th century a series of grandiose rail terminals were built at the ends of these routes. Only the Hamburger Bahnhof, today an art gallery, is still standing.

Because of the division of Germany, present-day rail traffic in Berlin has not returned to its pre-war levels. Nevertheless, in addition to the Bahnhof Zoo (in the West) and the Hauptbahnhof train station (in the East), plans are now being made for the construction of a large new long-distance train station on the grounds of the former Lehrter Stadtbahnhof in the Tiergarten district.

One reason the railroads have such a limited importance is partially due to the rapid development of air traffic. The great nostalgic zeppelins were built since 1915 in Staaken. In 1923 a small airport was inaugurated on the Tempelhofer Feld, which at that time was still outside of town. In 1926 Lufthansa was founded with the Tempelhof Airport as its home base. In 1936 Ernst Sagebiel designed the current semicircular complex, which was taken over by the US Army after the war. During the 1948/49 blockade of Berlin, the pilots of the air-lift landed here.

The city's status under the Allies forbade German airlines to fly into Berlin. Thus, when Tegel, the new airport, was dedicated in 1974, only foreign airlines were on hand. Since the reunification of Germany, the *yellow crane,* as Lufthansa is called after its logo, has flown from Tegel to its destinations around the world. At present, 400 flights per day take off from the airport. In Tempelhof, a series of regional airlines depart for Hamburg and other cities.

Ever since the first jets lifted off from Tegel, the airport has been a matter of dispute. Local residents complained of noise levels and air pollution. Nevertheless, the current Senate intends to expand Tegel extensively, since with six million passengers annually things have become increasingly tight on the runways. In addition, Schönefeld, the only airport on the city's edge, is bursting with three million passengers per year. Hence the decision to build a gigantic new airport south of the city, which could be finished around the turn of the millenium. It will turn Berlin into a major European intersection for air travel.

Nelles Guides

... get you going.

TITLES IN PRINT

Australia
Bali / Lombok
Berlin and Potsdam
Brittany
California
  Las Vegas, Reno, Baja California
Cambodia / Laos
Canada
  Ontario, Québec,
  Atlantic Provinces
Caribbean:
  The Greater Antilles
  Bermuda, Bahamas
Caribbean:
  The Lesser Antilles
China
Crete
Cyprus
Egypt
Florida
Greece - *The Mainland*
Hawaii
Hungary
India
  Northern, Northeastern
  and Central India
India
  Southern India
Indonesia
  Sumatra, Java, Bali,
  Lombok, Sulawesi
Ireland

Kenya
London, England and Wales
Malaysia
Mexico
Morocco
Moscow / St Petersburg
Munich *and Excursions to*
  Castles, Lakes & Mountains
Nepal
New York *and New York State*
New Zealand
Paris
Philippines
Prague - Czech Republic
Provence
Rome
Spain, *North*
Spain, *South*
Thailand
Turkey
Tuscany

IN PREPARATION (for 1995)

Israel
South Africa
U.S.A.
  The West, Rockies and Texas
U.S.A
  The East, Midwest and South
Vietnam

BERLIN and Potsdam
© Nelles Verlag GmbH, D-80935 München
  All rights reserved

Second Revised Edition 1995
ISBN 3-88618-043-3
Printed in Slovenia

Publisher:	Günter Nelles	**Editor in Charge:**	Marton Radkai
Chief Editor:	Berthold Schwarz	**Cartography:**	Nelles Verlag GmbH
Project Editor:	Jürgen Scheunemann	**Color**	
Translation:	Mitch Cohen,	**Seperation:**	Priegnitz, München
	Roger Rosko	**Printed by:**	Gorenjski Tisk

- 05 -

TABLE OF CONTENTS

PREPARATIONS

Climate and Travel Times

Berlin is located in the middle of Europe in the center of the North German Plain. Therefore, Berlin's weather is determined by the continental climate. The Atlantic's influence only prevails now and then. There are few great variations in the climate throughout the year. The best times for travel are between March and June or between late August and October. It's either too hot or too cold in the other months. In addition, during the winter, the biting east wind and the smog are bothersome.

Clothing

In Berlin you can wear anything that is practical, pleasing or downright crazy. If you really must get to know Berlin in the winter, you can hardly bring enough warm clothing along, whereas in summer it can't be airy and light enough. But in spring and summer too you shouldn't forget to bring a raincoat and a warm sweater. If you like going out in the evening you can dress more or less as you please, from casual to elegant, from fancy to shrill. Only a few bars, restaurants and discotheques require a more formal attire or evening dress, suit and tie.

Berlin in Statistics

Berlin is the largest German city, with an area of 883 sqkm, almost as large as the entire Ruhr region. It extends 38 km from north to south; all of 45 km from east to west. The greatest elevations are the 120-meter Teufelsberg (artificial) and the Grosser Müggelberg (115 m) in Eastern Berlin.

Currently there are 3,460,257 inhabitants residing in the city's 23 districts; of these, 2,168,586 are in the west and 1,291,671 in the east (June 1993). Only a bare 15 percent are over 65 years of age. By the way, there are 200,000 more women than men.

ARRIVING / TRANSPORTATION

Arriving by aircraft: Since the reunification of Germany, Berlin's skies are wider open than ever before; the Lufthansa flies to the Spree again and many other airlines have aquired landing rights in Berlin.

Berlin's three airports each perform different functions: People flying in from western German cities and countries of Western Europe as well as other parts of the world land in **Tegel (TXL)**, in northern Berlin. The smaller regional airlines land their turboprop aircraft at **Tempelhof (THF)**; and a portion of the international flights and travelers from Eastern Europe land in **Schönefeld** (SXL).

The central city can be reached form all three airports with public transportation. From Tegel, **bus route 109** runs to Bahnhof Zoo; **bus 199** or the **U 6 Tempelhof** brings travelers to the city center from Tempelhof; the **S-Bahn** connects **Schönefeld** to Berlin and to the U-Bahn Station "Jakob-Kaiser-Platz." A drive with the bus can take up to one hour.

By train: The ride to Berlin has become increasingly comfortable. There are rapid Intercity connections to Basel, Braunschweig, Frankfurt, Göttingen, Hamburg, Hanover, Karlsruhe and Cologne.

Due to the long division of Berlin there is no central train station. People coming in from West European countries and western Germany arrive at **Bahnhof Zoo**, although many trains also continue through to the **Hauptbahnhof** (the main station) in the eastern part of Berlin. All trains from East Europe and the eastern German federal states also stop there. Most trains arriving from the north also stop in **Spandau** and **Charlottenburg**. Travelers from the west and south can get out in **Wannsee** to load their cars on the train if they want to take them along.

By automobile or bus: Those wishing to get to Berlin quickly can drive on the

Autobahn from Hamburg, Hannover Frankfurt or Nürnberg; the more idyllic route runs over the regular highways in the former GDR. Of course, the road conditions are as bad as ever; the speed limit on its *Autobahns* is 100 kph!

Exiting the *Autobahn* you then take the Berliner Ring, continuing on into the city from there. If arriving from the north, drive via **Stolpe** right onto the *Stadtautobahn* or straight into the city center; from the west you drive via **Staaken** onto the Heerstrasse.

Motorists from the south reach the inner city through the former border control-point **Dreilinden** and then take the **AVUS**, which leads to the *Autobahn* junction at the **Funkturm** (radio tower). By the way: Dreilinden is still the place where hitchhikers flock to thumb their rides. The **bus station** (*Omnibusbahnhof*) at the radio tower is where the bus lines connecting Berlin to western Germany arrive. From the radio tower, the U-Bahn line 1 transports you to the city center within a few minutes.

Transportation within Berlin

The streets of the inner city are regularly jammed, and chaotic traffic often prevails around the Kurfürstendamm. Parking spots are rare, and even parking garages are often full – and expensive. Furthermore, Berlin drivers are aggressive, and taxi and bus drivers are often reckless. In Eastern Berlin the streets are emptier and parking spots are easier to find; but in exchange the roads are in extremely bad condition.

Taxis present an alternative: In the entire city there are about 7000 cabs, even so it's not always easy to flag one down. The basic price is a uniform DM 5.00 and this applies to all journeys shorter than 2 kilometers or not longer than 5 minutes; for each additional kilometer driven the charge is between DM 1.50 and DM 2.30 per kilometer (depending on the time of day and the distance traveled). Nights,

Sundays and holidays an extra charge is often added (usually DM 1.00). These fares apply only in Greater Berlin. For fares outside the city discuss the price with the driver beforehand.

Public transportation: Although both of the transportation offices, **BVG** (west) and **BVB** (east) still haven't merged by now, the Berlin transportation network has already grown back together. The two main nodal points are the **Zoological Garden** and **Alexanderplatz**. Several bus lines, suburban train (*S-Bahn)* and subway lines *(U-Bahn)* cross at both locations. The BVG has set up an extensive nighttime bus network (*Nachtbusnetz*) for night owls. In addtion, the U1 and U9 subway lines run all night on Fridays and Saturdays. For the most part the last subway trains run at midnight. The S-Bahns stop toward 1.20 a.m.

The **fares** are still clearly separate between East and West. Basically speaking, all tickets are valid for the entire network and for all forms of transport. In the West a two-hour ticket costs DM 3.50 and entitles you to any number of transfers. The 24 hour ticket is a better deal; for DM 13.50 it allows you to ride and transfer as often as desired. In the two parts of Berlin the reduced fare tickets only apply in that part of the city where they were purchased.

PRACTICAL TIPS

Acommodation

Berlin has approximately 35,000 hotel beds, however these are occupied year-round, and when there are large trade fairs or festivals they are booked out weeks ahead of time. It is therefore a good idea to make your reservations as early as possible.

LUXURY HOTELS: The best Berlin hotels in this category are:

Art Hotel Sorat, Charlottenburg, Joachimstaler Str. 28/29, Tel. 88 44 70. **Bristol Hotel Kempinski**, Charlottenburg,

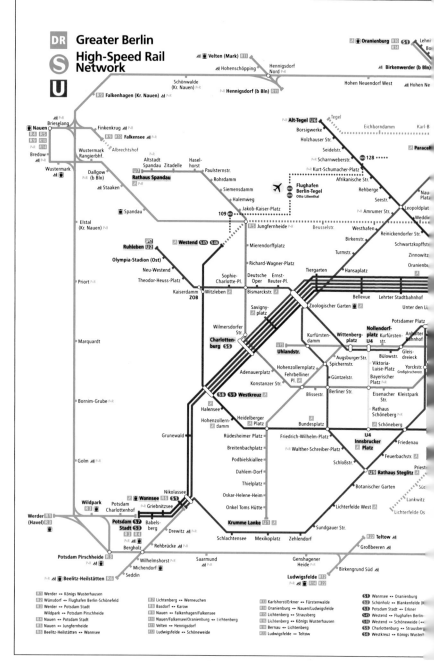

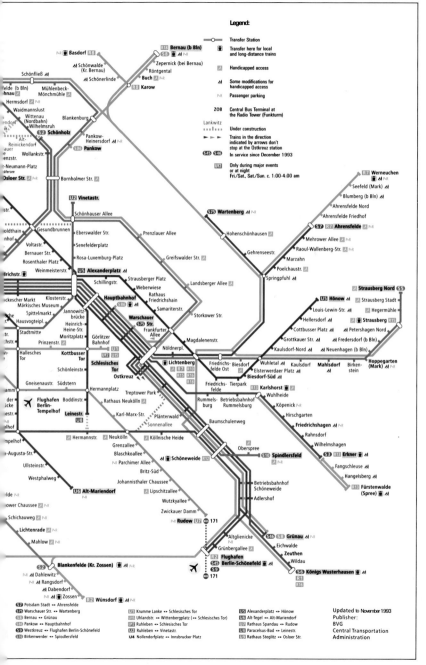

Kurfürstendamm 27, Tel. 88 43 40. **Curator**, Charlottenburg, Grolmannstr. 41-43, Tel. 88 42 60. **Berlin Hilton**, Mitte, Mohrenstr. 30, Tel. 238 20. **Grand Hotel Esplanade**, Schöneberg, Lützowufer 15, Tel. 26 10 11. **Grandhotel Maritim**, Mitte, Friedrichstr. 158, Tel. 232 70. **Inter-Continental**, Schöneberg, Budapesterstr. 2, Tel. 260 20. **Mondial**, Charlottenburg, Kurfürstendamm 47, Tel. 88 41 10. **Palace**, Schöneberg, Budapesterstr. 42, Tel. 25 49 70. **Radisson Plaza Berlin**, Mitte, Karl Liebknecht Str. 5, Tel. 238 28. **Residenz**, Charlottenburg, Meinekestr. 9, Tel. 88 44 30. **Riehmers Hofgarten**, Kreuzberg, Vorkstr. 83, Tel. 78 10 11. **Savoy**, Charlottenburg, Fasanenstr. 9-10, Tel. 31 10 30. **Schweizerhof**, Schöneberg, Budapesterstr. 21-31, Tel. 269 60. **Steigenberger**, Schöneberg, Los Angeles Platz 1, Tel. 210 80.

PENSIONS AND SMALLER HOTELS: **Hotelpension abc**, Charlottenburg, Grolmannstr. 32/33, Tel. 881 14 96. **Hotel Atlanta**, Charlottenburg, Fasanenstr. 74, Tel. 881 80 49. **Hotel Bregenz**, Charlottenburg, Bregenzer Str. 5, Tel. 881 43 22. **Hotel-Pension Diana**, Grunewald, Wernerstr. 14a, Tel. 826 10 77. **Hotel Pension Dittberner**, Charlottenburg, Wielandstr. 26, Tel. 881 64 85. **ECONTEL**, Charlottenburg, Sömeringstr. 24, Tel. 34 40 01. **Hotel-Pension Funkturm**, Charlottenburg, Wundstr. 72, Tel. 322 10 812. **Appartement im Grunewald**, Dahlem, Tempelhofer Damm 2, Tel. 785 70 77. **Hotel Sylvia**, Dahlem, Warnemünder Str. 19, Tel. 823 30 71.

YOUTH HOSTELS: The Berlin youth hostels are an alternative to hotels and pensions; information from the **Deutsches Jugendherbergswerk**, Landesverband Berlin e. V., Bayernallee 35, 14052 Berlin; Tel. 305 30 55.

ROOMMATE SERVICES: The most exciting way to become familiar with Berlin is available through the Berliner **Mitwohnzentrale** (roommate exchange)

which can arrange for rooms and apartments for several days or longer. Others are **Agentur Wohnwitz**, Wilmersdorf, Blissestr. 55; Tel. 861 82 22/ 42.

Check'in, Kreuzberg, Heimstr. 2; Tel. 694 32 90. **Mitwohnzentrale Ku'damm-Eck**, Charlottenburg, Kurfürstendamm 227/ 228; Tel. 88 30 51. **Zimmervermittlung Ost Berlin**, Prenzlauer Berg, Immanuelkirchstr. 11; Tel. 439 24 94. The tourist offices can also arrange rooms.

CAMPING: The **Deutscher Camping Club e.V.** (Geisbergstr. 11, 10777 Berlin; Tel. 24 60 71/72) provides information about camping and tent sites in the vicinity of Berlin as well as in the city.

Two campgrounds which are quite close to the metropolitan area but are located in an attractive setting are the **Campingplatz Haselhorst**, Spandau, Pulvermühlenweg; Tel. 334 59 55 and the **Zeltplatz** (camp-ground) **Kladow**, Spandau, Krampnitzer Weg 111, Tel. 365 27 97; parking places for RV's are also available.

Several of the more beautiful campgrounds include the **Zeltplatz** (campgrounds) on **Kleiner Müggelsee**, Tel. 656 18 60; the **Zeltplätze Zeuthen**, Tel. 685 82 49 and 685 94 45 as well as the "**Kuhle Wampe**" Youth Campground, Tel. 660 86 21.

Airlines
Aeroflot, Unter den Linden 51, Tel. 229 15 92; **Air Berlin**, Tegel Airport, Tel. 41 01 27 81; **Air France**, Europa Center, Tel. 26 10 51; **Alitalia**, Schöneberg, Tauentzienstraße 16, Tel. 24 01 81; **Austrian Airlines**, Schöneberg, Tauentzienstr. 16, Tel. 24 50 24; **British Airways**, Europa Center, Tel. 69 10 21; **DanAir**, Tegel airport, Tel. 413 30 28; **Euroberlin**, Kantstr. 165, Tel. 884 19 20; **Eurowings**, Tempelhof airport, Tel. 695 128 33; **Finnair OY**, Schöneberg, Budapester Str. 26a, Tel. 261 80 55; **Iberia**, Reservations, Tel. 261 70 01; **Japan Air Lines**, Europa Center, Tel 261 13 74;

KLM Royal Dutch Airlines, Schöneberg, Kurfürstendamm 17, Tel. 881 10 81; **Lufthansa**, at Kurfürstendamm 220, Tel. 887 55 30 06. Berlin-Mitte, Tel. 88 75 30 20. Reservations and information, Tel 88 75 88. Ticket sales, Tegel, Tempelhof and Schönefeld Airports, Tel. 410 43 33 (information); **Sabena**, Charlottenburg, Kurfürstendamm 179, Tel. 883 40 48; **SAS**, Charlottenburg, Kurfürstendamm 209, Tel. 881 70 11; **Singapore Airlines**, Charlottenburg, Kurfürstendamm 209, Tel. 883 20 16; **Swissair**, Charlottenburg, Kurfürstendamm 209, Tel. 883 90 01; **Tempelhof Airways**; Tempelhof Airport, Tel. 690 94 31; **Turkish Airlines**, Schöneberg, Budapester Str. 18b, Tel. 262 40 33/34.

Airports
Tegel: Tel. 410 11. **Tempelhof**: Tel. 695 10. **Schönefeld**: Tel. 609 10.

Banks
The following banks in the city offer a late service: **Commerzbank** (in Kempinski-Plaza), Uhlandstr. 181/183, Mon-Thur 9 am-1:30 pm, Fri 9 am-1 pm, Tue and Thur also 3:30-6:30 pm. Automatic Eurocard tellers at Rankestr. 1, Kurfürstendamm 59 and 102, Friedrichstr. 130.

Berliner Sparkasse, late service at: Rankestr. 33/34, Savignyplatz 9-10, Wilmersdorfer Str./corner Kantstr. and in the ICC Berlin: All are open Mon-Fri 9 am-6 pm; at Rankestr. 33/34 also Sat. 10 am-1 pm, and in the ICC Sat. 9 am-1 pm; at Alexanderplatz 2 from 10 am-1 pm. Automatic Eurocard tellers at Rankestr. 33/34, Kurfürstendamm 165, Savignyplatz 9-10, and in the Wittenbergplatz U-Bahn station.

The **Deutsche Bank** offers a late service at its branch in Otto-Suhr-Allee 6/16: Mon, Wed 9 am-3:30 pm, Tue, Thur 9 am-6 pm, Fri 9 am-12:30 pm. Automatic Eurocard tellers at Kurfürstendamm 28 and 182, Tauentzien 1, Hardenbergstr. 27 and Alexanderplatz 6.

Berlin's Districts (*Bezirke*)
The western part of Berlin has twelve, the eastern eleven districts. Since the introduction of new postal codes, the old postal delivery areas no longer exist. Following are the Berlin districts (in brackets the respective city sections or the well-known old sections which in part cover several districts).

WEST BERLIN: Charlottenburg (Halensee, Westend); **Kreuzberg** (61 and SO 36, the only city sections still known by their old delivery codes); **Neukölln** (Britz, Rudow, Buckow); **Reinickendorf** (Tegel, Lübars, Frohnau, Waidmannslust, Wittenau, Hermsdorf, Konradshöhe); **Schöneberg**; **Spandau** (Siemensstadt, Staaken); **Steglitz** (Friedenau, Lichterfelde, Lankwitz); **Tempelhof** (Buckow, Mariendorf, Lichtenrade); **Tiergarten** (Moabit), **Wedding**; **Wilmersdorf** (Grunewald, Schmargendorf); **Zehlendorf** (Grunewald, Dahlem, Schlachtensee, Wannsee).

EAST BERLIN: **Hellersdorf** (Kaulsdorf, Mahlsdorf); **Hohenschönhausen**; **Köpenick** (Friedrichshagen, Müggelheim); **Lichtenberg** (Friedrichsfelde, Biesdorf, Karlshorst); **Marzahn** (Ahrensfelde); **Mitte (Center)**; **Pankow** (Niederschönhausen); **Prenzlauer Berg**; **Treptow** (Adlershof, Baumschulenweg, Nieder- and Oberschöneweide, Johannistal); **Weissensee**.

Breakdown Assistance
ADAC Breakdown Service: Tel. 01802 / 22 22 22. **ACE Auto-Club Europe**: Tel. 192 16. **VCMD Verkehrshilfe** : Tel. 331 80 08.

Car Pools
Mitfahrzentrale in the Zoo Subway Station (Line 1 platform), Tel. 31 03 31, daily 8 am to 9 pm; **Mitfahrzentrale Ku'damm Eck** (3rd floor) Tel. 882 76 04, daily 8 am to 9 pm; **Mitfahrzentrale Sputnik**, Tel. 859 10 78; Mon-Fri 8 am to 9 pm; Sat 9 am-8 pm, Sun 10 am-6 pm.

Under this general telephone number eleven agents in the entire metropolitan area can be contacted.

Car Rentals

Avis, Int'l Reservations office, Tel. 0130 77 33; Charlottenburg, Budapester Str. 43, Tel. 261 18 81; Tegel Airport, Tel. 41 01 31 48; **City Auto Verleih**, Schöneberg, Lietzenburger Str. 29/ Nürnberger Str., Tel. 882 11 83 / 883 42 52. **Hertz** Reservation Center, Tel. 0130 21 21; Schöneberg, Budapester Str. 39, Tel. 261 10 53; Tegel Airport, Tel. 41 10 33 15; **InterRent-Europcar**, Charlottenburg, Kurfürstendamm 178-179, Tel. 881 80 93. Schöneberg, Kurfürstenstr. 101-104, Tel. 213 70 97; Tegel Airport, Tel. 41 01 33 54 / 410 133 68. **Sixt Budget**, Schöneberg, Budapester Str. 18a, Tel. 26 13 57; Tegel Airport, Tel. 410 28 86.

Consulates

American General Consulate, Zehlendorf, Clay-Allee 170, Tel. 892 40 28. **British General Consulate**, Charlottenburg, Uhlandstr. 7/8, Tel. 302 43 50. **French General Consulate**, Charlottenburg, Kurfürstendamm 211, Tel. 881 80 28/29.

Currency Exchange

Money can be exchanged in the banks mentioned above or in change booths at the Zoo Station (Bahnhof Zoologischer Garten), Mon-Sat 8 am-9 pm, Sun and holidays 10 am-6 pm, Tel. 881 71 17. Additional change booths at Joachimstaler Str. 1-3, Tel. 882 10 86, Mon-Fri 8 am-8 pm, Sat 9 am-3 pm, and Joachimstaler Str. 7-9, Tel. 882 63 71.

Emergencies

Police Emergency (Notruf): Tel. 110. **Fire Department** (Feuerwehr): Tel. 112. **Rescue Service** (Rettungsdienst): Tel. 112. **Emergency Pharmacy Service** (Apotheken-Notdienst): Tel. 011 41. **Emergency Physicians** (Ärztlicher Notdienst): Tel. 31 00 31. **Drug Emergency** (Drogen-Notdienst): Tel. 192 37. **Emergency Phone for Women** (Frauen-Notruf), Tel. 615 42 43 and 373 30 08. **Emergency Phone for Homosexuals**, (Schwulen-Notruf) Tel. 216 33 36. **Poison Emergency** (Giftnotruf): 302 30 22. **Emergency Veterinary Service** (Tierarzt): Tel. 011 41. **Telephone Counselling**, Tel. 111 01.

Festivals, Trade Fairs and Exhibitions

January/February: Grüne Woche, International Film Festival, Boat Exhibition.
March: International Tourism Fair (ITB), Moda Berlin (fashion), Lützowplatz Spring Festival.
April: Berlin Art Fair, Free Berlin Art Exhibition.
May: Theater competition.
June/July: French-German Folk Festival.
July: American-German Folk-Festival, Soviet-German Folk Festival.
August: International Broadcasting Exhibition (biannual).
September/ October: Bürodata, Berlin Festival Week, Octoberfest.
October/ November: Antiqua Berlin, Jazzfest, Young Authors' Conference.
December: Christmas Markets.
Further information available from the Austellungs-Messe-Kongress GmbH, Messedamm 22, 14055 Berlin (Charlottenburg), Tel. 303 80 and from the Berliner Festspiel GmbH, Budapester Str. 44-50, 10787 Berlin (Schöneberg) Tel. 25 48 90.

Guided City Tours

Traditional tours of the city, both small and large day-tours, excursions to Potsdam and nightclub tours are offered by the following enterprises.
Berliner Bären Stadtrundfahrt (BBS): Departures from Rankestr. 35/ Kurfürstendamm (Tel. 213 40 77).
Berolina Sightseeing: starts at Meinkestr.3/ Kurfürstendamm and at the corner of Unter den Linden/Universitätsstr. (Tel. 882 41 28).

Busverkehr Berlin (BVB): starts out at Kurfürstendamm 225, at *Joe am Ku'-damm* and the corner of Unter den Linden/Friedrichstrasse at the Lindenkorso (Tel. 882 68 47).

Severin und Kühn: Kurfürstendamm 216/ Fasanenstr. (Tel. 883 10 15).

In the last few years a series of independent associations and businesses have specialized in thematic tours. The **Kulturkontor** (Charlottenburg, Savignyplatz 9-10, Tel. 31 08 88) offers such specialized tours as "Berlin in the Twenties" or "Turn of the Century Berlin" and many others.

Similar to the Kulturkontor, the historians of **Stattreisen Berlin** (Wedding, Stephanstr. 24, Tel. 395 30 78) guide tourists onto unusual paths. Meeting points for the excursions are published in the city magazines. If you want to become familiar with Berlin by water you can, with the help of the **Geschichtswerkstatt** (Schöneberg, Goltzstr. 49, Tel. 215 44 50), board a ship on the Spree and experience Moabit, the old core of the city or the bridges of Berlin.

The tours of these three organizers are distinguished for their knowledgeable and frequently exciting style of presentation; furthermore the groups are conscientiously kept small so that time remains for specific questions.

Help for the Handicapped

In Berlin the **Telebus** offers transportation for handicapped and disabled persons, Tel. 88 00 31 31. Further services are offered by **Service-Ring Berlin**, Tel. 859 40 10, daily except Sun 10 am-6 pm or Tel. 924 21 18 daily except Sun 9 am-4 pm and by **Verband Geburts- und anderer Behinderter e.V.** which offers wheelchair rental, Tel. 341 17 97.

Lost-and-Found Offices

BVG-Fundbüro, Tempelhof, Lorenzweg 5, Tel. 751 80 21. **DB-Fundbüro**, Mitte, S-Bahn station Hackescher Markt, Tel. 29 72 06 21. **Zentrales Fundbüro West**, Tempelhof, Platz der Luftbrücke, Tel. 69 93 64 44.

Media

The heyday of the Berlin Press is a thing of the past. After a brief boom in 1989-1992 newspapers have begun dying in Berlin with many fighting for their lives. Today there are 9 daily newspapers left – still more than in any other city in Europe. Three city-magazines and the 12 radio stations (and 5 local TV stations) keep the Berliners well-informed.

After numerous innovations the *Tagesspiegel*, acquired in the meantime by the Holzbrinck group, has developed into the only supraregional Berlin newspaper. The paper, once referred to as Auntie Tagesspiegel on account of its feeble fussiness, today offers the best articles stylistically. Rather less liberal and serious are the Springer papers *Berliner Morgenpost, BZ* and *Bild*. Only the *Berliner Zeitung* has survived of the old East Berlin papers.

There is actually one Berlin newspaper that *does* transcend regional boundaries, the cheeky, leftist-alternative *Tageszeitung (taz)* which despite all financial emergencies and internal quarrels is as much as part of Berlin as the Victory Column. If you want information on the current program in the cinemas and theaters, then read the city-magazines *tip* and *zitty*, which appear bi-weekly. The new third city magazine *Prinz* is an import from west Germany but provides a good overview of parties and clubs.

The tourist office publication *Berlin Programm* also provides a good monthly survey of what's up. If the activities of the international community are what interest you, read *Checkpoint*, a very successful city magazine in English.

Multicultural City of Berlin

Foreigners visiting Berlin or people wanting to learn about the foreign cultures existing in the city can turn to the following addresses:

Anti-Racist Initiative e.V., in the Osloer Strasse factory, Wedding, Osloer Str. 12. **Senate Commission on Foreigners**, Schöneberg, Potsdamer Str. 65, Tel. 26 04 23 51 (Information). **German-Polish Association Berlin e.V.**, Steglitz, Lyedernallee 41a, Tel. 791 83 96. **Jewish Community of Berlin**, Charlottenburg, Fasanenstr. 97, Tel. 884 20 30. **Turkish Community of Berlin** (this is also the parent organization for various other Turkish associations), Kreuzberg, Adalbertstr. 4, Tel. 65 59 76. **House of World Cultures** (the former Kongresshalle), Tiergarten, J. Foster-Dulles-Allee 10, Tel. 39 40 31, exhibits and lectures. **Neighborhood House for Inter-Cultural Encounters ORA 34**, Kreuzberg, Oranienstr. 34. **Vietnam House**, Neukölln, Hobrechtstr. 8-9, Tel. 623 40 77. **Europe-Africa Center (EURAFRI)**, Schöneberg, Nollendorfstr. 21a, Tel. 216 20 89.

Postal Services

Postal Information, Tel. 251 06 69. **Post Office 120 in the Zoo Station**, Charlottenburg, Tel. 13 97 99, day-and-night counter. **Post Office in ICC Berlin**, Charlottenburg, Mon-Fri 9 am-1 pm and 1.45-4 pm, Tel. 34 09 22 56. **Post Office 519**, **Tegel Airport**, daily from 6.30 am-9 pm, Tel. 43 08 25 27.

Taxis

Tel. 690 22; Tel. 26 10 26; Tel. 21 01 01; Tel. 21 02 02; Tel. 96 44.

Telephone

The days are past when an East Berlin number was constantly engaged. However in only a few cases does Telekom continue to be unable to connect East and West together. In the meantime in both parts of the city there is a one-minute time unit for local calls. The telephone numbers supplied in this *Nelles-Guide*

have been brought up to date in January 1995. However, in the meantime some of the telephone numbers may have changed again – particularly in the east and in the areas surrounding the city. If in doubt, contact the telephone information (Tel. 011 88).

Tourist Information

In West Berlin the **Verkehrsamt** (tourist office) **Berlin** has locations in the Europa Center (Budapester Str. entrance) Tel. 262 60 31, open Mon-Sat from 8 am-10.30 pm, Sun 9 am-9 pm; at the Zoo Station, Tel. 313 90 63/64, open Mon-Sat 8 am-11 pm; at Tegel Airport, Tel. 41 01 31 45, daily 8 am-11 pm; at the Hauptbahnhof (main station) Tel. 279 52 09, daily 8 am-8 pm.

There is a new information center at the Brandenburg Gate (Tel 229 12 58). At the tourist offices you can obtain detailed materials and every sort of information. In addition, they can arrange for lodgings and, in Eastern Berlin, they will make reservations for tours of the city and provide advance sale tickets for performances.

Train Information, BVG and BVB

Deutsche Bahn, DB Travel Center at Bahnhof Zoo, Tel. 297 22 256 / 297 22 176. DB Travel Center Berlin-Lichtenberg, Tel. 297 42 934. Train information Berlin-Schönefeld, Tel. 297 47 580. Central train information, Tel. 194 19. Bus Station at the Radio Tower, Tel. 301 80 28. BVG Customer Service: Tel. 752 70 20 / 752 13 00.

AUTHORS

Eva Apraku studied German and art history; she worked for the Berlin *dpa* office and today is editor of the magazine *tip*.

Ellen Brandt studied history and began working freelance in the cultural desk of *Radio Free Berlin;* she also makes contributions to the magazine *tip* and the *Tagesspiegel*.

Matthias Eckoldt, born in Prenzlauer Berg, studied biology, German and history. He works as a freelance journalist for the weekly newspaper *Freitag* and the Berlin city-magazine *zitty*.

Reginald Hanicke studied history and political science in Berlin. He works as a freelance journalist and specializes in the history of individual districts.

Adrienne Kömmler, a freelance journalist, grew up in Prenzlauer Berg and was an editor at Berlin *Radio aktuell* following her studies in philosophy. Today she works for the *Berliner Morgenpost*.

Armin Lehmann, who is a native Berliner, studied history and German; he has written for the *Spandauer Volksblatt*, *dpa* and *tip*. Today he works for the *Tagesspiegel*.

Regina Mönch studied journalism and social therapy in Leipzig, wrote for the paper *die andere* which came out of the GDR civil rights movement, and was court reporter for the *Morgen*. She is now local editor for the *Tagesspiegel*.

Constanze Salm worked as an interior architect before becoming editor of the magazine *Feine Adressen Berlin*. Today she writes for the Berlin society magazine *topBerlin*.

Jürgen Scheunemann studied history in Berlin and Washington D.C. and now lives as a freelance journalist and translator. He was a staff writer on the *Tagesspiegel* and is now writing for magazines and newspapers, national and international. He is also the author of Berlin photo books and project editor of the *Nelles Guide USA*.

Birgit Schönberger moved from West Germany to Kreuzberg, did an internship at *Radio Free Berlin* after her study of German and now works as a freelance journalist.

Martin Schrader wrote for the *Hildesheimer Allgemeine Zeitung* and worked freelance in Berlin for the private

stations *Hit 103*, *RIAS*, *RIAS-TV*, for the *ZDF Studio Berlin* and the *Ostdeutscher Rundfunk (ORB)*.

Petra Steuer studied film direction at the Potsdam Film College. Today she works as a freelance journalist.

Hans-Joachim Wacker was co-founder of the Berlin cultural pages in the *tageszeitung* and has been cultural editor at *tip* since 1990, writing under the name "Qpferdach".

PHOTOGRAPHERS

Archiv für Kunst u. Geschichte 20,22, 28, 35L, 38, 44,132/133, 205
Bondzio, Bodo 10/11, 77, 80
Hartl, Helene 87R, 140
Landesbildstelle Berlin 32,33,36,39, 42, 43, 45, 47, 48, 49, 226
Maisel, Elisabeth. 12/13
Minehan, Mike 191, 194, 196, 197, 198, 200
Pansegrau, Erhard 2, 17, 40, 52, 53, 54/55, 56/57, 58, 68, 74, 76, 78, 100, 110, 112, 113, 115L, 117, 121, 124, 141, 147, 149, 154/155, 168, 169, 170, 184, 188L, 188R, 203, 223, 224, 233, backcover
Schneider, Günter 1, 8/9, 14, 16, 50, 62, 63, 66, 70, 84, 85, 88, 90, 92/93, 94, 96, 97, 102, 103, 107, 109, 115R, 116, 118, 120, 123, 125, 128, 134, 136, 143, 146, 156, 158, 160, 162, 163, 165, 166, 178, 180, 182/183, 186, 192, 195, 199, 204, 206, 210, 213, 214, 216, 220, 222, 227, 229, 230, 231, 232, 235, 237, cover
Schumann, Jens 67, 120, 137, 174, 176, 208, 211
Skupy, Hans-Horst 87L, 238
Steinberg, Rolf 26, 30, 35R
Vestner, Rainer 19, 24, 25, 65, 89, 150, 218/219